Joy In All Things

A Franciscan Companion

NEW INTERNATIONAL EDITION

Edited by
Br Damian Kirkpatrick SSF
fr Philip Doherty OFM Conv
Sr Sheelagh O'Flynn FMDM

CANTERBURY
PRESS
Norwich

© The Editors and Contributors 2002, 2009

Second edition published in 2009 by the Canterbury Press Norwich
(a publishing imprint of Hymns Ancient & Modern Limited,
a registered charity)
St Mary's Works, St Mary's Plain,
Norwich, Norfolk, NR3 3BH

www.scm-canterburypress.co.uk

British Library Cataloguing in Publication Data

A catalogue record for this book is available
from the British Library

The text of 'The Form of Life of Saint Clare' (pp. 48–67)
is taken from Clare of Assisi – The Lady, Early Documents,
edited and translated by Regis J. Armstrong OFM Cap
(New City Press, New York, London and Manila, 2006),
and is reproduced with permission.

ISBN 978–1–85311–747–3

Typeset by Regent Typesetting, London
Printed and bound in Great Britain by
CPI William Clowes, Beccles, NR34 7TL

Contents

Contents

Acknowledgements

By inviting the Franciscan Association of Great Britain to prepare the first edition of this Companion and Handbook, the Publishers brought together Brothers and Sisters of the Roman Catholic and Anglican congregations in a task which strengthened the ecumenical and fraternal relations between the two communions. The Editors warmly thank all the contributors for sharing their experience and giving their time, especially mentioning by name those beyond the shores of Great Britain: Murray Bodo OFM from the United States of America, the late Max Mizzi OFM Conv, and Pat Conlan OFM from Ireland.

Particular thanks are expressed to Mrs Peggy Taylor, widow of the late Bishop John Taylor, for permission to use her late husband's previously unpublished material, to Ignatius Kelly OFM, Paschal Worton SSF and Revd Dr David Peat for their contributions, and to Gina Eastman for invaluable secretarial help in aiding the completion of this book. For this second edition, the editors are grateful to the New City Press for permission to reproduce 'The Form of Life of St Clare'. Deo gratis.

The Portiuncula Chapel inside the
Basilica of Santa Maria degli Angeli

Preface

The wonder and delight of discovering Francis of Assisi stems from his deliberate and direct attempts to follow Christ, to take the Gospel to heart, to live out the Kingdom values, to seek to become fully human. Such is his appeal to all who, through the eight centuries since his life (1182–1226), have found his witness compelling, his story converting and his vocation radical – and hugely attractive. In all these senses Francis has come top of the poll in popularity in the league of saints identified in the western Church. When he heard the Lord call 'follow me', Francis knew it was going to cost him 'not less than everything'.

Francis' response was remarkable, and against the background of today's world, is amazingly relevant. As we can witness today, he saw the corrupting power of wealth, exploitation, violence and individuality. So he resolved to make the Lady Poverty the vehicle of a love affair; he spoke of the natural creation as his brothers and sisters; he discovered in the outcast the face of Christ; he began every new encounter with the greeting, 'peace to this house'; he begged that his prayer and his love might be as strong as that of Christ on the cross; he made his prayer into a bond of filial commitment, 'my God and my all!'

St Clare and that early company of young friends in his home town of Assisi in Italy were drawn like a magnet to follow Christ also. So Francis has attracted thousands upon thousands down the centuries in a movement within the Christian Church that continues to promote Gospel values, genuine simplicity of living, a humility through penance and a zeal for sharing the love of God. Today such a programme of mission is clearly relevant, urgent and vital to the whole future of planet earth.

The Franciscan family comprises so many congregations and secular vocations beyond counting! The editors, representing First Order friars, Second Order sisters of St Clare and Third Order regulars and secular, have linked to compile this resource and reference book. We trust that it may be useful to the English-speaking world, to inspire many to grow in love for God, to deepen commitment within their churches, and to extend the Christian witness in the broadest terms, for the good of all. Begin perhaps with a historical or practical question, or simply a heart that yearns for better things. The editors of this modest handbook, prepared as an ecumenical project, hope you will recover some of the joy of St Francis, discover the inner joy of life's deeper meaning, and uncover a 'Joy in all things'.

About the Contributors

Murray Bodo OFM is a Franciscan of the Province of St John the Baptist, Cincinnati, Ohio. A poet and the author of seventeen books, including the international best-seller, *Francis, the Journey and the Dream*, he is Visiting Professor of Poetry and Visiting Scholar in the Franciscan Institute at St Bonaventure University, New York. Fr Murray spends his summers in Assisi as a staff member and pilgrim guide for 'Franciscan Pilgrimage Programs'.

Patrick Conlan OFM was born in Limerick, Ireland, in 1940 and joined the Franciscans in 1958. Ordained in 1968, he did post-graduate work in theology, and was invited to help write the history of the Irish province. An expert on Irish medieval religious architecture, he also writes on Franciscan spirituality. Stationed at the Franciscan Centre for Peace and Reconciliation in Donegal, the best-known of his many books is *Franciscan Ireland*.

Austin Davis SSF has been a member of the Society of St Francis for thirty years. As well as having served in a number of houses of the Community, he has studied at the Franciscan Study Centre in Canterbury. He was recently appointed Master of the Eastbridge Hospital, an ancient medieval almshouse in the centre of the city of Canterbury, which acquired the Franciscan Gardens with The Greyfriars from the Dean and Chapter of Canterbury Cathedral in 2000.

Samuel Double SSF was born in London and ordained in the Anglican Diocese of Liverpool. After serving his curacy there he joined the Society of St Francis in 1974, serving in their houses in Manchester, Liverpool and Cambridge. Since 2002 he has been Provincial, based in Dorset.

Frances Teresa Downing is a member of the Poor Clare community in Arundel, Sussex, where she has held various posts over the years. By a special arrangement with her community, she currently teaches the Clare Course at the Franciscan International Study Centre, Canterbury. She is the author of *Living the Incarnation*, and *This Living Mirror*, as well as various articles of a Franciscan nature.

Guire Cleary was a Brother with the American Province of the Society of St Francis until 2007. He served as curator of the Mission San Francisco de Asis in San Francisco, California, the first Franciscan on their staff since 1846.

David Hayes retired as the Anglican rector of St Peter's and St Mildred's churches in Canterbury in 2007.

Tristam Holland joined SSF in 1967. He worked in the UK and in Zambia and, as General Secretary for fourteen years, regularly visited all the SSF Provinces around the world. He was a member of the Liturgical Commission of the Church of England and represented Religious Communities on the General Synod of the Church of England. He edited *Celebrating Common Prayer*, *Exciting Holiness* and other publications. He died in 2005.

Stephen Innes OFM Cap is presently a member of the Initial Formation Team of his Province in the UK. His field of interest is seventeenth-century Capuchin history. He is writing a biography of Father Cuthbert OSFC.

Bishop John Jukes OFM Conv, professed in the Order of Friars Minor Conventual in 1948, studied in Rome and was ordained priest in 1952. He went on to serve in a number of

English Friaries and was consecrated bishop in 1980. He is now retired and living in Aberdeenshire.

Damian Kirkpatrick SSF was born in London in 1941. After qualifying as an accountant and working for a short time with a missionary agency he joined the Anglican Franciscans in 1963 as a tertiary and in 1966 as a friar. He has served the Society of St Francis as a lay brother and as a priest in various chaplaincies, as Provincial and latterly as the community bursar. He is also currently Vicar of Lindisfarne in Northumberland.

The Revd Professor Andrew Linzey is Director of the Oxford Centre for Animal Ethics (www.oxfordanimalethics.com) and a member of the Faculty of Theology in the University of Oxford. He is also Honorary Professor at the University of Winchester and Professor of Animal Ethics at the Graduate Theological Foundation, Indiana. He has authored or edited more than twenty books including seminal works on theology and animals: *Animal Theology* (1994), *Animals on the Agenda* (1998), *Animal Rites: Liturgies of Animal Care* (1999), *Animal Gospel* (1999) and *Creatures of the Same God* (2007).

Maximilian Mizzi OFM Conv was born in Malta, but lived most of his life as a friar in Assisi where he developed a wide ecumenical ministry. Towards the end of his active life he created a Centre of Inter-Faith Dialogue in Assisi. He died in 2007.

Sheelagh O'Flynn of The Franciscan Missionaries of the Divine Motherhood hailed from Galway in Ireland. She taught in Nigeria, Zambia and Australia and spent thirteen years in Ireland working with young people as Vocations Directress for her Congregation. Sheelagh's ministry embraced spiritual direction, leading retreats and workshops on prayer and the spiritual life. She edited FMDM Voice for her congregation. In her last three years she journeyed with cancer and died peacefully in February 2009.

xiii

Martin Shaw is a Franciscan tertiary and an experienced leader of pilgrimages to Assisi. He carries Franciscan spirituality in his writing of poetry. He is also a singer and broadcaster. In 2005 he was consecrated Bishop of Argyll and the Isles in the Episcopal Church of Scotland.

John V. Taylor, poet, writer, artist, visionary and theologian, worked with the Church Missionary Society for thirty years, first in Africa and then as its General Secretary, until his appointment in 1975 as Bishop of Winchester, where his intellectual and spiritual leadership illuminated the diocese for ten years. His music and drama productions at the cathedral were legendary, and he used the media skilfully to communicate the Christian faith. He continued writing and preaching until his death in January 2001. John V. Taylor's story of St Francis is taken from his unpublished works, with the permission of his estate, with minor adaptations.

Philippe Yates OFM studied engineering at Cambridge University, UK, before entering the Franciscans in 1985. He was ordained a priest in 1992 and ministered in the London suburbs before continuing studies in Canon Law in Ottawa and Rome to gain his doctorate. He is currently Principal of the Franciscan International Study Centre in Canterbury.

I

Introduction

Murray Bodo OFM

Greetings in Christ!

Topos is the Greek word for place. It can be geographical, or abstract, as in the use Aristotle makes of it in his *Rhetoric*. There, *topos* is the place where one finds topics (again from *topos*) for argument. There is the *topos* of cause and effect, for example, or comparison and contrast. In this sense, *topos* is a place in the mind. In the same way, the *topos*, Assisi, is for me both a geographical place and a place in my soul. I've returned many times to Assisi in Italy; I return to Assisi in my soul almost daily. My soul's Assisi is the *topos* of the Franciscan charism.

It is the place of St Francis and St Clare. There, St Francis is born in 1182; there St Francis is born in me. There, the events of St Francis' life unfold; there, he models the events of my own life. There, St Clare joins the Brothers on Palm Sunday, 1212, and founds the Monastery of San Damiano, where the Poor Ladies (as St Francis called them) live the life of radical Gospel poverty. There, St Clare becomes the image of Lady Poverty, the Bride of Jesus Christ, who, Dante says, was the only one to ascend the cross with Jesus.

Topos: geography and geography of the soul. All my life geography has affected me so. That perhaps is why the poetry of Elizabeth Bishop draws me in, as in these lines from her poem, 'Crusoe in England' (E. Bishop, *Geography III*, New York: Farrer, Straus & Giroux, 1976, p. 16). Crusoe dreams of

                    other islands
    stretching away from mine, infinities
    of islands, islands spawning islands,
    like frogs' eggs turning into polliwogs
    of islands, knowing that I had to live
    on each and every one, eventually,
    for ages, registering their flora,
    their fauna, their geography.

I fall into Bishop's word-maps the way I fall into the geography of Assisi. Geography, the inner and outer polarities of my soul. Assisi is the *topos* of the unfolding of my Franciscan life. Assisi is the town of St Francis; it is also the town he left to live with the lepers on the plain below Assisi. Assisi is a safe, walled, medieval town; it is also the town out of which Francis strode in order to *descend* to the poor, the marginal, the outcasts. Assisi is the town of St Francis dying in the Bishop's palace; it is also the town where he asked to be carried *outside* the city walls to lie naked on the ground, stripped like Christ of everything, in order to die where he first lived and worked with the lepers. Like the cell which St Francis encourages his friars to carry with them, his town, this *topos*, is a cell I can enter anywhere, any time.

For St Teresa of Avila the cell within is an interior castle; for Dante it is a dark wood that leads to a seven-storey mountain from which one ascends to the white rose of eternity. For me it is Assisi and its environs in the Umbrian valley. It is the *topos* of St Francis' centre from which he set forth on his missionary journeys. It is the place where Francis and the Brothers gathered on the plain below Assisi each year on the Feast of Pentecost to tell the stories of their itinerant journeys, confess their sins to one another, and send each other forth two by two to preach and witness to the Gospel for another year. It is the *topos* of story, and story is the *topos* of Franciscan spirituality.

It is the place where Franciscans go to discover how to pray and how to live. Like the Gospels themselves, the stories of the Brothers, the so-called Little Flowers of St Francis, are the *topoi* where we define who we are, from the two *Lives of St Francis* by Thomas of Celano, through *The Legend of the Three Companions*, *The Legend of Perugia*, *The Mirror of Perfection*, the Major and Minor Life of St Francis by St Bonaventure, to the Western Classic entitled, *The Little Flowers of St Francis*.

Instead of methodology for prayer and contemplation Franciscans have stories that reveal the way stories do, through the *topoi* of plot and theme, character and conflict, climax and denouement. Stories engage the imagination, the emotions, the heart. Francis and Clare of Assisi, and their companions old and new, are the stuff of story, an inexhaustible source of narrative, as the following pages reveal.

2

Telling the Stories

The story of St Francis (1182–1226)
+John V. Taylor

The province of Umbria forms a broad fertile plain in the centre of Italy through which the River Tiber runs south towards Rome. Along the eastern rim of this plain lie the Apennine Marches, and one of those great mountain shoulders heaved up above the valley is called Monte Subasio. On its lower slopes, facing west across the rich plain, stand several small fortified towns, of which the most famous by far is Assisi.

It was a prosperous little place even in the days of ancient Rome. An ancient temple of the goddess Minerva looks out over the central square. The poet Propertius, who wrote about the ecstasies and disillusionments of love, was born there in about 51 BC.

Six feet below the level of this central square today lie the paving stones of the Roman forum and the bases of the public buildings of that classical age. The great highway from Rome to the north-east, the Via Flaminia, swept past Assisi just below in the broad valley, and the legions marched by on their way to the conquest of the world. Now, as then, it is a walled city jealously guarding the spur of hillside to which it clings. In the Middle Ages it was dominated by the Rocca or castle-fortress of the feudal overlord. Only eight years before the birth of St Francis of Assisi, the Emperor Frederick Barbarossa, the Red Beard, established himself for a while within this castle and renovated its walls.

Down in the little town, however, the citizens were restive, remembering that they were, like most other ancient towns

I

of Italy, an independent city-state. They had their feudal aristocracy, but there was a new class of rich merchant traders, increasing in power and civil liberty. These merchant leaders were organized in guilds, whose great halls overlooked the central square. This new middle class called themselves the Majores, or greater folk, in contrast to the Minores or lesser fry, who made up the poorer and powerless class in the Commune.

One of the Majores, a member of the Clothiers Guild, was Pietro Bernadone of the Mariconi family, a hard-working, hard-dealing trader in fine broadloom cloth. He was often away from home to do business in the great fairs of Europe, in which fortunes could be made or lost very quickly. It may have been on such a journey that he sealed a business alliance with a family in Provence by marrying their daughter, the gentle Pica. At all events it was Pietro's fancy to give his eldest son the nickname 'Francesco', the little Frenchman, though his baptism name was Giovanni. He learned to speak and sing in French as well as in that mixture of Latin and Umbrian Italian which all the children in the town used.

Francesco took after his mother more than his father. In their home, which tradition places on the site of the Chiesa Nuova, the Lady Pica's more gracious influence brought out his natural gaiety and wit, and cultivated that delight in music and beauty of all kinds and that deep courtesy towards all other beings which was his special charm. The first glimpse of Francis which reliable history gives us is as a boy, helping in his father's shop. When a strolling beggar came whining at the open door: 'Alms for the love of God,' it was a busy, inopportune moment and the man was gestured away. But the beggar had not gone far before Francis ran after him to give what cash he had in his satchel, vowing that he would never refuse any request made in the name of God.

As he grew older his daring originality won him a place of natural leadership among the more flamboyant young sons of the fashionable set. With them he loved to flaunt his extravagant, exaggerated finery to shock and to fascinate the

workaday citizens of Assisi. Francesco would sling his lute
before him and stroll with a few companions along the smaller
streets, singing in a voice that was always strangely powerful in
so slight a frame as his, the popular serenades from Provence
which he loved to the end of his days. This was the heyday of
the troubadours, weaving a mantle of chivalrous romance and
idealized passion around the bloody realities of the Crusades.
Blondin had sung for Richard Coeur de Lion only three years
earlier, and now Francis was in love with loveliness itself and
moved by longings greater than he could understand. One day
he would call himself God's troubadour.

When Francis was 16 the great Innocent III became Pope
at the early age of 37. He was to become the most powerful
European since Charlemagne, and at once he resolved to
break the sovereignty of Charlemagne's successors, throwing
the Imperial forces and their Lombard mercenaries out of
Italy. In Assisi the people of the Commune rose against their
overlord and, when he fled, began to break down the wall
of the Rocca. Civil discord raged and the feudal nobles, who
prized their city's freedom as much as any, appealed to neighbouring Perugia for troops to restore law and order.

It was a tactical mistake. Perugia was the traditional enemy
and, exulting in the pageantry and adventure of his first taste
of a fight, Francis rode out with the citizen army of Assisi
to drive back the Perugian force. By the old Roman bridge
over the Tiber, now dedicated to St John, they engaged in a
prolonged skirmish among the vines. At the end of the day
the Perugians had won and young Francis was taken prisoner with others from his city and locked up in the citadel of
Perugia. His fellow captives noted how the cocky high spirits
of this youngster kept them all cheerful during twelve months
in prison. When one of them asked him if he was off his head
to be so optimistic he retorted: 'Why shouldn't I be lively?
One day the whole world will bow down to me.'

Yet the arrogance of this latter-day Joseph could also turn
to quick sympathy. They noticed also how specially attentive
Francis was to one morose and unattractive fellow prisoner

who had no other friends. But high spirits are sustained at a price. When peace was patched up and the captives returned, Francis found himself in a state of profound depression. For the first time in his life the beauty of the world failed to move him, and the love of it seemed an empty devotion. His old confidence in himself and in the basic goodness of life deserted him. An invisible hand was laid heavily upon him. 'All things betray thee who betrayest me.'

Meanwhile the struggle between Pope and Emperor was still raging. One leader of Innocent III's forces was Walter of Brienne, a romantic figure who captured the hearts of many young recruits. Francis too, when he was 22, fell under the spell of hero-worship and joined a band of Assisian youths to ride south to Spoleto to offer their service to this Walter. The proud father Pietro Bernadone fitted out his son with a sumptuous kit. All was brilliant fantasy and, during the night before their departure, Francis dreamed of a triumphant return and a dazzling lady love who would become his bride, though who she might be he had no idea.

Next morning the little troop was sent on its way with wide acclaim. Somewhere near the small town of Spello, Francis became aware of one of his fellow riders who was withdrawn and shamed by his shabby outfit that compared so poorly with the rest. So he persuaded him to accept his own resplendent armour – which was not at all the purpose for which his father had so lavishly provided it.

At Spoleto where they were to meet Walter of Brienne, Francis had another dream. A voice asked him: 'Francis, whom is it better to serve, a lord or his vassal?' 'Surely,' Francis replied, 'it is better to serve the lord.' 'Why then,' came the answer, 'do you make a lord of him who is servant?' The next day Francis told his dismayed companions that he must leave them to return home. It is easy to see how desperately hard that was. Francis was never afraid of looking a fool, but this appeared to be cowardice. And he could in no way understand why or for what purpose he had to turn back. It says a great deal for his integrity that those of his friends who had remained behind in Assisi welcomed him back and let him take up the old life as king of their revels. But a new note had crept into his extravagance. It consisted in giving things away. Francis was becoming obsessed by the poor and his distance from them. He wandered the countryside, seeking out small abandoned chapels, or the hermitages of the Benedictine monks, to find solace in prayer for the struggle that was raging in his mind. He specially loved the Carceri, a cluster of cells perched among the ilex and sycamores on the slopes of Monte Subasio a few miles above Assisi which in his day was little more than a group of caves around a spring of water. The memory of Christ's passion became the focus of his devotion and always moved him to tears. In later years he was remembered as one who wept easily for the sorrow and the joy of God.

Desperately uncertain what his future should be, Francis went to Rome, to pray near to the tombs of the Apostles Peter and Paul, as devout folk did. A beggar was standing outside St Peter's and, impetuous as ever, Francis exchanged his fine clothes for the poor man's rags and stayed there against the church wall till evening, learning what it was like to beg one's living. It gave him a strange excitement and an unexpected sense of liberation. Francis had begun the trick of standing the world on its head and turning all its values upside down.

Back in Assisi, during the familiar escapades with his friends, he fell into a reverie and they, looking back to where they had left him standing, called out 'Look at Francesco! He must be in love. Who is she, amico?' With a dart of passionate intensity he called back: 'She is more noble and beautiful and rich than any you have set eyes on.' He was still ignorant of her name, but he was soon to learn it: The Lady Poverty. In his quest for her, as he was riding just outside Assisi, his horse suddenly swerved. There on the path before him stood a leper begging alms. The disease was rife then in Europe and a colony of the poor outcasts lived nearby in the charitable hospice of San Salvatore. The fastidious young gallant was nauseated, but an aching compassion made him dismount, thrust all his cash into the sufferer's hands and raise the crippled fingers to his lips. The leper returned the kiss of peace and Francis felt a sweetness flood his whole being.

Now he had found something to do. Almost daily he visited the leprosy hospice to show loving service to its inmates. His inner anxiety lifted and the old delight in life returned more vividly than ever. He was learning the secret of joy.

One day when Francis was 24 or 25 he found the path that led down from the southern gate to a half-ruined chapel dedicated to St Damian, kept by an old priest whose tiny house was built against its wall. As he knelt with his eyes fixed on the painted crucifix he heard the voice of Christ saying: 'Francis, go and repair my house which is falling into ruin.' Literal as always in his response to the words of Jesus, Francis sprang up, thrust what money he had into the hands of the priest, telling him to buy oil to keep a lamp of love burning before the crucifix, and ran back up the hill to the city gate to his father's store. There he chose several bales of scarlet broadcloth, slung them across the saddlebow of his own horse and rode off along the Spoleto road to Foligno market. He sold the cloth and, never doing anything by halves, sold his horse as well before trudging the ten miles back to the chapel of San Damiano. The old priest, sensing trouble, refused to take the money. So Francis tossed it in through the window and then coaxed him into letting him live there. Each day he climbed the steep lane back to the city to beg for building materials to carry back to the little chapel, and what he could not obtain as charity he bought with some of the proceeds from the sale of the cloth.

Pietro Bernadone had been away on another of his trading tours when all this was happening. He returned to find the whole town buzzing with the scandal of how his cloth had been taken and sold. His fellow merchants reported, perhaps with some gleeful relish, how that precious son of his had become the laughing stock of the streets as he begged from door to door, and how the jeering children, believing he had gone out of his mind, had pelted him with mud and rotten fruit from the market stalls. Pietro stormed down to San Damiano to fetch his boy home, but Francis gave him the slip and a few days later was back at his begging and his building as before.

The gossips in every back street were agog with the drama. 'Pietro has dragged his son back into their house and locked him in the cellar.' 'Then the Lady Pica released him and he's gone straight back to San Damiano.' 'Now Pietro has petitioned the magistrates to banish Francis from the city, for he can't endure the shame another week. But they've refused to do anything so drastic, so he's taken the case to the Bishop's ecclesiastical court.'

Pietro demanded restitution from his own child for the bales of cloth and the horse. He was baffled and uncomprehending. And Francis saw that what he was confronting was not simply an angry parent, but a whole society. He stripped off all his clothes and laid them at Pietro's feet saying: 'I shall return not only the money that is his. Here also are the clothes I have had from him. Hitherto I have called Pietro Bernadone father; now I will say only, "Our Father, who art in heaven."' Then the good Bishop Guido wrapped his own cloak round Francis to hide his nakedness. When Francis finally left the court he was wearing a tattered tunic and hood which a workman had discarded and a length of rope as a girdle.

Francis needed time to take stock. He journeyed to the hill city of Gubbio where he lodged with an unnamed friend while he considered his new-found clarity of purpose. The liberty of possessing nothing and being possessed by nothing was too precious ever to be lost again. As he explained it later to Bishop Guido: 'My lord, if we keep property we shall need arms to defend ourselves, and we shall constantly be involved in litigation and feuds, and this will often prevent us from loving God and our neighbours. Therefore we desire to possess no temporal goods in this world.'

He returned to San Damiano to continue the work of

restoration. The steeply-pitched barrel vault of the chapel is typical of all the small shrines which Francis is said to have built with his own hands. When this one was completed he started to restore others in the same way. The old church of St Peter in Assisi was the next to command his attention, and then, by chance it seemed, he came upon the very ancient and broken chapel of St Mary of the Angels, deep in the woods that covered the valley. It is believed to have been built in the fourth century by pilgrims returning from the Holy Land. It stood in a little portion of land, or Portiuncula, belonging to the Benedictines from Monte Subasio. So Francis started to put the Portiuncula chapel in order. And there, on the Feast of St Matthias, 24 February, he heard the priest read at Mass: 'As you go, preach, saying, "The Kingdom of God is at hand." Get you no gold nor silver nor brass in your purses, nor scrip for your journey, or two coats or shoes or staff. And when you come into a house, salute it saying, "Peace be to this house."' From that moment onwards Francis would greet everyone he met with the words, 'Good people, the Lord give you peace' – or, more simply, 'Pax et bonum' which has become the motto of Assisi. But what struck him even more forcibly was the clear command to preach. Up till now his life had been taken up with prayer, begging, building. Francis obeyed the Gospel command.

No one was more surprised than he when his street preaching turned the old popular ridicule into instant popular acclaim. Soon he could move nowhere without a crowd pressing about him. People had never heard anything so fresh and free from formality and dogma, nor anything so passionately sincere, because his supreme sermon was the life he lived. Moreover, he was actor, poet, singer, jester, all surrendered in one perfect instrument.

Among those who heard this extraordinary public preaching was Chiara Favarone, the young fair-haired daughter of one of the nobles of the feudal aristocracy. Her family naturally rejected as madness this young fanatic's challenge to their logic of money and power, but Chiara (or Clare) kept her own 13-year-old thoughts to herself.

At this time one of the lay canons of the cathedral, Peter Catanio, being learned in theology and church law, was secretly approached by the head of another aristocratic family, Bernard of Quintavalle, seeking confidential advice. This Bernard was on the point of renouncing all his wealth to throw in his lot with Francis, but still wondered whether to trust his own judgement. As they talked in the canon's house, it transpired that he also had been waiting for someone else to move before declaring himself a convert to Francis and his way of life. So together they came to him, offering to give away their possessions to become wandering preachers like himself.

For Francis the only right way was to obey the Gospel. This is why the earliest portraits so often depict him holding the book, though he forbade his brotherhood to own even that as their property. So now he took the two men to the church of St Nicholas in the main square where he left them on their knees while he went and opened the Gospel book on the altar. The first words on which his eye fell were: 'If you would be perfect, go sell what you have and give to the poor and you will have treasure in heaven.' He opened at random a second time: 'If any man will come after me, let him deny himself and take up his cross and follow me.' Yet a third time Francis opened the Gospel. 'And he commanded them that they should take nothing for the way.' Radiant he turned to Bernard and Peter, his first two followers, saying: 'Brothers, this is our life and our rule.'

The report flew through the streets of Assisi. 'Bernard of Quintavalle and Dr Peter Catanio have sold up their homes and are distributing every penny they possess in the piazza San Georgio.' A priest called Sylvester accosted Francis, complaining: 'If you've got all this money to throw away how come you gave me such a low price for the stones I sold you for your building repairs?' Francis filled his two hands with coins from the pile and thrust them on the astonished priest. Utterly taken aback, he went off with the money in his satchel and strange thoughts in his head. A few days later he was offering himself to join Francis as the third companion. They slept rough among the old olive groves in the countryside below the city, while they continued Francis' service of the lepers and his building programme, preaching around the neighbourhood as he did. But their main occupation in those first days together was prayer, sometimes reciting the offices together – and now in Sylvester they had a priest – and sometimes breaking out in their own less formal songs. They became known as God's jesters. One chronicler said, 'They could rejoice so much because they had abandoned so much.'

The next to come to them through the trees was a sturdy farmer's boy, Giles. Then, as their preaching rounds spread more widely, others came in quick succession: Angelo Tancredi, son of a nobleman, whom Francis had known from boyhood; the tall and eloquent Masseo; the pious young nobleman, Rufino, who had been trained as a knight; the simple, clownlike Juniper; Leo, the pure and loyal friend; John and Sabbatino; and the sceptical Pacificus who, on first meeting Francis, put him to the test. 'What can I do for you?' asked Francis. 'Give me your tunic,' replied Pacificus. At once his habit was stripped off and placed over the stranger's head, thus investing him as a member of the Order.

When the brothers numbered twelve, Francis felt the time had come to seek the Pope's blessing on their way of life. He had already found a name for his Order; choosing the title of the lesser fry in that society, the Minores, he called his movement 'The Lesser Brothers' – the Friars Minor. They walked to Rome and made their way to the Lateran Palace, where Francis went in as their spokesman and tried to catch the attention of the great Innocent III, but he was mistaken for a beggar and put aside. That night, it is said, Innocent dreamed that his own palace and cathedral were tottering, but were saved from collapse by the strong shoulder of that same ragged beggar.

The next day Francis and his companions were summoned to an audience. Members of the papal court objected that the way of life Francis was proposing was impossibly severe and a distortion of the Gospel, but the Pope saw further. He dismissed the brothers with the words: 'Go forth, and as the Lord shall inspire you, preach repentance to all men. When Almighty God has multiplied you in numbers and grace, come to me again, rejoicing, and I will grant you more than this.'

It may have been on the return journey from Rome that Francis turned aside to go deep into the mountain country above Rieti, where a grotto above the village of Poggio Bustone was already a favourite retreat. There he sought strength to meet the natural reaction of doubt and fear. He returned with a strong assurance of sins forgiven and of God's hand on the future. 'Let not our simple ways dismay you,' he said to the brothers, 'for the Lord has shown me a multitude of men desiring to put on the habit of our holy vocation. The French are coming, the Spaniards are hastening, the Germans and the English run.'

Back in Assisi, Francis saw that, if his brothers were to travel farther afield on their preaching missions, they needed a permanent home to return to. At first they found a disused stone cowshed among the meadows of Rivo Torto, the twisting stream conveniently close to the lepers' hospice in the valley. But when an uncivil peasant drove his ass into the place, Francis accepted humiliation and rejection as the greatest joy – this was always his way – and at once remembered the little portion of Benedictine property around the chapel farther along the valley. The abbot who owned the place agreed to let them have it in exchange for one basket of fish from the river every year. So the Portiuncula chapel in the woods which he had himself repaired a few years before became forever the mother house of the world-wide Franciscan order. Today it stands ringed round, not by tall forest trees, but by the pillars of a massive baroque Basilica. Yet, apart from painted frescoes and an added turret, it is the same simple sanctuary that it was 800 years ago.

∾

The preaching of Francis himself became more powerful and magnetic than ever. An eyewitness reported: 'He began to preach wonderfully of despising the world, and of holy penance and voluntary poverty, of the self-stripping of Christ in the passion. He seemed to those who heard him as a man from another world, whose heart was set on heaven and his face turned upward, seeking to draw others with him.' But such freedom and love for God and all God's creatures was fostered through heroic self-discipline. One night, when he was wrestling against a strong tide of sexual passion in himself, he ran from his cell to fling himself naked onto the thorns of several wild rose bushes. The roses still grow in the garden of the Portiuncula, but ever since that night they have been thornless, it is said.

He walked now the length and breadth of central Italy, not only to organize his movement, but to seek solitude for prayer in lonely caves and hermitages. One can imagine this young man teasing Brother Masseo at a crossroads when he asked over-solemnly how they should know which was the way God wished them to take. 'I command you under holy obedience, spin round and round until I call "Stop", and whichever way you are facing then we shall take.' At Greccio, one of Francis' beloved mountain retreats, he sought permission from the Pope to reverse the ban that had been placed on the old Nativity plays, and at the Christmas celebration he placed a manger in the area by the wayside, and laid a child in it, with an ox and ass tethered beside it; and a great congregation marvelled at the poverty of Christ and his mother.

There are a multitude of stories, true or legendary, of the genius and power of this little poor man. There is a ring of truth in the incident of the sermon to the birds. Noticing a flock of birds in a field between Bevagna and Cannara, Francis declared in his fanciful way: 'I am going to preach to these our sisters.' As he walked among them none flew off, so he spoke to them for some time of their reason to be grateful for God's care. Then he made over them the sign of the cross and they departed, singing and chattering.

Rather more legendary is the story of the wolf that haunted the forested mountainsides around Gubbio, and attacked people who ventured forth, and how Francis brought it, tamed and repentant, into the city square. Such parables of his extraordinary influence over the worldly spirit of his day brought secular men and women to dedicate themselves to a simple disciplined life in the Third Order.

The great Basilica raised as a mausoleum for Francis' body in Assisi contrasts strangely with that poverty which he ever tried to emulate. It speaks of the tragedy of St Francis and the struggle which dragged on for ten years from 1216 to 1226. There were some able and influential men who were moved by immense admiration for Francis' achievements, yet were blind to all that he stood for. Such were the great Cardinal Hugolino, Bishop of Ostia, and the clever Brother Elias, surnamed Bombarone. It was he who, after Francis' death, raised the money – a fortune – to build the upper and lower churches and the monastery precincts, a fitting symbol of his systematizing mind. At one level he and the Cardinal Hugolino were right. A simple injunction to live by the Gospel and a habit of spontaneous response to new situations is well enough for a community of twelve friends. But when an Order numbers thousands, with missionaries in every land from England to the Holy Land, many of whom have never met Francis or come under his spell, it becomes necessary to appoint a hierarchy and make detailed and less absolute rules. Francis saw the simplicity and freedom of his movement threatened. The powerlessness and vulnerability he so greatly prized were being replaced by efficiency and legalism.

After only the first three years of this sad conflict, Francis, who had been frustrated many times in his wish to go further afield, like his own missionaries, insisted at last on trying to preach to the Muslim power in Egypt. He came first to the Crusading army that was besieging Damietta. This soon disabused him of any romantic enthusiasm for the code of chivalry. Yet one of the Crusading bishops was hard put to it to dissuade many of his troops from joining the Franciscan Order. Though Saladin's successor, the Sultan Malik al Kamil, had given orders that any Christian was to be killed on sight, Francis made his way to the court. The two met in touching courtesy and, when Francis had preached, he and his companion were invited to live on at the palace. Had there been fewer Crusaders and more than one Francis, the story of Christian–Muslim relations would have been vastly different. For of these two men Kipling's words ring strangely true:

> O, East is East and West is West,
> And never the twain shall meet,
> Till Earth and sky stand presently
> At God's great judgement seat.
> But there is neither East nor West,
> Border nor Breed nor Birth,
> When two strong men stand face to face,
> Tho' they come from the ends of the earth.

From Egypt Francis visited Palestine and walked in the steps of Christ among the Holy Places. Returning to Italy he found division and disloyalty among the Brothers, worse even than he had been told. For five more years the struggle went on. At the General Chapter each Pentecost, his simple but absolute Gospel rule was questioned and further compromised. He might have carried the day by sheer weight of personal authority, but he refused to shift his ground from the vulnerability and non-aggression which were the inward counterpart of poverty. One day in 1223 he came and stood again, silently pleading with uplifted arms, before the crucifix in the chapel of San Damiano. After a long time he asked for ashes and poured them over himself intoning the Miserere. Then he left without a word.

The following summer, 1224, after the difficult Pentecost Chapter was over and thousands of brothers were dispersing all over Europe, he resolved to go for retreat to a solitary mountain in Tuscany, Mount La Verna, a gift to his order from the Count Orlando who lived in a castle nearby. This time he was too ill to make the journey on foot. Anxiety and physical exhaustion had taken their toll. His eyes suffered painfully from trachoma, yet he planned to fast and pray for the six weeks up to the Festival of St Michael and All Angels. With his most trusted companions – Leo, Masseo and Angelo – he made the ascent. He had a little cell made somewhat apart from the others, approached by a plank bridge across a chasm in the rock. Only Leo was allowed to come there to bring him food.

From that high lookout he seemed to survey the whole world. He prayed for the Brothers in all the lands to which they had carried his message. He prayed for their continuing faithfulness to the rule of poverty. 'Lord, I commit to thee the family thou has given me. I cannot lead them any more myself.'

But, as ever, his preoccupation was with the suffering of Christ. Leo heard him exclaim: 'Weep hills, weep mountains! Rocks rend yourselves, valleys heave deep sighs, because Love is not loved.' As the weeks of vigil wore on, Francis began to pray more boldly: 'Lord Jesus, I beg of thee two favours before I die – that I may feel in my soul and body the suffering that thou didst endure in thy passion; and that I may receive in my heart that exceeding love for us sinners by which thou wast inflamed.'

What happened early the next morning was retold by the companions as he related to them. As he prayed he saw a six-winged seraph coming slowly from heaven bearing the image of a crucified man. As he gazed, Francis was filled with fear, joy, sorrow and wonder, and at once in his hands and his feet and his side wounds began to appear, red and bleeding, with the heads of the nails sticking out. It was during this time that Francis broke into one of his spontaneous songs of praise which he immediately after transcribed on a sheet of parchment. Then, sensing that his beloved Leo felt that this strange glory had distanced them from each other, Francis turned the parchment over and wrote on the other side: 'The Lord bless you and keep you; the Lord show his face to you and have on mercy on you. The Lord turn his countenance to you and give you peace. Brother Leo, may our Lord bless you.' And through the letters of Leo's name he drew the T-shaped cross and handed the parchment to him.

Soon after his painful journey back to the Portiuncula, Francis stayed for a while at the Convent with the Poor Clares. He was nearly blind, could not walk unaided and was desperately sick, but his voice remained strong and clear. After a dream of great spiritual encouragement, he wrote his Canticle of Praise for All Creatures, giving praise to God for all aspects of creation, calling them his Sisters and Brothers.

Soon he was to encounter Brother Fire more intimately. Cardinal Hugolino arranged for him to consult an oculist in his beloved Rieti to see if the severe pain in his eyes could be alleviated. According to the practice of those days, the doctor undertook to cauterize his temples. As Francis prepared for the ordeal, he spoke to the brazier in which the iron was heating: 'O my Brother Fire, among all creatures most noble and useful, be courteous to me in this hour, for I have ever loved thee for love of him who created thee.'

The operation was useless and brought no relief. Yet Hugolino urged him on to visit other doctors in Siena. But it became all too obvious that Francis was dying. Brother Elias brought him back to Assisi to lodge in Bishop Guido's house. He rallied enough to be moved down to the Little Portion in the valley. Halfway down the hill, Francis asked them to stop so that he might look back at Assisi. There he blessed the little town. 'Blessed be thou by God, O holy city, because many true servants of God shall dwell in thee and through thee many will be elected to the Kingdom of eternal life. Peace be with thee.'

Now everyone in the city was thinking of little else but the small chapel hidden in the haze of the valley. They knew that at his request Francis had been laid on the bare ground under the trees. He had kept faith with his Lady Poverty to the end.

It was the evening of 3 October 1226. He was only 44. A multitude of larks were singing in the sky above him; and, as he died, men said, the bell of San Stephano up in the city tolled of its own accord. Since then, other bells have rung in his memory. By day and night the hours are struck on two of them, one at each end of Assisi: from the great Basilica which Elias had built and, a moment later, a clear silvery voice joins in from the convent church of Santa Chiara beside the old San Georgio square where Clare's body lies and where her sisters continue her life of prayer and simplicity.

Yet it is not in splendid buildings that their spirit is to be found, but in every living thing that proclaims the humility and the freedom and the fragility of the eternal love. This is the wisdom and the power of God – 'as sorrowful, yet always rejoicing, as poor yet making many rich, as having nothing and yet possessing all things'.

The story of St Clare (1194–1253)
Frances Teresa OSC

And so at last we come to Clare, the help-mate, the 'little plant of the Blessed Father Francis' (Rule of Clare, 1.1), the woman of courage and silence, the one who understood Francis better than anyone else, perhaps even, better than he did himself. Clare was the one who shared and never forgot that original vision of Gospel living, who had been called by the same Holy Spirit to the same form of life, as the friars once reminded Francis when she wanted him to visit San Damiano and he never got round to it. Clare, every bit as much as Francis, was taken up by the Church after her death and presented as a model for others, and in the process her originality and her genius were so eroded that she was, for many years, numbered among the saints of the Benedictine Order. Clare, every bit as much as Francis, remains for us as the image of a faithful love which endures whatever comes, one who shared as profoundly in his sufferings as she had shared in his inspiration.

Clare was born into the aristocratic Offreduccio family of Assisi in 1194, so Francis was about thirteen years the elder, a big enough gap that he could be her mentor, a small enough gap that she could be his true companion. In the great social upheaval when Francis and his friends were picketing the Rocca and smashing its walls and its might, Clare and her family fled to the 'traditional enemy' Perugia and found refuge with another noble family. There she met two other small girls, Filippa and Benvenuta, and the three became life-long friends. These little girls grew up and followed Clare to San Damiano, Benvenuta in the September, and Filippa (after some persuasion by Clare) about four years later. To the end, they were her closest companions; to Filippa she confided her great dream about herself and Francis (Canonization Process, 3.29), and these two friends were as faithful as she was herself, to the vision and the dream.

Finally the Offreduccio family made its way back from Perugia to Assisi, to the family house next to San Rufino cathedral, which Clare's grandfather had re-built (and a document exists to this day which he signed with other nobles of Assisi, undertaking that their houses would not become taller than the cathedral). There she was trained by her mother, Ortolana (which means the gardener) to 'raise up those members of his body who were failing' (3Ag, 8). This was the time of Francis' dramatic confrontation with his father and his total renunciation before Bishop Guido. It was the time when he was learning how to speak to the people and when the citizens of Assisi were changing their minds about him. All this was the stuff of local news which Clare surely heard. We also know that she had listened to him preach in the cathedral one day and had been much moved. As far as we know, her earliest link with him had been when she was about 12 and had sent money to him and his brothers while they were repairing the Portiuncula chapel.

Years later, as part of the process of canonization, the

Church sought the testimony of those who had known Clare as a young girl. Some invaluable evidence was given by Ioanni de Ventura, who had been a family servant in the household and a nightwatchman. He speaks of her respectfully as 'madonna Chiara' indicating her noble status, and gives us the names of her father, grandfather and great-grandfather: Favarone di Offreduccio di Bernardino. Medieval society thought of itself as having been made by God in three parts, composed of those who prayed, those who fought and those who worked. Ioanni de Ventura makes it clear that Clare's family were among the *bellatores*, the fighters. The men were naturally violent, as her story will reveal, they were combative and aggressive, although for about a hundred years or so men had begun to learn the skills and delights of writing poetry and song. The nobility were now to be found among the troubadours and singers of Southern France whose songs were sung throughout Western Europe. Yet this poetic imagination imposed its own restrictions, especially on the women who became symbols of unattainable love, and who were required to live up to their image in numerous ways. So fathers, brothers and uncles were passionate defenders of their women's virtue while their own imaginations were flooded with tales of the Holy Grail and the knightly quest. Among the qualities required of women were beauty, courtesy, wisdom and good reputation – all qualities attributed to the young Clare.

At 17 or 18 Clare was potentially a great success in any arena – but she had already chosen her own. She had heard Francis preach several times and he had heard of her reputation and longed to win her for Christ – not realizing that Christ had already spoken for himself. Beatrice, Clare's younger blood sister, tells us (Canonization Process, 12.2–3):

> After St Francis heard of the fame of her holiness, he went many times to preach to her, so that the virgin Clare acquiesced to his preaching, renounced the world and all earthly

things and went to serve God as soon as she was able. After that she sold her inheritance and part of that of the witness (Beatrice) and gave it to the poor.

Among the aristocratic families of central Italy at that time there had been a shift from the Germanic custom of the husband paying a 'bride price' to that of the bride bringing a dowry to the marriage. This dowry was sometimes, though not necessarily, handed over to the girl on the death of her father, and sometimes at the time of marriage and sometimes when the girl reached marriageable age, and it would most likely have been 'moveable' goods, jewellery, clothes and so on. These Clare sold and gave the proceeds to the poor.

On Palm Sunday morning in 1212, as she had arranged with Francis, Clare went to Mass in the cathedral, beautifully dressed in her best and richest clothes. This was her farewell to secular life. Shyly, she did not go up to receive her palm and the irascible old bishop, who was so good to them both, brought it down to her in her place. That night, Clare left her family home, as Sister Cristiana tells us (Canonization Process, 13):

> Because she did not want to leave through the usual exit (perhaps because of Ioanni de Ventura?), fearing her way would be blocked, she went out by the house's other exit which had been barricaded with heavy wooden beams and an iron bar so it could not be opened even by a large number of men. She alone, with the help of Jesus Christ, removed them and opened the door. On the following morning, when many people saw the door opened, they were astonished at how a young girl could have done it. Asked how she knew these things she replied that she, the witness, was in the house at that time . . .

She went down the narrow streets and out of the Porta Moiana which was not shut because it was under repair. From there she ran across the wooded plain to the Portiuncula where

Francis and the brothers were waiting for her (Canonization Process, 12):

> Then St Francis gave her the tonsure before the altar in the church of the Virgin Mary called the Portiuncula, and then sent her to the church of San Paolo de Abbadesse.

This was a Benedictine monastery, then about four kilometres from Assisi, though now a suburb of that city. Its powerful privileges of sanctuary had recently been re-confirmed by Innocent III and included excommunication for those who used violence in that place. Clare's position there is unclear, but she was not a postulant. Since she had no dowry it is possible that she stayed there as a servant, really surrendering herself to her call to leave all *nobilitas*, all privilege, and share with Christ in his self-emptying, like him 'taking the form of a servant'. The parallel with Francis' story is clear (1Cel, 16):

> Eventually he arrived at a cloister of monks, where he spent several days covered only with a cheap shirt, serving as a scullery boy in the kitchen.

We can safely take it that Clare was aware of these echoes. She and Francis were on a shared and parallel quest. Each recognized their own calling in the other and they grew together in their understanding of the will of God as a result.

The assumption that Clare was some kind of servant at San Paolo is reinforced by the monastery's complete lack of support for her – in spite of their massive and powerful privileges around the right of sanctuary. To cling to the altar cloth is the classic action of claiming sanctuary, but it brought her no response from the monastery. The standing army, kept for the purpose of defending the privileges of sanctuary, was not mobilized on her behalf. Just as Francis had been led among the lepers by God, so Clare had now embarked on a life-long journey into *vilitas*, or powerlessness, though at that stage she can have had no idea how it would work out in the years to come. The *Legend* tells us what happened next (*Legend of Clare*, 9):

> After the news reached her relatives, they condemned with a broken heart the deed and the proposal of the virgin, and banding together as one, they ran to the place, attempting to obtain what they could not. They employed violent force, poisonous advice and flattering promises, persuading her to give up such a worthless deed that was unbecoming to her class and without precedence in her family. But taking hold of the altar cloths, she bared her head, maintaining that she would in no way be torn away from the service of Christ. With the increasing violence of her relatives, her spirit grew and her love – provoked by injuries – provided strength. So for many days, even though she endured an obstacle in the way of the Lord, and her own relatives opposed her proposal of holiness, her spirit did not crumble and her fervour did not diminish. Instead, amid words and deeds of hatred, she moulded her spirit anew in hope until her relatives, turning back, were quiet.

The liturgy at the Portiuncula had not introduced Clare into the monastic life, but into the life of a penitent. As far as we know, she made no other profession, even though for many years she lived under the Rule of St Benedict. It is hardly surprising that she was not happy at San Paolo and, as Beatrice tells us (Canonization Process, 12):

> St Francis, Brother Philip and Brother Bernard took her to the church of Sant'Angela di Panzo, where she stayed for a little time, and then to the church of San Damiano where the Lord gave her more sisters for her direction.

At both San Paolo and at Sant'Angela, Clare was simply a penitent, like Francis and the brothers. At Sant'Angela, however, her younger and closest sister Catherine joined her, which created even greater family uproar, for she was only 16 (*Legend of Clare*, 25):

> Twelve men, burning with anger and outwardly hiding their evil intent, ran to the place and pretended to make a peaceful entrance. Immediately they turned to Agnes (as Catherine was later called) – since they had long ago lost hope of Clare – and said: 'Why have you come to this place? Get ready to return with us immediately.' When she responded that she did not want to leave her sister Clare, one of the knights in a fierce mood ran towards her and, without sparing kicks and blows, tried to drag her away by the hair while others pushed her and lifted her in their arms. At this, as if she had been captured by lions and been torn from the hands of the Lord, the young girl cried out: 'Dear sister, help me! Do not let me be taken from Christ the Lord!'
>
> While the violent robbers were dragging the young girl along the slope of the mountain, ripping her clothes and strewing the path with the hair they had torn out, Clare prostrated herself in prayer with tears, begging that her sister would be given constancy of mind and the strength of humans would be overcome by divine power. Suddenly Agnes' body lying on the ground seemed so heavy that the men, many as they were, exerted all their energy and were not able to carry her beyond a certain stream. [. . .] After the long struggle, Clare came to the place and asked her relatives to give up such a conflict and to entrust Agnes, half-dead on the ground, to her care. After they departed with bitter spirit at their unfinished business, Agnes got up joyfully and gave herself perpetually to the divine service. In fact, blessed Francis cut off her hair with his own hand and directed her together with her sister in the way of the Lord.

From this moment on, Clare ceased to be a solitary penitent and began to move into a new form of life in community.

Bishop Guido gave them the little church of San Damiano which Francis had repaired, and there she found peace of soul. Pacifica soon joined her, together with Benvenuta. They would have been more like what we today would consider a diocesan congregation, living in community with the knowledge and approval of the local bishop, under the direction of a lay penitent, Francis, but following no approved rule. The earliest account of their lives is that of Jacques de Vitry, Bishop of Acre in the Holy Land, who stopped in Perugia on his way to his new See. Jacques had been very involved with the Beguine movement in Liège, and was always interested in new forms of consecrated life. He seems to suggest that both the brothers and the sisters worked in local hospices, returning to their monasteries at night. Certainly, there is a strong oral tradition in Assisi that Clare and her sisters worked among the lepers. Since this was such a powerful factor in early Franciscan life, it is not impossible. On the road from Portiuncula to Rivo Torto, there is a small chapel called La Maddalena, which was the chapel of the women lepers. It is not far from San Damiano and if Clare and the others did indeed go out to work with lepers, this could well have been their centre of operations.

In 1216, Clare came to the crisis point in her journey. Some years earlier, Cardinal Hugolino had been deputed by the Pope to organize and regularize the many, very varied, groups of religious women in and around the Valley of Spoleto. This he did with great acumen and enthusiasm, writing constitutions for them based on the Rule of St Benedict, establishing strict enclosure and placing the communities on a firm financial basis. When he finally came to San Damiano on his travels, and met Clare, he was bowled over by her. Was it at this point that he conceived the idea of a new Order of religious women, founded by himself with Clare at its head? Modern research strongly suggests that this was so (see, for example, the work of J. Grundmann, Raoul Manselli, Marco Bartoli, and Maria Pia Alberzoni, among others). Francis, meanwhile, had been caught up in the post-conciliar situation and, like Clare, had given his energies to implementing its decrees. (It is in this connection that we need to read the stories about him cleaning up churches, or the accounts of Clare making altar linen and sending it to the local churches. These actions were part of their contribution to restoring the honour given the Eucharist.) Hugolino's dream threatened two fundamental aspects of Clare's way of life: her commitment to poverty and her link with Francis and the brothers.

To take the last first: when she had gone to San Damiano, Francis had given her and Agnes a form of life which was almost certainly based on that verbally approved for the brothers by Innocent III in 1209/1210. Although other Rules were to come and go in her life, for Clare this was what she had promised Francis and this was the form of her life to the end. She began to live up to her early promise of obstinacy! Clare considered that she and her sisters were of one group with Francis and his brothers. This was the medieval understanding of the phrase 'to promise obedience', which Clare used of her action in the Portiuncula on that Palm Sunday night. So to be channelled off into the Order of St Benedict meant an abandonment of what she and the others had undertaken before God, and paid so high a price for with their families. It is possible that Francis had never really believed the sisters to be able to live the kind of radical dispossession that was open to the brothers in their mendicant way of life. This is probably what Clare was referring to in the Rule (Ch 6) about Francis seeing for himself that they were able to rejoice in being despised, in bearing hardship, scorn and all sorts of troubles. Perhaps he did not believe in the project but believed in Clare. Whatever was in his mind, it seems that he was not fully aware of the repercussions for Clare in accepting Hugolino's proposal. She saw clearly that she would cease to be a simple penitent living the Gospel in poverty, and become a religious with all the expectations of the time. Francis, we are told, almost forced her to become abbess, that is, the superior of a religious community and to this day we do not really know the inner substance of their dialogue.

The second matter, poverty, needs to be placed within the changing situation of the poor in medieval society. In the rural society of the high Middle Ages, poverty had largely affected individuals living in the country, but the development of the towns and cities had changed all that. Now there was an urban poor living with a frightening lack of resources or support. M. Mollatt ('La notion de la pauvreté au Moyen Age', in *Revue d'Histoire de l'Eglise de France*, 52, 1966) tells us:

> The static and individual misery of the country was changed into the collective misery of the city. The rural poor were generally disadvantaged people who were well-known locally and helped by their own families. The urban poor became, in a sense, anonymous, often homeless with no other refuge than that which others in the same situation would share with them.

This new kind of poverty posed new problems for the Church. Those groups which sought to return to the basics of the Gospel came to understand the option for poverty as fundamental, rather as Helder Camara in our own day has spoken of the need for the Church to be seen to share the poverty of the dispossessed and not to hand out the Word of God to those who are dying of hunger without also – and first – giving them bread for the body. 'Naked to follow the naked Christ' became the slogan and watchword expressing the radical absolutism of those committed to these new insights. Poverty became a way of preaching through action, especially in a world where monasticism was not notably poor, or not poor as the poor understood it. To the destitute in the cities, the communal poverty of the new movements was far more convincing than the personal poverty of the monasteries. This was certainly part of Francis' approach to poverty – there are numerous stories which illustrate his conviction that anything he had and used was only lent him until he met someone poorer who would, by definition, have the greater claim. There was a strong dimension of social awareness in both Francis' and Clare's understanding of poverty, as well as being an expression of total trust in his heavenly Father – as Francis had so publicly committed himself to do. From the start, Francis and his companions wanted to share the conditions of the most marginalized (Rule of 1221, 9.3):

> They must rejoice when they live among people considered of little value and looked down upon, among the poor and powerless, the sick and lepers, and the beggars by the wayside.

This kind of option was more difficult for Clare and her sisters, but it was important to her that their little place remained a modest construction and did not grow into a large monastery like San Paolo. In the beginning Clare and the sisters lived just the same kind of poverty as the early brothers. Although it is questioned, there is little reason to doubt that Clare petitioned Innocent III for some sort of Privilege of Poverty; although this may have carried little juridical weight, the fact of its existence would have been enough for Clare at that time. This privilege would have provided the precedent for Hugolino, as Pope Gregory IX, when he later came to re-confirm the Privilege of Poverty in the form we know it today. This was in 1228, perhaps on the same occasion as his great struggle with Clare about poverty after Francis' death. If so, it would seem that Clare was the clear victor that day, a victory for which she paid dearly in terms of being ignored and overlooked in the future. While she did accept the Constitutions of Gregory in 1216–1219, and she did accept becoming abbess, at the same time these two things were no part of her vision. She never made her peace with the Rule of St Benedict or with Hugolino's Constitutions. So much was this so that Innocent IV tried again in 1247 to find a text which she and many other communities could accept, in which he acknowledged the link with the friars but made no mention of her vision of poverty as the way to union with Christ. Much to his surprise, there was almost universal rejection of this text, beginning with Clare in Assisi and her friend and correspondent Agnes in Prague, and many others united themselves to their protest. As a result Innocent very soon withdrew his Rule, and Clare settled down to finalize a text of her own. This was a wholly new work for a woman and it would be good to know more about the process of writing this Rule, for it is clear, concise, says exactly what she wants, and strikes an inspired balance between the requirements of canon law of that time and the vision of Gospel living to which she had given her life. Not only that, but it is a Rule which works and which is still observed today by the Poor Clares who follow her.

In this Rule, with regard to poverty, she says (Rule of St Clare, 6.10–15):

> And I, together with my sisters, have always been careful to observe the holy poverty which we promised the Lord God and the blessed Francis, and in the same way the abbesses who shall succeed me in office, and all the sisters, are committed to observing it inviolably right to the end, committed, that is, to not accepting having possessions or ownership either of themselves or through another, or even anything that could reasonably be called property except as much land as necessity requires for the integrity and seclusion of the monastery, and this land may not be cultivated except as a garden for feeding the sisters.

This simple text was the fruit of long years of struggle and refinement. From 1216 and Hugolino's expanding vision of his new order, until the end of her life, she had to pursue this vision almost alone. Hugolino begged her to accept property and security, and she refused, earning his great displeasure. This was probably in 1228 when, having become Pope Gregory IX the previous year, he came to Assisi for

Francis' canonization. From that moment on, and still more after 1230, Clare moved into greater silence, became marginalized in a wholly new way. Conflicts developed between the friars who wanted to follow the directives of the Council, to teach in the schools and universities, to live in community and become a supple, available task force at the Church's disposal, and those on the other hand who longed for the days when they were brothers living in unity, when they had nothing and were happy, when they felt they were true minors and really poor, following the poor Christ. Clare remained in close touch with all those early brothers who had been her friends since the beginning, men like Leo, Rufino her cousin, Angelo who was Provincial at the time of her death, Juniper for whom she had a special affection, Philip who was chaplain to the sisters for so long, Pacificus the troubadour, as well as Bernard, Giles and many others. Above all, she kept in touch with Elias.

1226 brought Clare the major loss of Francis. Not long before he had sent her and her sisters his last will and testament:

> I, brother Francis, the little one, wish to follow the life and poverty of our most high Lord Jesus Christ, and of his most holy mother, and to persevere in it until the end, and I ask and counsel you, my ladies, to live always in this most holy life and poverty.

For Clare, these words could rank second only to the Gospel itself, and she clung to them most faithfully to the end of her life. How they must have sustained her in the conflicts to come!

By the Chapter of 1230, the Order was deep into argument and dissension. Things were so difficult that the assembled Provincials appealed to Gregory IX for some rulings. In response he wrote the decree *Quo elongati*, making numerous radical decisions for the friars in the light of his long friendship with, and presumed understanding of, Francis. Gregory's decisions focused around the relationship of Gospel and Rule, which for Francis (and Clare) were synonymous. Gregory broke this identification. In addition, he made a number of lesser rulings, including forbidding the brothers to visit the Poor Ladies. In response, Clare sent away the brothers who begged food for them too, an action which brought a swift retraction from the Pope!

From this time on, Clare and the early brothers were increasingly beleaguered as they tried to be faithful to the 'life and poverty of our most high Lord Jesus Christ, and of his most holy mother, and to persevere in it until the end'. From this time onwards, we see Clare in relation to the Order as a lonely, rather tragic figure, holding faithfully, and at great cost, to her original commitment. In a way which must surely have been wholly unanticipated, she found herself marginalized even by those whom she regarded as her brothers. It was an intense experience of *vilitas*, accentuated by her poor health. She entered further and further into the experience of the Suffering Servant whom she loved so deeply, and like him, her prayer was answered. The people of Assisi knew this well and appealed for her intercession, seeking miracles without hesitation – and without disappointment. One incident only, from the summer of 1241, can be mentioned here, chosen because it is still celebrated each year in the city of Assisi (Canonization Process, 3.19):

> The greatly feared Vitalis d'Aversa had been sent by the Emperor with a great army to assault Assisi. Since he had asserted that he would not leave Assisi until he had taken it, Lady Clare was told in order to prevent this danger. After she had heard this, the Lady – confident of God's power – called all the sisters, had them bring some ashes and covered her unveiled head with them.
>
> Then the Lady placed ashes on the heads of all the sisters and commanded them to go to prayer so the Lord God would free the city.

She learned next day that Vitalis had left by night with all his army.

In spite of her distance from some of the brothers, Clare, for the last years of her life, was a major figure on the religious scene of Europe. She was widely known and revered, not least for her support of Agnes of Prague (with whom she formed a close friendship and to whom she wrote some precious letters); and the expansion of her form of life contributed to this. By the time she died, Clare was connected in one way or another with over 200 communities. Yet within the wider Order, she was less and less central. Increasingly the friars became a mendicant Order of clerics and lay brothers and the sisters a rather unwelcome task, requiring the *cura monialum* – the care of the nuns – which so many men's orders at that time were trying to shed. As a true Franciscan, Clare seems to have devoted her energies to her own call and to her community at San Damiano. Her health became worse and worse, though we do not know enough to make a diagnosis across so many years. Miracles attended her continually, and her influence was immense. She was 'the teacher of the continent' says the Bull of Canonization.

Clare died in 1253, only a couple of days after her Rule, or form of life, had finally been approved by Innocent IV, capturing in legal form her love and dedication to the poverty of our Lord Jesus Christ, and her commitment to the band of brothers Francis had generated. By 1260, her community had yielded to pressure from Assisi and moved within its walls. In 1262, Pope Urban IV wrote another Rule and imposed it on all the communities of Poor Ladies across the world. Clare's form of life, however, spread widely, beginning with houses in France as early as 1217 and continuing to this day, for there are now several flourishing communities in Africa and Asia.

Early Franciscan sources
The Editors

St Francis left a considerable collection of writings, in addition to the Rule which he wrote in 1209, and again in 1221
and revised in 1223, and the prayers which are introduced
in Chapter 7. The earliest is a Letter to the Faithful (1 and 2
Lt F) written for that early group of penitents who came to
him for instruction in the Gospel life. It has been related to,
and therefore taken up as, an introduction to the Rule of the
Secular Franciscan Order. He wrote letters to the Clergy, to
the Custodians of the Lesser Brothers, to the Rulers of the
People and a Rule for Hermitages. He also wrote twenty-eight
Admonitions, containing reflections and teachings on biblical
themes. In 1225–6 he prepared a Letter to the Entire Order
and finally, in the year of his death, the Testament which
begins, 'The Lord gave me, Brother Francis, thus to begin
doing penance in this way: for when I was in sin, it seemed
too bitter for me to see lepers. And the Lord himself led me
among them . . .'

Following their deaths the stories of Francis and Clare
began to spread, both orally and in written form. Some of the
more significant writings are noted here.

Behind *The Legend of the Three Companions* is thought
to be the witness of Br Angelo of Tancredi who knew Francis
and his family from childhood. He shared the time of impris-
onment with Francis in Perugia in 1203, and attested to his
stigmata after the saint's death. Also associated with this
work are Rufino and Leo, and the three, along with Masseo,
are buried in four niches down in the crypt of the Basilica
around the altar and tomb of St Francis. The Chapter of the
Brothers in 1244 requested an account of the life and miracles
of St Francis, and thus it provides an early sketch of the Order
in its earliest times.

The Mirror of Perfection is believed to be less authentic, or
more problematic for scholars. Paul Sabatier was the first to

produce an edition in 1897 from discovered early manuscripts, said to be under the authorship of Br Leo. Throughout, the writer is expressly encouraging the brothers to follow that light thrown onto the pages of the Gospel by their holy father Francis.

The collection known as *The Legend of Perugia* was discovered in the fourteenth century, and probably provided material for Celano's Second Life. It is thought that this may be the work of Leo, Rufino and Angelo, and that it had been part of a larger compilation included with *The Legend of the Three Companions*.

Br Thomas of Celano was a priest and a scholar who was commissioned to write the first formal and official biography, known as the *First Life of St Francis* (1Cel), in about 1228. Not always accurate, it appears he did not consult the early followers, Leo, Angelo and Rufino. His *Second Life of St Francis* (2Cel) was prompted by the 1244 Chapter's request for material about Francis, and appeared around 1248. It is concluded by some that Celano wrote the first biographical work about St Clare.

In 1260 the General Chapter of the Friars at Narbonne issued a directive, 'we order that a good "Legend of St Francis" be written, based on all those already in existence', and as Minister General at the time Bonaventure was entrusted with the task. It was felt that there had been significant changes in the development of the Order and that the founder needed to be presented to the next generation in a way that distinguished the saint from their own less heroic witness, and as the need grew to transform the fraternity into an Order. *The Major Life of St Francis* (LM) was completed in 1263 and replaced Celano's and all other writings as the official Life. Nevertheless his sources must have been primarily from Celano. It was not written with a historical accent and there is evidence of some magnification of earlier accounts, such as may be observed in his detailed description of the stigmata. His clear motivation which can be traced through his work was to restore a measure of order in the ranks of the community, and so he presents Francis as a mediator of peace and reconciliation. A *Minor Life of St Francis* (LMin) was written for liturgical use and is very much shorter, compassing seven brief chapters.

The earliest manuscript of *The Little Flowers* (Fior), in Latin, is dated 1396, and goes out of its way to expand the popular devotion to the saint, describing in many stories how Francis and some of the early friars witnessed to the simplest and direct following of Gospel precepts in the way of the Incarnate and Crucified Christ. The names of Leo, Masseo, Giles and Clare are associated with this collection, having been passed down through several generations. It has become the best-known collection of stories and anecdotes of Francis and his followers, told in a lovely but colourful medieval style. It has been translated into several languages.

3

Living the Gospel: the Rule of St Francis and its Development

+John Jukes OFM Conv

Influence of the Rule of 1223

One of the most significant documents to illuminate the life of the world-wide Church is the thirteenth-century Rule of St Francis of Assisi. In this relatively short document there is encapsulated the inspiration and example of St Francis in his desire to follow Jesus Christ, the poor and suffering saviour, as closely as he could. For almost eight hundred years, the Rule has been a foundation of the life of the brothers who followed Francis in his own time down to the many thousands who belong to the First Order of St Francis in its many forms throughout the world today. Partly through the text of this Rule, St Francis inspired the other Rules written by St Clare of Assisi who followed him in the life of poverty and self-denial. The Rule of St Francis also acts as a guide for the members of the Third Order Regular, women and men. Furthermore, it serves as an inspiration to those dedicated individuals of what is known today as the Secular Order or Third Order of St Francis, who, while staying in the world, shape their lives according to the principles that Francis established in following Jesus Christ in his poverty and suffering.

We are most fortunate in having the actual document giving the text of the Rule of Life of the Friars Minor, approved by Pope Honorius III in 1223. However, to help us understand that text, we need to know something of the way in which that Rule came to be composed.

The Primitive Rule

As the earliest biographer of St Francis, Thomas of Celano, notes, 'When blessed Francis saw the Lord God was daily increasing their numbers, he wrote for himself and his brothers present and future simply and in a few words, "a form of life and rule".' He used primarily words of the holy Gospel, longing only for its perfection. He inserted a few other things necessary for the practice of a holy way of life. Then he went to Rome with all his brothers, since he greatly desired that the Lord Pope Innocent III confirm for him what he had written. The Pope gave his approval to this simple Rule either in 1209 or 1210 (sometimes referred to as the Primitive Rule). It acted as a focal point for Francis and his small band of brothers who were seeking to live according to the simplicity of the Gospel.

The Primitive Rule probably contained many challenging verses, directly lifted from the Gospels themselves, exhorting the brothers to put their whole trust in God's provision for their bodily needs, and how to live in the divine presence, power and purity, as expressed, for instance, in the Beatitudes and the direction to take up the cross day by day.

Attempt to expand the Rule

Francis was immensely successful in inspiring others to follow Jesus. Inevitably, as the fraternity grew, a greater need for some form of further regulation developed. By the year 1221 the Order had grown to such an extent that there were several thousand friars. A Rule was therefore developed which is known as the Unapproved Rule (RegNB) which consisted of 24 chapters. However, this Rule was found to be too long, detailed and without sufficient focus upon the urgent needs of the brethren, and so amendments to it were made and the text shortened.

Adoption of the Rule of 1223

Eventually the new Rule (RegB) was submitted to Pope Honorius III, who on 29 November 1223 placed his seal upon the revised text. This actual document still exists and is preserved in the sacristy of the Basilica of St Francis in Assisi, the church in which Francis' body was eventually buried. It consists of 12 chapters and has an attractive quality, as it attracts, challenges and encourages. It also warns against the harsh imposition of its demands, preferring to give to the brother opportunity to volunteer his response of poverty and to avoid judgementalism. 'But let them be meek, peaceful, modest, gentle and humble, speaking courteously to everyone, as is becoming' (Chapter 3). When it was necessary to correct an occasion of failure, the minister is to act 'with a heart full of mercy', imposing a penance but with charity, 'for anger and disturbance impede charity in themselves and in others' (Chapter 7).

Even the terms used by Francis and given to those in authority within the Order avoided hierarchical attitudes: for example, general minister and provincial minister were the leaders of the fraternity, yet 'it must be that ministers are the servants of all the brothers' (Chapter 10). Each group of brothers living in a friary was to have a 'guardian', again avoiding terms which suggest superiority, like abbot or prior, with their implication that one is first or over others. In other writings of Francis, he instructs those in authority to be deeply forgiving in their dealings with the friars, as was the teaching and witness of Christ in the Gospels.

Here is the full text in its twelve chapters.

Bull of Pope Honorius III

Honorius,
Bishop, Servant of the servants of God,
to His Beloved Sons,
Brother Francis and the other brothers

of the Order of the Lesser Brothers,
Health and Apostolic Benediction.

The Apostolic See is accustomed to grant the pious requests and favourably to accede to the laudable desires of its petitioners. Therefore, beloved sons in the Lord, attentive to your pious prayers, We confirm with our Apostolic Authority, and by these words ratify, the Rule of your Order, herein outlined and approved by Our predecessor, Pope Innocent of happy memory, which is as follows:

Chapter I
In the Name of the Lord:
The Life of the Lesser Brothers Begins

The Rule and Life of the Lesser Brothers is this: to observe the Holy Gospel of Our Lord Jesus Christ by living in obedience, without anything of one's own, and in chastity. Brother Francis promises obedience and reverence to our Lord Pope Honorius and his successors canonically elected and to the Roman Church. Let the other brothers be bound to obey Brother Francis and his successors.

Chapter II
Those Who Wish to Adopt This Life,
and How They Should be Received

If there are any who wish to accept this life and come to our brothers, let them send them to their provincial ministers, to whom alone and not to others is permission granted to receive the brothers. Let the ministers examine them carefully concerning the Catholic faith and the sacraments of the Church. If they believe all these things, will faithfully profess them, and steadfastly observe them to the end; and if they have no wives, or if they have wives who have already taken a vow of continence and are of such an age that suspicion cannot be raised about them, and who have already entered a monastery or have given their husbands permission by the authority of the bishop of the diocese, let the ministers speak to them the words of the Holy Gospel that they go and sell all they have and take care to give it to the poor. If they cannot do this, their good will may suffice. Let the brothers and the minister be careful not to interfere with their temporal goods that they may dispose of their belongings as the Lord inspires them. If, however, counsel is sought, the minister may send them to some God-fearing persons according to whose advice their goods may be distributed to the poor.

Then they may be given the clothes of probation, namely, two tunics without a hood, a cord, short trousers, and a little cape reaching to the cord, unless, at times, it seems good to these same ministers, before God, to act otherwise. When the year of probation has come to an end, they may be received into obedience promising always to observe this rule and life. On no account shall it be lawful for them to leave this Order, according to the decree of our Lord the Pope, for, according to the Gospel: no one who puts a hand to the plough and looks to what is left behind is fit for the kingdom of God.

Those who have already promised obedience may have one tunic with a hood and another, if they wish, without a hood. And those who are compelled by necessity may wear shoes. Let all the brothers wear poor clothes and they may mend them with pieces of sackcloth or other material with the blessing of God. I admonish and exhort them not to look down upon or judge those whom they see dressed in soft and fine clothes and enjoying the choicest food and drink, but rather let everyone judge and look down upon himself.

Chapter III
The Divine Office, Fasting,
and How the Brothers Should Go About in the World

Let the clerical (brothers) recite the Divine Office according to the rite of the holy Roman Church excepting the psalter, for which reason they may have breviaries. The lay (brothers), however, may say twenty-four Our Fathers for Matins, and five for Lauds; seven for each of the Hours of Prime, Terce, Sext, and None, twelve for Vespers, and seven for Compline. Let them pray for the dead. Let them fast from the feast of All Saints until the Lord's Nativity. May those be blessed by the Lord who fast voluntarily during that holy Lent that begins at the Epiphany and lasts during the forty days which our Lord consecrated by His own fast; but those who do not wish to keep it will not be obliged. Let them fast, however, during the other (Lent) until the Lord's Resurrection. At other times they may not be bound to fast except on Fridays. During a time of obvious need, however, the brothers may not be bound by corporal fast.

I counsel, admonish and exhort my brothers in the Lord Jesus Christ not to quarrel or argue or judge others when they go about in the world; but let them be meek, peaceful, modest, gentle, and humble, speaking courteously to everyone, as is becoming. They should not ride horseback unless they are compelled by an obvious need or an infirmity. Into whatever house they enter, let them first say: 'Peace be to this house!' According to the Holy Gospel, let them eat whatever food is set before them.

Chapter IV
Let the Brothers Never Receive Money

I strictly command all my brothers not to receive coins or money in any form, either personally or through intermediaries. Nevertheless, the ministers and custodians alone may take special care through their spiritual friends to provide for the needs of the sick and the clothing of the others according to places, seasons and cold climates, as they judge necessary, saving always that, as stated above, they do not receive coins or money.

Chapter V
The Manner of Working

Those brothers to whom the Lord has given the grace of working may work faithfully and devotedly so that, while avoiding idleness, the enemy of the soul, they do not extinguish the Spirit of holy prayer and devotion to which all temporal things must contribute.

In payment of their work they may receive whatever is necessary for the bodily support of themselves and their brothers, excepting coin or money, and let them do this humbly as is becoming for servants of God and followers of most holy poverty.

Chapter VI
Let the Brothers Not Make Anything Their Own;
Begging Alms; the Sick Brothers

Let the brothers not make anything their own, neither house, nor place, nor anything at all. As pilgrims and strangers in this world, serving the Lord in poverty and humility, let them go seeking alms with confidence, and they should not be ashamed because, for our sakes, our Lord made himself poor in this world. This is that sublime height of most exalted poverty which has made you, my most beloved brothers, heirs and kings of the Kingdom of Heaven, poor in temporal things but exalted in virtue. Let this be your portion which leads into the land of the living. Giving yourselves totally to this, beloved brothers, never seek anything else under heaven for the name of our Lord Jesus Christ.

Wherever the brothers may be and meet one another, let them show that they are members of the same family. Let each one confidently make known his need to the other, for if a mother loves and cares for her son according to the flesh, how much more diligently must someone love and care for his brother according to the Spirit! When any brother falls sick, the other brothers must serve him as they would wish to be served themselves.

Chapter VII
The Penance To Be Imposed on the Brothers Who Sin

If any brother, at the instigation of the enemy, sins mortally in regard to those sins concerning which it has been decreed among the brothers to have recourse only to the provincial ministers, let him have recourse as quickly as possible and without delay. If these ministers are priests, with a heart full of mercy let them impose on him a penance; but, if the ministers are not priests, let them have it imposed by others who are priests of the Order, as in the sight of God appears to them more expedient. They must be careful not to be angry or disturbed at the sin of another, for anger and disturbance impede charity in themselves and in others.

Chapter VIII
The Election of the General Minister of This Fraternity and the Chapter of Pentecost

Let all the brothers always be bound to have one of the brothers of this Order as general minister and servant of the whole fraternity and let them be strictly bound to obey him. When he dies, let the election of his successor be made by the provincial ministers and custodians in the Chapter of Pentecost, at which all the provincial ministers are bound to assemble in whatever place the general minister may have designated. Let them do this once in every three years, or at other longer or shorter intervals, as determined by the aforesaid minister. If, at any time, it appears to the body of the provincial ministers and custodians that the aforesaid general minister is not qualified for the service and general welfare of the brothers, let the aforesaid brothers, to whom the election is committed, be bound to elect another as custodian in the name of the Lord.

Moreover, after the Chapter of Pentecost, the provincial ministers and custodians may each, if they wish and it seems expedient to them, convoke a Chapter of the brothers in their custodies once in the same year.

Chapter IX
Preachers

The brothers may not preach in the diocese of any bishop when he has opposed their doing so. And let none of the brothers dare to preach in any way to the people unless he has been examined and approved by the general minister of this fraternity and the office of preacher has been conferred upon him.

Moreover, I admonish and exhort those brothers that when they preach their language be well considered and chaste for the benefit and edification of the people, announcing to them vices and virtues, punishment and glory, with brevity, because our Lord when on earth kept his words brief.

Chapter X
The Admonition and Correction of the Brothers

Let the brothers who are the ministers and servants of the others visit and admonish their brothers and humbly and charitably correct them, not commanding them anything that is against their soul and our rule. Let the brothers who are subject, however, remember that, for God's sake, they have renounced their own wills. Therefore, I strictly command them to obey their ministers in everything they have promised the Lord to observe and which is not against their soul or our Rule.

Wherever the brothers may be who know and feel they cannot observe the Rule spiritually, they can and should have recourse to their ministers. Let the ministers, moreover, receive them charitably and kindly and have such familiarity with them that these same brothers may speak and deal with them as masters with their servants, for so it must be that the ministers are the servants of all the brothers.

Moreover, I admonish and exhort the brothers in the Lord Jesus Christ to beware of all pride, vainglory, envy and greed, of care and solicitude for the things of this world, of detraction and murmuring. Let those who are illiterate not be anxious to learn, but let them pay attention to what they must desire above all else: to have the Spirit of the Lord and its holy activity, to pray always to him with a pure heart, to have humility and patience in persecution and infirmity, and to love those who persecute, rebuke and find fault with us, because the Lord says: Love your enemies and pray for those who persecute and calumniate you. Blessed are those who suffer persecution for the sake of justice, for theirs is the kingdom of heaven. But whoever perseveres to the end will be saved.

Chapter XI
The Brothers May Not Enter the Monasteries of Nuns

I strictly command all the brothers not to have any suspicious dealings or conversations with women, and they may not enter the monasteries of nuns, excepting those brothers to whom special permission has been granted by the Apostolic See; and they may not be godfathers to men or women, so that scandal may not arise among the brothers or concerning them on account of this.

Chapter XII
Those Going Among the Saracens and Other Non-Believers

Let those brothers who wish by divine inspiration to go among the Saracens or other non-believers ask permission to go from their provincial ministers. The ministers, however, may not grant permission except to those whom they see fit to be sent.

In addition to these points, I command the ministers through obedience to petition from our Lord the Pope for one of the Cardinals of the Holy Roman Church, who would be the governor, protector and corrector of this fraternity, so that, being always submissive and subject at the feet of the same Holy Church and steadfast in the Catholic Faith, we may observe poverty, humility, and the Holy Gospel of our Lord Jesus Christ as we have firmly promised.

It is forbidden, therefore, for anyone to tamper with this decree which we have confirmed, or rashly dare to oppose it. If anyone presume to attempt this, let him know that he shall incur the anger of Almighty God and of his blessed Apostles Peter and Paul.

Given at the Lateran, the twenty-ninth day of November, in the eighth year of Our pontificate.

Development of the Rule

Such was the standing of the Rule and its significance to the brothers that there has never been a direct change to the Rule itself. Rather, as the number of friars grew and their experience of the world and serving the Church increased, the friars adopted the device of writing other documents, often known as Constitutions, which dealt with newly arising questions of how to live the way of life originally traced out by Francis in the first quarter of the thirteenth century. Each of the families of the Franciscan First Order today, that is the Order of Friars Minor, the Conventual Friars (OFM Conv) and the Capuchin Friars (OFM Cap), therefore observe this Rule as interpreted by their respective constitutions and other legal documents. Such additional material marks the changes necessary to adjust the life of the community to the changes in the Church and the needs of people the friars are called to serve. The basic Rule, however, remains untouched as the permanent inspiration and guide to the friars to the way in which they should follow the inspiration they received from the Little Poor Man of Assisi.

The Rule of Poor Clares

The Rule of St Francis was so powerful and his example so significant that Clare, with her companions who left the security of their own homes to follow in the way of Francis, used the Rule as a basis for developing their own rules of life and the documents that would guide them in meeting the challenges of the thirteenth century, in which the Second Order, the Order of Poor Clares, was established. Clare and her companions faced a rather different challenge from Francis and his brothers. From the earliest days, because of the social restraints of the time, Clare and her followers, whilst inspired by St Francis in their living out of a life of poverty, abnegation and self-help, were not freely able to wander about the world of their time. Therefore they adopted a settled and enclosed form of life, which has endured to this present time. Many efforts were used to induce Clare and her immediate followers to abandon the total self-denial and refusal to own property that she wished for herself and her sisters. After much discussion, and indeed difficulty, Clare eventually, and just before her death, obtained from the Pope the permission and privilege to live without property in her community. Down to this day there are a number of communities of Poor Clares who follow in the same line of total rejection of property as introduced by Clare and her sisters. This means that they simply occupy and use such places in which they lead their own enclosed life of prayer and self-denial. St Clare's Rule is very much poised on this point, yet takes much of its inspiration from the original Rule of St Francis.

The Third Order Rules

The attractiveness of the life and person of Francis of Assisi, with the obvious dedication and self-denial of Clare, had a great influence upon those who were not free to abandon their home duties or their work in society. In time, many did choose to follow as professed religious in community according to a Third Order Rule. However, many others, attracted to the Franciscan witness but remaining in their secular context, took to themselves the inspiration given them by Francis to follow Christ in poverty and humility. These men and women adopted various forms of Rule which became known as the Rules of the Third Order of St Francis. The Order was first known as the Order of Penitents. Today they are known in the Roman tradition as the Secular Franciscan Order (SFO), the Anglican branch taking the name Tertiary (TSSF). These Rules have received considerable amendment over time but they are united in their general approach of encouraging the followers of the Rules to live lives of Gospel simplicity, poverty, self-sacrifice, and taking on a discipline of prayer. It is intended that they may thus be marked with the Franciscan notes of humility, love and joy.

Conclusion

The theme running through the Rules of all three Orders based on the inspiration of Francis is that of humility and self-denial, following Jesus Christ in the obscurity of his private life before he embarked upon his public ministry. The Rules are an essential point of departure in that they offer a fixed point from which those who feel moved and called to live a more direct response to the Gospel of Jesus Christ, may refer in working out the manner and style in which they are to attempt this inspiration and vocation.

4

The Rule of St Clare

An Introduction
Frances Teresa OSC

The Rule of St Clare had a much longer and more difficult period of development than the two rules of Francis, although she seems to have been spared one dimension which he must have found particularly painful, namely that much of Francis' opposition came from his own friars. Clare, as far as we know from the sources, had her sisters solidly behind her, but she encountered opposition from that quarter where Francis experienced most support, namely the papacy. It is a tribute to Clare's remarkable tenacity and stability of vision that she was happy with the final redaction of her Rule, or at least, as we would say today, she felt she could live with it, although in fact she died within 48 hours of receiving the pope's approval.

A short history of legislation for Clare

When Clare began her life at San Damiano, she was given a *forma vitae* by Francis. The text of this is lost but two possibilities present themselves. One is that it was an adaptation of the so-called Proto-Rule of Francis, that text which Innocent III approved for him in 1208. Another is that the Form of Life he gave her was based on what we now call the Rule for Hermitages. Certainly it would be more accurate to say that Clare was living *in eremo*, in hermitage, like the brothers in the Carceri, on La Verna or at Fonte Colombo than to say she was living in enclosure as we know it today. Of the ten verses in Francis' Rule for Hermitages, almost every one has its counterpart in the Rule of Clare. This is too much to be mere chance, and we may conclude that it is echoed in Clare's Rule because it was a significant part of the sisters' daily life. So it is not too fanciful to ask whether the Rule for Hermitages was not the basis of the Form of Life which Francis gave Clare and Agnes.

However, there must have been more, perhaps a covering letter, for Clare gives us a precious fragment in Chapter 6 when she quotes Francis:

> Because by divine inspiration you have made yourselves daughters and handmaids of the most high, most exalted King, the heavenly Father, and have taken the Holy Spirit as your spouse, choosing to live according to the perfection of the holy Gospel, I resolve and promise for myself and for my brothers always to have the same loving care and special solicitude for you as for them. (RegCl, 6:3–4)

This does not read like a rule of life but more like words of inspiration and encouragement, and containing the precious promise that he would always consider the sisters as on the same basis as the brothers. We know how important this was to Clare and how she clung to it all her life in the face of considerable opposition both from the papacy and (sometimes) from the brothers themselves.

Soon after this, in 1217, Cardinal Hugolino took up his task as legate to the many groups of religious women in north Italy. There is no room here to develop this story, simply to say that he wrote a set of Constitutions for them, based on the Rule of St Benedict, and in 1228 he finally persuaded Clare to accept them at San Damiano in exchange for the Privilege of Poverty, which, effectively, undermined Hugolino's key item of setting these communities on a firm financial basis.

After Clare had been at San Damiano for about ten years, Francis drafted his Rules which we know today as the Regula non bullata and the Regula bullata, or by their dates 1221 and 1223. Clare was very astute and well understood how official systems function and how to negotiate with them – in many ways better than Francis. She realized that if she was to gain papal approval for her form of life, then while it enshrined her vision it also had to be expressed in language that made sense canonically. To this end, she took Francis' approved Rule of 1223 and used it as the basis for her own. This had the advantage of stressing again that the sisters and brothers were one group.

At the same time, she also needed to take note of the canon law of her time, which was being re-codified and organized in the aftermath of the Fourth Lateran Council. The Constitutions of Hugolino and the later 1247 draft of Innocent IV needed to be woven in too. All these were incorporated into her text, which is still marked by two key elements: great inner liberty and Clare's immense respect for the maturity of her community. She envisioned community life as something based on shared responsibility, a mature attitude towards authority, and compassion for each other's needs. All this was new in legislation for women, as a quick glance at Hugolino's Constitutions will make plain, but then Clare was, as far as we know, the first woman to write a rule for other women. There were other women's Rules, such as Caesarius of Arles' for Radegunde and Abelard's for Heloise, but they were both a man's insight into women's requirements and how women lived. With Clare's text, we have a rule for women which – in order to function well – demands a house of mature women living in a culture of dialogue. Throughout, Clare is concerned to give legal articulation to her vision in such a way that the Church can approve it. Central to this vision is the understanding that the sisters and brothers are organically one, and that they are wholly committed to most high poverty.

We might ask what this really means in practice. First, it means that I am always a pilgrim, a stranger, as the apostle says. Second, through fidelity to most high poverty, we become 'faithful souls', that *fidelis anima* so dear to Francis and Clare:

It is now clear that the soul of the faithful person, the most worthy of all creatures because of the grace of God, is greater than the heavens itself, since the heavens and the rest of creation cannot contain their Creator; only the faithful soul is his dwelling place and throne, and this only through charity, which the wicked lack. (3rd letter to Agnes of Prague, 21–22)

The content of the Rule

The whole of Clare's Rule is substantially contained in the first sentence of Chapter 1 – all the rest is application and commentary!

The form of life of the Order of the Poor Sisters that blessed Francis established is this: to observe the Holy Gospel of our Lord Jesus Christ by living in obedience, without anything of one's own, and in chastity. (Rule of Clare, 1.1)

In this first chapter, she speaks of:

Clare and the Gospel.
Clare and Francis.
Clare and the Church.
Clare and the Order.
Clare and the future.

Then she goes on to define how to join the sisters and how to live from then on. In the centre, Chapter 6 (although the chapter divisions were made later), she enshrines two precious texts that Francis had written for them in the early days. After this she offers us a sustained reflection on the meaning and application of *sine proprio* – having nothing of one's own – and she expands this into a number of related and more spiritual areas:

Finally in Chapter 11 she deals with the cloister and various practical matters. Chapter 12 of the Rule deals with the visitator, the chaplain, the cardinal protector, their duties, privileges and rights. Much of this would have been the canon law of the time or its equivalent. It is very difficult, across eight hundred years, to form a clear picture of the way Clare and her sisters lived or what sort of enclosure they observed. She tells us that after profession the sisters do not go out except for a reasonable, useful, manifest and approved cause, but that is very much wider than the legislation of Hugolino. Then she ends her Rule as she began, speaking about the gospel, about our Lady and about the poverty and humility of Jesus Christ.

This is a text of great wisdom, yet full of practicality and realism. Time and again Clare says 'however . . .', leaving details to those on the spot, aware of the different demands of climates and cultures, concerned only that the sisters be able to pursue that for which they have been called. The Rule of Clare is a document of amazing originality, which has not always been fully appreciated. Although Innocent IV approved it, he did so for San Damiano only, and the sad irony is that within ten years the pope (Urban IV) had superseded it with another Rule, more monastic and less well adapted to Clare's vision. Although Clare's Rule was known and honoured, it is only recently, with the growth of scholarship and the revision of the Constitutions, that it has regained its central place in Poor Clare legislation.

The Form of Life of St Clare
Regis J. Armstrong OFM Cap

Introduction

The last years of Clare's life were characterized by her struggle to have her vision of religious life approved by the Church. In order to understand her *Form of Life* for the Poor Ladies, it is helpful to read those which preceded it, those of Cardinal Hugolino and Pope Innocent IV, which were based on the Benedictine Rule and the canonical legislation of the twelfth and early thirteenth centuries. Clare's insistence on her own *Form of Life* no doubt came from years of attempting to live the vision Francis inspired in her within the limits of these documents, imposed as they were by men who did not comprehend the uniqueness of her vision. It is remarkable that Clare became the first woman to write a religious rule and, in so doing, inaugurated a totally new epoch for women in the life of the Church.

Although it had been overlooked among the relics of Clare until 1893, the original document with the papal bull of Innocent IV is still preserved in the Protomonastery of St Clare in Assisi. The manuscript contains two phrases handwritten by the pope: '*Ad instar fiat! S.* [So be it!]' and '*Ex causis manifestis michi et protectorii mon[asterii] fiat ad instar* [For reasons known to me and the protector of the monastery, so be it!]'. The first of these is the formula of approval given by Innocent IV who uses the first letter of his baptismal name, Sinibaldo, as his signature; the second is a clause explaining the uniqueness of the document. In the margin of the papal bull, someone else has written: '*Hanc beata Clara tetigit et obsculata (!) est pro devotione pluribus et pluribus vicinis* [Blessed Clare touched and kissed this many times out of devotion]'.

The Form of Life of Clare of Assisi

Innocent,
Bishop, Servant of the servants of God,
to his beloved daughters in Christ,
Clare, Abbess, and the other sisters
of the monastery of San Damiano in Assisi,
Health and Apostolic Blessing.

The Apostolic See is accustomed to accede to the pious requests and to be favourably disposed to grant the praise-worthy desires of its petitioners. Thus, We have before Us your humble request that We confirm by Our Apostolic authority the form of life that Blessed Francis gave you and which you have freely accepted. According to [this form of life] you should live together in unity of spirits and in the profession of the highest poverty. Our venerable brother, the Bishop of Ostia and Velletri, has seen fit to approve this way of life, as the Bishop's own letters on this matter define more fully, and We have taken care to strengthen it with Our Apostolic protection. Attentive, therefore, to your devout prayers, We approve and ratify what the Bishop has done in this matter and confirm it in virtue of Our Apostolic authority and support it in this document. To this end We include herein the text of the Bishop, word for word, which is the following:

Rainaldo, by divine mercy Bishop of Ostia and Velletri, to his most dear mother and daughter in Christ, the Lady Clare, Abbess of San Damiano in Assisi, and to her sisters, both present and to come, greetings and a fatherly bless-ing.

Beloved daughters in Christ, we approve your holy pro-posal in the Lord and we desire with fatherly affection to impart our kind favour upon your wishes and holy desires, because you have rejected the splendours and pleasures of the world and, following the footprints of Christ Himself and His most holy Mother, you have chosen to live bodily enclosed and to serve the Lord in the highest poverty that, in freedom of soul, you may be servants of the Lord. Acceding to your pious prayers, by the authority of the Lord Pope as well as our own, we, therefore, confirm forever for all of you and for all who will succeed you in your monastery, and we ratify by the protection of this document this form of life, the manner of holy unity and of the highest poverty that your blessed Father Saint Francis gave you for your observance in word and in writing. It is as follows:

Chapter I
In the Name of the Lord Begins the Form of Life of the Poor Sisters

The form of life of the Order of the Poor Sisters that Blessed Francis established is this: to observe the Holy Gospel of our Lord Jesus Christ, by living in obedience, without anything of one's own, and in chastity.

Clare, the unworthy handmaid of Christ and the little plant of the most blessed Father Francis, promises obedience and reverence to the Lord Pope Innocent and his successors canonically elected, and to the Roman Church. And, just as at the beginning of her conversion, together with her sisters she promised obedience to the Blessed Francis, so now she promises to observe the same inviolably to his successors. And the other sisters shall always be obliged to obey the successors of Blessed Francis and Sister Clare and the other abbesses canonically elected who succeed her.

Chapter II
Those Who Wish to Accept This Life and How They are to be Received

If, by divine inspiration, anyone should come to us desiring to accept this life, the abbess is bound to seek the consent of all the sisters; and if the majority have agreed, she may receive her, having obtained the permission of the Lord Cardinal Protector. If she judges she should be received, let [the abbess] examine her carefully or have her examined concerning the

Catholic faith and the sacraments of the Church. And if she believes all these things and is willing to profess them faithfully and to observe them steadfastly to the end; and if she has no husband, or if she has one who has already entered religious life with the authority of the Bishop of the diocese and has already made a vow of continence; and if there is no impediment to her observance of this life, such as advanced age or some infirmity or mental disorder, let the tenor of our life be thoroughly explained to her.

If she is suitable, let the words of the holy Gospel be addressed to her that she should go and sell all that she has and take care to distribute the proceeds to the poor. If she cannot do this, her good will shall suffice. Let the abbess and her sisters take care that they be not concerned about her temporal affairs, so that she may freely dispose of her possessions as the Lord shall have inspired her. However, if some counsel be required, let them send her to some discerning and God-fearing persons, according to whose advice her goods may be distributed to the poor.

After her hair has been cut all around and her secular clothes set aside, she may be permitted three tunics and a mantle.

Thereafter, she may not go outside the monastery except for a useful, reasonable, evident, and justifiable purpose. When the year of probation is ended, let her be received into obedience, promising to observe perpetually the life and form of our poverty.

Let no one receive the veil during the period of probation. The sisters may also have little mantles for convenience and propriety in serving and working. In fact, let the abbess, with discernment, provide them with clothing according to the diversity of persons, places, seasons and cold climates, as in necessity she shall deem expedient.

Young girls who are received into the monastery before the age established by law may have their hair cut all around; and, after putting aside their secular clothes, let them be clothed in religious garb, as the abbess sees fit. However, when they reach the age required by law, let them, clothed in the same way as the others, make their profession. Both for these and the other novices, the abbess shall carefully provide a mistress from among the more discerning sisters of the entire monastery, who shall form them diligently in a holy way of life and proper behaviour according to the form of our profession.

Let the form described above be observed in the examination and reception of the sisters who serve outside the monastery. These sisters may wear shoes. No one may live with us in the monastery unless she has been received according to the form of our profession.

Out of love of the most holy and beloved Child wrapped in poor little swaddling clothes and placed in a manger and of His most holy Mother, I admonish, beg, and encourage my sisters always to wear poor garments.

Chapter III
The Divine Office and Fasting,
Confession and Communion

Let the sisters who can read celebrate the Divine Office according to the custom of the Lesser Brothers. They may have breviaries for this reason, reading without singing. Those who, for some reasonable cause, occasionally are not able to recite their hours by reading them, may, like the other sisters, say the Our Father.

Let those who do not know how to read say the Our Father twenty-four times for Matins; Lauds five times; seven times for each of the hours of Prime, Terce, Sext and None; twelve times, however, for Vespers; seven times for Compline. For the dead let them also say the Our Father seven times with the Eternal Rest for Vespers; twelve times for Matins, because the sisters who can read are obliged to recite the Office of the Dead. When a sister of our monastery shall have passed on, however, let them say the Our Father fifty times.

Let the sisters fast at all times. They may eat twice on the Nativity of the Lord, however, no matter on what day it happens to fall. The younger sisters, those who are weak, and

those who are serving outside the monastery may be merci-
fully dispensed as the abbess sees fit. But let the sisters not be
bound to corporal fasting in time of manifest necessity.

Let them go to confession, with the permission of the abbess,
at least twelve times a year. Let them be careful not to intro-
duce other talk unless it pertains to the confession and the
salvation of souls. Let them receive Communion seven times,
namely, on the Nativity of the Lord, Thursday of Holy Week,
the Resurrection of the Lord, Pentecost, the Assumption of
the Blessed Virgin, the Feast of Saint Francis and the Feast of
All Saints. It is lawful for the chaplain to celebrate inside [the
enclosure] to give Communion to the sisters, the healthy or
the sick.

Chapter IV
The Election and Office of the Abbess:
The Chapter, and the Officials and the Discreets

The sisters are bound to observe the canonical form in the
election of the abbess. Let them quickly arrange to have the
General Minister or the Provincial Minister of the Order of
Lesser Brothers present. Through the Word of God, let him
dispose them to perfect harmony and the common good in
the election to be held. Let no one be elected unless professed.
And if a non-professed is elected or otherwise somehow given
to them, she may not be obeyed unless she first professes our
form of poverty.

At her death let the election of another abbess take place. If
at any time it should appear to the entire body of sisters that
she is not competent for their service and common good, these
sisters are bound as quickly as possible to elect another as
abbess and mother according to the form described above.

Let whoever is elected reflect upon the kind of burden she
has undertaken on herself and to Whom she must render an
account of the flock committed to her. Let her also strive to
preside over the others more by her virtues and holy behav-
iour than by her office, so that, moved by her example, the

sisters may obey her more out of love than out of fear. Let her avoid exclusive loves, lest by loving some more than others she give scandal to all. Let her console the afflicted. Let her also be the last refuge for those who are troubled, lest the sickness of despair overcome the weak should they fail to find in her health-giving remedies.

Let her preserve the common life in everything, especially in whatever pertains to the church, the dormitory, refectory, infirmary and clothing. Her vicaress is bound to preserve it in the same way.

The abbess is bound to call her sisters together at least once a week in the chapter, where both she and her sisters should humbly confess their common and public offences and negligences. There let her consult with all her sisters concerning whatever concerns the welfare and good of the monastery, for the Lord frequently reveals what is better to the youngest.

No heavy debt may be incurred except with the common consent of the sisters and by reason of manifest necessity, and let this be done through the procurator. Let the abbess and her sisters, however, be careful that nothing be deposited in the monastery; for such practices often give rise to troubles and scandals.

In order to preserve the unity of mutual love and peace, let all who hold offices in the monastery be chosen by the common agreement of all the sisters. In the same way, let at least eight sisters be elected from the more discerning whose counsel the abbess should be always bound to use in those matters which our form of life demands. Moreover, if it seems useful and expedient, the sisters can and should at times remove the officials and discreets and elect others in their place.

Chapter V
Silence, the Parlour and the Grille

Let the sisters keep silence from the hour of Compline until Terce, except those who are serving outside the monastery. Let them also continually keep silence in the church, the dormitory and the refectory only while they are eating. At all times, however, they may be permitted to speak with discernment in the infirmary for the recreation and service of the sick. Nevertheless, they may always and everywhere communicate whatever is necessary, briefly and in a quiet voice.

The sisters may not be permitted to speak in the parlour or at the grille without the permission of the abbess or her vicaress. Let those who have permission not dare to speak in the parlour except in the presence and hearing of two sisters. Moreover, let them not presume to go to the grille, unless there are present at least three sisters appointed by the abbess or her vicaress from the eight discreets who were elected by all the sisters for the council of the abbess. Let the abbess and her vicaress be themselves bound to observe this form of speaking. Let this happen very rarely at the grille but never at the door.

Let a curtain be hung inside the grille which may not be removed except when the Word of God is preached or when a sister is speaking with someone. Let the grille have a wooden door which is well provided with two distinct iron locks, bolts and bars, so that it can be locked, especially at night, with two keys, one of which the abbess may keep and the other the sacristan. Let it always be locked except when the Divine Office is being heard and for the reasons given above. A sister may not under any circumstance speak to anyone at the grille before sunrise or after sunset. Inside the parlour let there always be a curtain which may not be removed.

No one may speak in the parlour during the Lent of Saint Martin and the Greater Lent, except to a priest for Confession or for some other manifest necessity, which is left to the prudence of the abbess or her vicaress.

Chapter VI
Not Having Possessions

After the Most High Heavenly Father saw fit by His grace to enlighten my heart to do penance according to the example and teaching of our most blessed father Saint Francis, shortly after his own conversion, I, together with my sisters, willingly promised him obedience. When the Blessed Father saw we had no fear of poverty, hard work, trial, shame or contempt of the world, but, instead, we held them as great delights, moved by piety he wrote a form of life for us as follows:

> Because by divine inspiration you have made yourselves daughters and handmaids of the most High, most Exalted King, the heavenly Father, and have taken the Holy Spirit as your spouse, choosing to live according to the perfection of the holy Gospel, I resolve and promise for myself and for my brothers always to have the same loving care and special solicitude for you as for them.

As long as he lived he diligently fulfilled this and wished that it always be fulfilled by the brothers.

In order that we as well as those who were to come after us would never turn aside from the holy poverty we had embraced, shortly before his death he repeated in writing his last wish for us. He said:

> I, little brother Francis, wish to follow the life and poverty of our most high Lord Jesus Christ and of His most holy Mother and to persevere in this until the end; and I ask you, my ladies, and I give you my advice that you live always in this most holy life and poverty. And keep careful watch that you never depart from this by reason of the teaching or advice of anyone.

As I, together with my sisters, have ever been solicitous to safeguard the holy poverty which we have promised the Lord God and blessed Francis, so, too, the abbesses who shall succeed me in office and all the sisters are bound inviolably to observe it to the end, that is, by not receiving or having possession or ownership either of themselves or through an intermediary, or even anything that might reasonably be called ownership, except as much land as necessity requires for the integrity and proper seclusion of the monastery, and *this land may not be cultivated except as a garden for the needs of the sisters.*

Chapter VII
The Manner of Working

Let the sisters to whom the Lord has given the grace of working work faithfully and devotedly after the Hour of Terce at work that pertains to a virtuous life and the common good. [Let them do this] in such a way that, while they banish idleness, the enemy of the soul, they do not extinguish the Spirit of holy prayer and devotion to which other temporal things must contribute.

At the Chapter, in the presence of all, the abbess or her vicaress is bound to assign the work that each should perform with her hands. Let the same be done if alms have been sent by anyone for the needs of the sisters, so that an acknowledgement of them be made in common. Let all such things be distributed for the common good by the abbess or her vicaress with the advice of the discreets.

Chapter VIII
The Sisters Shall Not Appropriate Anything as Their Own; Begging Alms; The Sick Sisters

Let the sisters not appropriate anything to themselves, neither a house nor a place nor anything at all; instead, as pilgrims and strangers in this world who serve the Lord in poverty and humility, let them confidently send for alms. Nor should they be ashamed, since the Lord made Himself poor in this world for us. This is that summit of the highest poverty which has established you, my dearest sisters, heiresses and queens of the kingdom of heaven; it has made you poor in things but exalted you in virtue. Let this be your portion which leads into the land of the living. Clinging totally to this, my most beloved sisters, do not wish to have anything else in perpetuity under heaven for the name of our Lord Jesus Christ and His most holy mother.

Let no sister be permitted to send letters or to receive or give away anything outside the monastery without the permission of the abbess. Let it not be permitted to have anything that the abbess has not given or allowed. Should anything be sent to a sister by her relatives or others, let the abbess give it to her. If she needs it, she may use it; otherwise, let her in all charity give it to a sister who does need it. If, however, money is sent to her, let the abbess, with the advice of the discreets, provide for the needs of the sister.

Concerning the sick sisters, let the abbess be strictly bound to inquire with diligence, by herself and through other sisters, what their illness requires both by way of counsel as well as food and other necessities, and let her provide for them charitably and kindly according to the resources of the place. Because all are bound to serve and to provide for their sisters who are ill as they would wish to be served, let them be bound as if they were bound by some illness. Let each confidently make her needs known to another. For if a mother loves and cares for her child according to the flesh, how much more attentively should a sister love and care for her sister according to the Spirit?

Those who are ill may lie on sacks filled with straw and may use feather pillows for their head; those who need woollen stockings and quilts may use them. When these sick sisters are visited by those who enter the monastery, they may briefly respond with some good words to those who speak to them. But the other sisters who have permission may not dare to speak to those who enter the monastery except in the presence and hearing of the two discreets appointed by the abbess or her vicaress. Let the abbess and her vicaress themselves be bound to observe this form of speaking.

Chapter IX
The Penance to be Imposed on the Sisters Who Sin; The Sisters Who Serve outside the Monastery

If any sister, at the instigation of the enemy, has sinned mortally against the form of our profession, and, if after having been admonished two or three times by the abbess or other sisters, she does not amend, let her eat bread and water on the floor before all the sisters in the refectory for as many days as she shall have been obstinate. If it seems advisable to the abbess, let her be subjected to even greater punishment. Meanwhile, as long as she remains obstinate, let her prayer be that the Lord will enlighten her heart to do penance. The abbess and her sisters, however, must beware not to become angry or disturbed on account of another's sin, for anger and disturbance prevent charity in oneself and in others.

If it should happen, may it never be so, that an occasion of trouble or scandal should arise between sister and sister through a word or gesture, let her who was the cause of the trouble, before offering the gift of her prayer to the Lord, not only prostrate herself humbly at once at the feet of the other and ask pardon, but also beg her simply to intercede for her to the Lord that He forgive her. Let the other sister, mindful of that word of the Lord, 'If you do not forgive from the heart, neither will your heavenly Father forgive you,' generously pardon her sister every injury she has done to her.

The sisters who serve outside the monastery may not delay for long unless some manifest necessity requires it. Let them conduct themselves virtuously and say little, so that those who see them may always be edified. Let them strictly beware of having suspicious meetings or dealings with others. They may not be godmothers of men or women lest gossip or trouble arise because of this. Let them not presume to repeat the gossip of the world inside the monastery. Let them be strictly bound not to repeat outside the monastery anything that is said or done within which could cause scandal.

If anyone should innocently offend in these two matters, let it be left to the prudence of the abbess mercifully to impose a penance on her. But if she does this through a vicious habit, the abbess, with the advice of her discreets, may impose a penance on her according to the nature of the fault.

Chapter X
The Admonition and Correction of the Sisters

Let the abbess admonish and visit her sisters, and humbly and charitably correct them, not commanding them anything that is against their soul and the form of our profession. Let the sisters, however, who are subjects, remember that they have renounced their own wills for the sake of God. Therefore, let them be firmly bound to obey their abbess in all the things they have promised the Lord to observe and which are not against the soul and our profession.

Let the abbess, on her part, be so familiar with them that they can speak and act with her as ladies do with their handmaid. For this is the way it must be: the abbess should be the handmaid of all the sisters.

Moreover, I admonish and exhort the sisters in the Lord Jesus Christ to beware of all pride, vainglory, envy, avarice, care and anxiety about this world, detraction and murmuring, dissension and division. Let them be always eager, however, to preserve among themselves the unity of mutual love which is the bond of perfection.

Let those who do not know how to read not be eager to learn. Let them direct their attention to what they should desire above all else: to have the Spirit of the Lord and Its holy activity, to pray always to Him with a pure heart, and to have humility, patience in difficulty and infirmity, and to love those who persecute, blame and accuse us, for the Lord says: Blessed are those who suffer persecution for the sake of justice, for theirs is the kingdom of heaven. But whoever perseveres to the end will be saved.

Chapter XI
The Custody of the Enclosure

Let the portress be mature in her manner of acting, discerning, and of a suitable age. Let her remain in an open cell without a door during the day. A suitable companion may be assigned to her who may take her place in everything whenever necessary.

Let the door be well secured by two different iron locks, with bars and bolts, so that, especially at night, it may be locked with two keys, one of which the portress may have, the other the abbess. During the day let it never be left without a guard and securely locked with one key.

Let them most diligently take care to see that the door is never left open, except when this cannot be conveniently avoided. Let it never be opened to anyone who wishes to enter, except to those who have been given permission by the Supreme Pontiff or our Lord Cardinal. The sisters may not allow anyone to enter the monastery before sunrise or to remain within after sunset, unless demanded by a manifest, reasonable and unavoidable cause.

If a bishop has permission to celebrate within the enclosure, either for the blessing of an abbess or for the consecration of one of the sisters as a nun, or for any other reason, let him be satisfied with as few and virtuous companions and assistants as possible.

Whenever it is necessary for other men to enter the monastery to do some work, let the abbess carefully assign a suitable person to the door, who may open it only to those designated for the work and to no one else. Let the sisters be extremely careful at such times not to be seen by those who enter.

Chapter XII
The Visitator, the Chaplain
and the Cardinal Protector

Let our Visitator always be taken from the Order of the Lesser Brothers according to the will and command of our Cardinal. Let him be the kind of person who is well known for his integrity and good manner of living. His duty shall be to correct any excesses against the form of our profession, whether these be in the head or in the members. Taking his position in an open area that he can be seen by others, let him speak with all and with each concerning what pertains to the duty of the visitation as he sees best.

We ask as a favour of the same Order a chaplain and a clerical companion of good reputation, of prudent discernment, and two lay brothers, lovers of a holy and upright way of life, in support of our poverty, as we have always mercifully had from that Order of Lesser Brothers, in the light of the piety of God and our blessed Francis.

Let the chaplain not be permitted to enter the monastery without a companion. When they enter, let them remain in an open area, in such a way that they can always see one another and be seen by others. They may enter for the confession of the sick who cannot go to the parlour, for their Communion, for the Last Anointing and the Prayers of the Dying.

Moreover, for funeral services, and on the solemnity of Masses for the Dead, for digging or opening a grave, or even for making arrangements, suitable and sufficient outsiders may enter, according to the prudence of the abbess.

Let the sisters be strictly bound always to have as our Governor, Protector and Corrector that Cardinal of the Holy Roman Church who has been delegated by the Lord Pope for the Lesser Brothers, so that, always submissive and subject at the feet of that same holy Church and steadfast in the Catholic faith, we may observe in perpetuity the poverty and humility of our Lord Jesus Christ and of His most holy Mother and the Holy Gospel we have firmly promised. Amen.

Given at Perugia, the sixteenth kalends of October, in the tenth year of the Pontificate of Lord Pope Innocent IV.

Therefore, no one is permitted to destroy this document of our confirmation or oppose it recklessly. If anyone shall presume to attempt this, let him know he will incur the wrath of Almighty God and His holy Apostles Peter and Paul.

Given at Assisi, the fifth of the Ides of August, in the eleventh year of our Pontificate.

5

Essentials of Franciscan Spirituality

Stephen Innes OFM Cap

The Oxonian Franciscan, Friar Roger Bacon, wrote in his *Tractatus de Geographica*: 'To discover the shape of the earth, one must sail toward the west to reach the east.' If we are to investigate the orbit of what is called 'Franciscan Spirituality', then according to Bacon's insight, we must be prepared to embrace the globe of our topic to discover its centre and circumference, to distinguish what is essential and what is non-essential, to grasp the characteristic shape of the whole.

The first issue that arises in any treatment of Franciscan Spirituality is to know whether or not we are justified in claiming that there is such a thing. In the search for a resolution to this query, we will come to a better understanding of what is meant by a 'spirituality' and thereby prepare the foundation for the edifice of vision and virtue that we wish to identify as specifically 'Franciscan'.

In recent times, the notion of specialized spiritualities has been seriously challenged. Louis Bouyer, for example, denies the instance of a particular spirituality in favour of one Christian spirituality without any distinctions (*Introduction to Spirituality*, tr. Mary Perkins Ryan, London: DLT, 1963, pp. 20–1). G. K. Chesterton, by contrast, had no hesitation in sensing the variations of congenial spiritualities and their distinctive characteristics when he penned these appropriate lines: 'In a better sense than the antithesis commonly conveys, it is true to say that what St. Benedict had stored St. Francis scattered; but in the world of spiritual things what had been stored into the barns like grain was scattered over the world as seed' (*St. Francis of Assisi*, London: Hodder & Stoughton, 1964, p. 116).

With the conviction that there is a synthesis which we call 'Franciscan Spirituality', can we begin to delineate its special features? Yes, but not yet! For surprisingly there is not unanimous agreement on the specific features of Franciscan Spirituality, and still less a consensus to what are its essential elements. But if we are going to discern any precise idea about those spiritual features and ideals that we can properly call 'Franciscan', then the right place to start is with *The Writings* of Francis and the first accounts of his life. These two sources, the instruction Francis gives and the example he sets, would appear to be the valid starting point for our quest. In recent years such an approach has gained much support. There was a time, however, when the traditional approach to Franciscan Spirituality spurned the writings and biographies in favour of the thoughtful digestion of the philosophical vision presented by St Bonaventure, Duns Scotus and the other Franciscan masters. Today's approach stresses the basic and essential value of the writings and the first biographies to get at the real core of Franciscanism. These two approaches may be considered as complementary, and if we prefer to access first through the one rather than the other, that does not imply uninterest or a lack of respect for the christocentrism constructed by the Bonaventurean School.

The writings of Francis naturally have a singular priority in leading us to discover the mind and intentions of the saint; what kind of person he was, what was important to him; what ideals and values he cherished and taught as a teacher of Christian life and spirituality. Paul Sabatier wrote at the end of the nineteenth century: 'The writings of St. Francis are assuredly the best means of acquaintance with him' (*Life of St. Francis*, tr. Louise Seymour Houghton, New York: Charles Scribner's Sons, 1905, pp. 351–2). But the writings are not an organized or systematic record which easily reveals the person of Francis with his mind and intentions. Whilst they do provide us with an irreplaceable inroad to the spirit of Francis, the writings have to be supplemented by the earliest, biographical accounts which we have of Francis and his first Friars. A brief survey of this hagiographical data reveals two basic portraits of Francis: the one is associated with the 'official' biographies and the other with the *florilegia*. The one paints a picture of a Saint, his conversion, his foundation of an Order, his ministry, miracles, stigmata, death and glorification; the other depicts a disaster story of a holy prophet in the discovery of an ideal and its betrayal by the Church, a sorrowful denouement and final crucifixion after a deathbed appeal to preserve his ideal intact. These different portraits and their origins are at the core of the so-called 'Franciscan Question', as are the personalities and circumstances that surround their composition. The search for an authentic portrait of Francis and a true picture of the spirituality he bequeathed to the Church and to the world has been above all the controlling force of modern Franciscan scholarship.

So what are some of the essential features of Franciscan Spirituality? Christianity is not just a body of dogmas to be received nor a moral code to be guarded, it is rather a faith to be lived in imitation of Jesus Christ. This is probably why G. K. Chesterton wrote: 'Christianity has not been tried and found wanting; it simply has not been tried!' But then he added: 'Only Francis of Assisi has tried it and has not been found wanting!' Francis was not first and foremost an ecclesiastical reformer, nor was he a missionary or theologian. He was all of these. But he was firstly a disciple of Jesus and a follower of his Gospel teaching.

The imitation of Christ – discipleship

In his pursuit of an all-embracing commitment to Christian discipleship, Francis sought to live evangelical perfection and to incarnate the person of Christ into his life (LM, Pro). He understood, moreover, that imitation is the truest form of veneration, so that the configuration to Christ which we observe in Francis' life concerns not external conduct, but an inner conformity of spirit. The true disciple of the Lord is not a replica, but a faithful follower whose desire it is 'to observe the holy Gospel' and 'to walk in his [Christ's] footsteps'. Francis was so conformed to Christ through a heroic living of the Gospel that he was taken for 'another Christ' by his contemporaries (1Cel, 115; LMin, 6, 7). This surely reminds us that the imitation of Christ is of the very essence of Francis' spirituality as it is of Christianity itself. First and foremost, Francis was a disciple of Christ, the Christ of the Gospel. In fact, what distinguishes Francis from the other saints is that he lived after the manner of the Gospel; he did not just know the Gospel, he did it.

Above all, the Crucified Christ was central to Francis' experience of Gospel living, so much so that the cross formed the crossroads of his life. Clearly, we can say that Francis pursued a personal relationship with Christ to the extent that his life only had meaning in relation to the Incarnate, Crucified Son of God (2Cel, 105). In the gift of the stigmata, Francis experienced in his own body the agony of the cross. So intensely did he devote himself to the imitation of Christ that he became another Crucified (1Cel, 90; 2Cel, 211; LM, 14.1–6).

What were the means by which Francis came to such a familiar knowledge of Christ and imitation of him? They were basically twofold: personal prayer and obedience to the Church.

Prayer

To look at Francis' prayer is to discover something of his inner spirit. Francis is regarded as a contemplative, since he lived in the unitive way most of his life and his whole make-up was geared to mystical union with God. Such was the intensity of Francis' personal prayer life that he himself became a living prayer (1Cel, 71; 2Cel, 95). But Francis' prayer was not simply a vertical ascent to God. He did not flee from the world, nor did he despise the world. Francis embraced the world, delighting in the works of God's hands, loving God in all his creatures (2Cel, 165). In this way, Francis' spirituality had a distinctive horizontal dimension wherein he saw the world to be 'sacramental', bearing the traces of God's goodness and love. In a very real way Francis was a brother to Nature and a true friend of the Earth. Above all, it was the goodness of God invested in creation, and the humility of God manifested in the Incarnation, that drew Francis' reverence and advanced the prayer-vision of his soul's journey into God. These characteristics of Francis' prayer life have a definitive place at the core of his spirituality.

Church

Another means of knowing Christ for Francis was the Church. His loyalty and devotion to the Church are unequalled and indeed unchallenged. For whilst Francis' conscience was completely bound to the inspiration he received from the Lord, it was just as firmly bound to the Church founded by Christ and to its Supreme Pastor and hierarchy (RegB, 1; 1Cel, 32, 33; 2Cel, 16). We recognize a fundamental tension in that Francis was guided directly by God, yet he was also bound to the mediation of God's will for him through the Church. Francis saw clearly what the Church of his age was like, yet he realized full loving submission to the Church and its life. He sought its approval for his Order and its Rule of Life (RegB, 12.3). If at the heart of Christianity is the belief that the Word was made flesh, then the Church in its *Magisterium* represents in every age the continuation of the Incarnation (RegNB, 19.1–3).

An address given by Paul Sabatier at Kensington Town Hall on 4 April 1908 was entitled 'The Originality of St Francis of Assisi' (in *St Francis of Assisi: Essays in Commemoration 1982*, St Bonaventure: Franciscan Institute, 1982). According to Sabatier, the 'originality' of Francis consisted in his being 'catholic', but catholic in such a way that we struggle not merely to keep up with him, but even to keep him in view. This attitude can only be understood in the light of faith and is honoured through devotion.

Obedience

Most of all, Francis' catholicity is specified and identified in his obedience to the Church. Because Francis clung to the person and mystical body of Christ, his concept of obedience was eminently ecclesiastical. In this respect, Francis was a keen observer of the Fourth Lateran Council of 1216. Undoubtedly, in direct response to the reforms introduced by the Council, he preached a personal crusade, whereby he endeavoured to implement the Council's disciplinary legislation on the celebration of the Eucharist, the Sacraments and the Divine Office. Similarly, Francis' concept of obedience for his friars was innovative in so far as it was exercised within the twofold framework of conscience and the Rule. Moreover, he ignored the traditional language for the office of superiors, preferring the use of titles like 'minister' and 'servant'. Whilst the Friars had the freedom of the world for their 'cloister', it was the regulation of obedience which controlled their lives. As with the Master, obedience was set in the context of a personal relationship and surrendered for service. Hereby, Francis encountered a central core of the Christian faith and with uncompromising simplicity made it a lived experience for himself and his friars, and indeed, a distinctive feature of his spirituality.

Poverty

Of course, to live the Gospel demands an inner self-sacrifice of anything that makes for security, comfort and control (see Mt 16.24; 19.21; Lk 14.26). In this Francis was lifted to the plane of the Incarnation, wherein the Son of God dispossessed himself of himself in life and death, and called his disciples to follow him so as to be filled with the Spirit, and thereby embrace the providence of God in the prayer 'My God and my All'. Francis was a man so possessed of God that Joseph Lortz rightly says of him: 'God is the intellectual and spiritual air in which Francis lived and moved. God is the living, sublime *Thou* who actually addresses him, challenges him, loves him, and to whom Francis responds with love, service and worship. His being rests in God; he lives from God' (Joseph Lortz, *Francis, the Incomparable Saint*, St Bonaventure, NY: The Franciscan Institute, 1986, p. 67). Because Francis was so full of God, he had the capacity to dispossess himself of everything that was not of God. For Francis, the practice of poverty was not so much an ascetical exercise as something that touched the roots of his being in his relationship to God, others and the world at large. Poverty is fruitful when it is expressed in the freedom of fraternal relationships and in the meeting of the needs of others and allowing others to respond to one's own. Poor in spirit, Francis chose to associate with indigent poor, the marginalized, the leper and the beggar by the wayside. Moreover, in relation to humility, Franciscan poverty is a liberating force for the spirit: 'Holy Poverty puts to shame all greed, avarice, and all the anxieties of this life. Holy humility puts pride to shame, and all the inhabitants of this world and all that is in the world' (Salutation of the Virtues, 11, 12).

Inner liberty born of voluntary poverty and humility makes for the joyous disposition of minority (2Cel, 148; LM, 6.12–15; SP, 43). Only the true 'minor' possessed of the Spirit of God can attain true joy together with peace of mind and tranquillity of heart (VPLaet). Poverty, minority, peace and joy are inextricably linked to the Franciscan vocation and person and thereby constitute essential features of Franciscan Spirituality.

Penance

At the heart of Francis' Christian outlook was the adoption of the 'spirit of the Lord' and the conquest of the 'spirit of the flesh'.

In this sense Francis understood 'a life of penance' or 'doing penance' primarily as Gospel *metanoia*, which implies the complete and unceasing renewal of mind and heart so as to receive the 'spirit of the Lord' (Testament, 1). Obviously, Francis did not neglect the external practice of penance: fasting, mortification and self-denial to the highest degree, but he readily saw the constant need for conversion from self and self-concern to a life dedicated to the worship and praise of God in gratitude for all that we have received from him.

Preaching the Gospel

Francis of Assisi is regarded as one of the contemplatives of the Church and he made full allowance for the contemplative element in Franciscan life. But on the resolution of a dilemma that haunted him for some time, he chose to adopt the 'mixed' life, combining prayer with the apostolate of preaching (LM, 42, 12.1–2; Fior, 16). And whilst Francis was a zealous preacher (1Cel, 23; TestMin, p. 10), he also knew the power of silent witness, urging those friars whom he sent among the Saracens 'to engage in neither strife nor controversy, but to be subject to every human creature for God's sake, and simply confess that they are Christians' (RegNB, 16). The secret of the seraphic spirit which infused Francis and his first followers was a life sacrificed for the love of God, immersed in the Gospel, teaching by witness, word and example. Clearly, the central feature of Franciscan mission is not some form of activity, but a manner of life and the development of a particular way of Christian living (see E. Esser, OFM, *The Order of St. Francis*, tr. I. Brady, OFM, Chicago: FLIP, 1959, p. 45).

The challenge

Ultimately, Francis' love, holiness, humility, penance, poverty, obedience, joy and whatever else may characterize him should not be singled out for special or particular treatment as if in isolation from his personality, his character, his very being. His person, his life, his ideals and values, his sanctity, constitute his very being and it is the spiritual fabric of his whole being that we must try to capture if we are to know something of the essentials of Franciscan Spirituality. There are few saints who can speak to us as easily and directly as Francis. Yet in the final analysis we cannot capture the quicksilver of his personality, nor observe the heroic authenticity of Francis' life, unless we are prepared in some measure to be confronted and enthralled by his words and deeds, which provide for us the first glimmerings of what is essential to Franciscan Spirituality.

6

Living as a Franciscan

In community
Samuel Double SSF

Francis was not able to find his true self either in the family business or as a soldier, or indeed in the pleasure pursuits of his peer group in the town of Assisi. He did not feel at home in the security offered by his father. He also found himself at odds with his Christian contemporaries. He could submit neither to the restrictions of a monastic Rule nor to the outward remoteness of the public worship of the day. He stood alone, broken by his encounters with all these things. He felt misunderstood and isolated.

From such background he had a series of conversion experiences, and as he looked into the face of one suffering from leprosy, things began to fall into place. He discovered himself in a community of disabled people.

The opening paragraphs of the Testament of St Francis briefly describes the path by which Francis discovered his concept of community as a way of life. 'The Lord gave me, Brother Francis, thus to begin doing penance in this way: for when I was in sin, it seemed too bitter for me to see lepers. And the Lord himself led me among them and I showed mercy to them. And when I left them, what had seemed bitter to me was turned into sweetness of soul and body.' After his encounter with those suffering from leprosy, he writes that 'God inspired me with such faith in his churches' in which to pray, and then in priests who administer the Sacraments, in the Scriptures – particularly the Gospels. Finally, 'the Lord gave me some brothers'.

The experience of isolation

Bill has been a regular at our Friary at Hilfield in Dorset. Over many years he has made use of Giles House, the night shelter, and shares in the life of the Community for a few days at a time. He is not homeless in the strict sense of the term, since he often arrives from a bedsit in one of the nearby towns. However, he is rootless in that he has little experience of the network of relationships which normally make a person feel 'at home'. Addiction to alcohol is a symptom of his problem, but the causes are less easy to pinpoint. One of them certainly is a sense of isolation, a deep loneliness which leads him always to be moving on, to a restlessness and unhappiness from which alcohol is a temporary means of escape.

It is generally recognized that loneliness is a significant issue for many in our western society, not just for people like Bill, but in all walks of life. In the UK the percentage of those living on their own, particularly of single men, has grown steadily over recent decades, and it is a trend that is expected to continue. The emancipation of many women in recent times has brought further opportunity for independent living, but with it some loss of security. An ever-mobile population, an increase in family breakdown, and a greater length of life are all playing their part in creating a society of loners. Underneath all these things, however, there lies in our contemporary culture an exaltation of personal autonomy which is corrosive of any idea that we should belong to each other, or find happiness and fulfilment through interdependence. It is ironic that, in a world in which so much energy is being put into communication – through travel, the media and the Internet – the tendency is towards isolation.

Loss of institutions

Loneliness is not an invention of our time. There is an element of loneliness in every human heart. Yet we are essentially social beings and we find our identity in those groups to which we belong, be it our family or our church, our political party, our work partners, our sports club. What is new is that such 'institutions' are becoming weaker and more ephemeral. It is harder, for instance, for trade unionists to live out the rhetoric of being 'brothers and sisters' when people change jobs so frequently that they can barely build the network of interdependent relationships which in the past made those 'family' terms a reality. Returning to Liverpool after twenty-six years, to the closely-knit parish where I served as a curate, I was made deeply aware of the loss of community which has happened since; not just the church, but all the 'institutions' – the local shops and pubs, the pensioners' groups, the youth organizations, were all struggling.

A Franciscan vision

In the light of such fragmentation and isolation it is significant that, at the heart of the early Franciscan movement in the thirteenth century, there was a powerful vision of belonging, of relatedness, of family. Many of the Franciscan sources from that time witness to the strength and intimacy of the fraternity: 'They loved one another from the heart and each one served and took care of the other, as a mother serves and cares for her son. The fire of love burned so intensely in them that they would have willingly sacrificed their lives not only for the name of our Lord Jesus, but also for one another' (*Legend of the Three Companions*, 11). Such a closeness of fellowship must have been one of the reasons for the extraordinary growth of the Order in the first decades of its existence, and for the fact that they were commonly known as 'the Brothers'. It continues to be an essential part of the Franciscan charism.

Roots of fraternity

Franciscan fraternity has its roots in the Gospel of Jesus Christ, who called men and women into fellowship with him, and through that, into a new way of belonging. Such experience transcended other relationships, most especially the strong ties of blood: 'whoever does the will of my Father is my brother and sister and mother' (Mt 12.50). The early Church was remarkable for its living out of and expressing this relationship so that the poor were honoured, the hungry fed, and the lonely welcomed: 'See how these Christians love one another' (Tertullian, *Apology*, 39). Whenever there has been renewal in the life of the Church there has also been a rediscovery of brotherhood/sisterhood.

Marks of fraternity

Where do we find such fraternity? Not all 'families' are benign; no doubt there is a strong sense of belonging and loyalty among thieves, and a fundamentalist church can feel like an intimate fellowship – to those inside it! In the same way some natural families can be deeply destructive, towards both those within and those without. The sort of brother/sisterhood which lies at the heart of the Franciscan Way is based upon, first of all, the knowledge, however tentative, that we are sons and daughters, and on the experience, however fragmentary, of being loved, forgiven, accepted and cherished by God. Through knowing Brother Jesus, and being drawn into an ever-deeper relationship with him, Francis discovered his true sonship and his brotherhood to all around him. The relationship increasingly absorbed his attention and became the focus of his devotion: 'Oh how glorious it is to have a holy and great Father in heaven! O how holy, consoling to have such a beautiful and wonderful Spouse! O how holy and how loving, gratifying, humbling, peace-giving, sweet, worthy of love, and above all things, desirable: to have such a Brother and such a Son, our Lord Jesus Christ, who laid down his life for his sheep . . .' (Letter to all the Faithful, 14). True brother/sisterhood is based not upon mutual attraction, common task or shared interest, let alone on fear of the outsider, but on the recognition and acceptance of a membership of a community to which we are assigned, and where we enjoy fraternal relationships which are pure gift.

The fellowship of wounds

Fraternity flourishes where people are willing to be vulnerable to each other. One of the most powerful experiences of belonging for some people comes through membership of Alcoholics Anonymous (or of another of the 'Anonymous' groups derived from it). At each meeting individuals share something of their experiences, their hopes and their fears, and above all their admission, in the face of their addiction, that alone they are powerless to do anything to resolve the situation. Often in a meeting there is an honesty of confession, a depth of repentance and a sense of forgiveness which goes beyond anything which usually happens in the liturgy, and there is consequently a sense of fellowship which puts the polite acquaintance of some church congregations in the shade. Likewise, it is often the case that those who have gone through an experience of great trial – such as comrades in arms, survivors from an accident, or bereaved relatives – find a fellowship through their suffering and loss; they find a new kind of family.

Places of encouragement

Francis encourages his brothers to be open with each other and gentle with each other's wounds. He willingly, almost joyfully, confesses his own failure and weakness, and when a brother cries out in hunger, Francis not only brings him food but eats with him, lest he be shamed before the others for being unable to manage the simplicity of their life. He urges one who is Minister to show special love to the weaker brother: 'If he would sin a thousand times before your eyes, love him more than me so that you may draw him to the Lord; and always be merciful with brothers such as these' (Letter to a Minister, 2).

Those who live in community know that it is often when vulnerability and weakness are acknowledged and accepted that our life together is renewed; our wounds can become the opportunities for us to discover again that we are brothers and sisters. Conversely, those communities which are intolerant of failure of any kind usually experience a growing shallowness, an unreal fraternity. This does not mean that anything goes, or that destructive patterns of behaviour should be ignored. There is a real danger in any community which is primarily concerned with the avoidance of rocking the boat, keeping the show on the road, or just projecting an image of respectability and niceness. Brother/sisterhood which 'bears the marks of the Lord Jesus' will recognize and embrace the tensions of the life together, and the conflict and reconciliation that that will involve. Jean Vanier, the founder of L'Arche, the community of those with learning difficulties, has said: 'In community we discover our deepest wounds . . . and the mystery of forgiveness'.

Welcoming the stranger

Generous belonging together, true fraternity, is able and willing to reach out and welcome others, to provide hospitality to the stranger. We may be quite good at seeing as our brother or sisters those to whom we are attracted, those who share our own outlook and values. It is more difficult to extend that recognition to the outsider, to the one who threatens us or with whom we strongly disagree. Almost every Christian congregation claims to be friendly – 'we are a family church here'; that may be so, but it can be hard for the stranger to feel accepted and welcomed, especially if they are a bit different from the rest of the congregation, or on the edge of society. Francis managed to see through the 'otherness' of the outsider, the stranger, the robber, the infidel, the leper, to the brother or sister who stood before him, and to share with them the gift of belonging which he himself knew. Franciscan houses which are true to their patron will be places where the visitor finds a fraternity, however imperfect or fragmented, a fraternity which, like that of Francis, is rooted in Jesus Christ, and which gives a glimpse of life beyond loneliness, a foothold in a fellowship, and a hint, a hope, of a homeland.

In the world
The Editors

Contemporary Franciscan attitudes

The values which we prize from the early Franciscans are gleaned from the life of Francis and Clare and their early companions, set against the secular forces which dominated thirteenth-century Europe. We discover surprising parallels with those conditions, then and now, that influence many thriving areas of our own contemporary world. One of the source documents of those early days, *The Legend of the Three Companions*, describes a background where love and fear of God are not apparently in the conscious minds of people, and 'lust for the flesh, greed for the world and pride of life was so widespread that the whole world was engulfed in these three malignancies' (II.88). It is hoped that modern western people have to some extent matured, yet deep wells of greedy and selfish behaviour linger with little concern for penitence.

Grounded in the Fatherhood of God

To understand the ground of Francis' witness to his own contemporaries, it should be recognized that everything was affected by his prayerful perception of God as Father and his vision of every person and every thing as a brother and sister. That dominant recognition of the whole of creation as one community resulted in his respectful attitudes towards all that the Father had made. Nothing could be excluded, because they were loved into being by the Father's will. The more he entered into the contemplation of God, accepting every creature as being under God's providential care, the more he lived with the joy and the pain of God's created world.

Celtic links with Italy

There is evidence that Francis visited the local Celtic monastery at Bobbio founded by the seventh-century saint, Columbanus, and his missionary monks from Ireland and Britain. Their spirituality, particularly their emphasis on the sacredness of creation and the importance to God of all creatures, may well have assisted Francis' own growing perceptions of the true relationship with the Father-creator of each of the species of the natural world.

Commodities or community?

When Francis was named the Patron Saint of Ecology by Pope John Paul II in 1979, this brought to focus the absolute necessity to reverse the growing common assumption that the resources of the world were simply commodities to be exploited by human beings. The efforts of the UN Conference on Environment and Development held at Rio de Janeiro in 1992 seriously brought to our attention vast conservation requirements. This has awakened a degree of commitment to what is still only a slow brake upon our modern tendency to misuse the resources of the planet and threaten its life for future generations. At the political level, the follow-up work undertaken to restore the ozone layer in the earth's atmosphere, to reduce the carbon dioxide pollution in the air we breathe, and to conserve the richness of the soil and the population of trees, has been slow indeed. Much remains at stake but it is heartening to see, for instance, the number of small children learning something of the basic attitudes of ecology in today's classrooms, and the relief organizations campaigning hard for essential reforms in the world trade laws. Such practical signs offer a measure of hope for future generations.

Choices

However, consumerism becomes an ever-increasing pastime under the pressures of a free global economy, heavily armed with beguiling advertisements. To yield to such pressures and their distracting forces will often be at the expense of losing any capacity to wonder at and enjoy the freer delights of the natural world. Our need for obsessive busyness obscures our ability to achieve peace of mind. As we take advantage of what is offered through technology, so we discover we have lost our capacity to live with inconvenience, with insecurities and without solutions. As we reach for boundaries of safety, we create barriers of discrimination and lose that attractive inclusiveness which marks the Kingdom that Jesus proclaims and Francis emulated so attractively and convincingly.

Fruits of contemplation

The fruit of Francis' contemplation was to see every aspect of life in relational terms, where everyone and everything had its place under the Fatherhood of God. His well-known mantra, 'My God and my all', the prayer Francis sustained through a whole night under the roof of his neighbour, Bernard of Quintavalle, carries clear expressions of welcome and extended openness. More correctly his prayer is to be translated 'My God and all things', which better describes how every moment of the day would introduce him to a brother or a sister, be it a leprosy sufferer or a worm about to be trodden underfoot. He had the gift of showing immediate empathy.

A personal commitment

The compassionate heart of Francis was derived from his growing relationship with God's Son, the man Jesus Christ, whom he emulated with his whole heart and mind. In his times of contemplation Francis gained a rare closeness of identification with Jesus, imitating him as far as he found possible. His daring to take up his cross daily led to his bearing many humiliations and sufferings. That witness has encouraged the Church, and very many outside, to become 'instruments of peace' in a multitude of postures in our contemporary world with all its injustices and crises and crea- turely needs.

Peace issues

Most people are concerned to promote peace, and in a variety of ways pray for peace: peace between nations, within nations and local communities, in the work-place, in families, and that elusive 'inner peace' which comes and goes seemingly beyond our personal control. Working for peace – a fundamental Franciscan pursuit – remains a priority because of Francis' recognition that nothing is more important than relationships. Christ's sacrificial life and death was for the sake of reconciling people to his Father and to one another. Franciscans will be at the forefront of justice and peace programmes and campaigns, from the highest levels of Franciscans International, the non- governmental organization based beside the United Nations in New York and also in Geneva, to the local levels in the house to house collections organized by Christian Aid and Caritas. At every level peace is more likely to be made through loving sacrifice rather than smoothing over the cracks. Peacemakers, according to the Beatitudes, are specially owned by Jesus as children of God.

There are many opportunities today to work for a reconcil- ing peace based in the forgiveness of the cross. The two short essays that follow express growing contemporary thinking on some of these ways. Francis' message is both urgent and relevant, and calls for a response that is vital and challenging within our precious but fundamentally fragile world today.

Dialogue with other faiths
Maximilian Mizzi OFM Conv

In past centuries the attitude of Christian Europe towards the Muslims did not reflect the spirit of the Gospel, which is centred on the command of the Lord 'to love one another'. Muslims have been looked upon as a politico-military power. Muslims identified Christendom with the Crusades. War and conflict were the only dialogue between the followers of the two religions.

St Francis was the first Christian ever to go to the non-Christians, to Muslims. In a prophetic vision he looked upon the Muslims not as 'the enemies of the cross' to be conquered by means of war and violence, but as brothers to be brought to the light of Christ by the means of the preaching of the Gospel in all humility and submission to them. In his first Rule Francis writes, 'the brothers who go to the Muslims can behave themselves among them spiritually in two ways. One way is to avoid quarrels and disputes and be subject to every human creature for God's sake (1 Pet 2.13), so bearing witness to the fact that they are Christians. The other way is to proclaim the word of God openly, when they see that it is God's will' (Regula non Bullata 16).

The Second Ecumenical Vatican Council opened a new chapter in the history of the Church. By means of the ecumenical movement and inter-religious dialogue, the Roman Catholic Church has put aside centuries of misunderstanding, prejudice and intolerance, not only towards the other Christian denominations but also towards the followers of the other world religions, including Islam.

The Declaration on the Relationship of the Church to non-Christian Religions of Vatican II declares, 'Upon the Muslim too, the Church looks with esteem. They adore one God, living and enduring, merciful and all-powerful, maker of heaven and earth and Speaker to man.'

Muslims today are involved in a peaceful dialogue with the

Church and are playing a very important role in contributing to world peace, religious freedom and reconciliation. Similar fruits of the Spirit are in evidence in Assisi today, where, from a small branch house of the Friars, has risen a Centre of Inter-Faith Dialogue. Indeed, such centres are beginning to spring up all over the world.

The tragic events of 11 September 2001 in the USA have not at all changed the good relationship between Islam and Christianity. The terrorist attacks, even though they were committed in the name of Islam, have nothing to do with Islam. Terrorism and violence cannot be made in the name of any religion. In the event, those tragic events have generally increased concern each for the other and a common effort for lasting peace. More than ever before, people are challenged to face terrorism and violence in the spirit of St Francis and by following his example. In January 2002, as in the year 1986, Christians and Muslims and other religious leaders from all over the world gathered in Assisi to pray for peace, thus setting an example of mutual respect, love and harmony.

Franciscan concern for animals
Andrew Linzey

Almost everyone knows the stories of St Francis of Assisi and animals – how he, for example, befriended the wolf, bought back the lamb destined for slaughter, saved worms from being crushed underfoot, and preached to the birds. Even though these stories have caught the popular imagination, as witnessed by the familiar paintings of Francis surrounded by animals, many theologians have had difficulty in interpreting them. They are usually ignored, or glossed over, or regarded as legendary accretions. That the stories seem strange to us says as much about ourselves, and our understanding of the Gospel, as it does about St Francis.

In fact, these stories exemplify the heart of the Gospel preached by St Francis. That Gospel is about the love of God the Creator, which sustains all living beings – not just the human ones. It follows that if God is the common Creator of all then we are also related to all other beings as fellow creatures. As St Bonaventure writes of Francis: 'When he considered the primordial source of all things, he was filled with even more abundant piety, calling creatures no matter how small, by the name of the brother and sister because he knew they had the same source as himself'. Pre-Darwin, and the discoveries of evolution, St Francis grasped the insight that there is a kinship between all life; we are to celebrate fellow creatures because God's love extends to all beings, animate or inanimate, within creation.

It may be thought, however, that preaching to other creatures is going too far. But Francis' actions can only be understood in the light of the dominical injunction to preach the Gospel to all creation. As God is the Creator of all, so all things are to be included within the work of salvation. By befriending and protecting animals, Francis manifested in his life the very divine generosity which he believed to be at the heart of the cosmos. 'He overflowed with the spirit of charity,' writes his early biographer Thomas of Celano, 'pitying not only men who were suffering need, but even the dumb brutes, reptiles, birds, and other creatures without sensation.' Called to imitate Christ, it follows that humans should show a Christ-like generosity to other creatures.

The theological significance behind the stories of St Francis and the animals consists mainly in this: as we grow in union with, and love for, God the Creator, so we should likewise grow in communion with, and love of, God's other creatures. Far from being some kind of aberration, or distortion of the Gospel, concern for animals is a sign of true spirituality. If we wish to honour God the Creator, so we should honour fellow creatures. Other creatures are not just 'out there' to be used as humans think fit; rather, we are intimately connected with them, and should celebrate and rejoice in what God has created. Francis' famous 'Canticle to Brother Sun' is a tremendous theophany of creation in praise of its Creator.

As David Kinsley comments, 'for Francis, what we refer to as "dumb nature" is far from dumb; it is eloquent in singing and testifying to the beauty of its creator'.

Franciscan theology speaks powerfully at a time when there is increasing ethical concern about our use of the environment and our treatment of animals in particular. It challenges the still common view that animals are simply resources, commodities, machines or things here for us. To see animals in that way constitutes a kind of spiritual impoverishment. It is to fail to grasp that since creation is precious to the Creator, so it ought also to be precious to us – especially since we are made in God's image and have the responsibility to care for it as God intended. Specifically, to inflict suffering, or to kill without justification, is an abuse of the Christ-like care we should exercise over creation.

Not least of all, Francis' convivial and respectful attitude towards animals should be seen as a prefiguring of that state of peaceableness within creation which Christians believe will be established at the end of time. Bonaventure perceptively writes of how 'it was that by God's divine power the brute beasts felt drawn towards him and inanimate creation obeyed his will. It seemed as if he had returned to that state of primeval innocence, he was so good, so holy'. Franciscan theology challenges the traditional acceptance of violence as normal either between human beings, or between humans and other creatures. Francis has become a modern icon for those who strive to live without violence, even and especially violence to other creatures. 'St Francis is before us as an example of unalterable meekness and sincere love with regard to irrational beings who make up part of creation', suggested Pope John Paul II in his sermon in Assisi on 12 March 1982. 'We too are called to a similar attitude', he continued, evoking the lines from the encyclical *Redemptor Hominis*. 'Created in the image of God, we must make him present among creatures "as intelligent and noble masters and guardians of nature and not as heedless exploiters and destroyers".'

∼

People who want to explore further will find Edward Armstrong's work *St Francis: Nature Mystic* (Berkeley, CA: University of California Press, 1973) a helpful text as well as the more recent book by Roger Sorrell, *St Francis of Assisi and Nature* (Oxford: Oxford University Press, 1988).

Paul H. Santmire's *The Travail of Nature: The Ambiguous Ecological Promise of Christian Theology* (Minneapolis: Fortress Press, 1985) provides an impressive analysis of the legacy of Francis and other seminal Christian theologians, and Michael Robson offers a perceptive account of St Francis and animals in his biography *St Francis of Assisi: The Legend and the Life* (London: Geoffrey Chapman, 1997). In many ways, however, St Bonaventure's *Life of St Francis*, edited by Ewert Cousins (New York: Paulist Press, 1978) cannot be bettered as a thoroughgoing theological interpretation of Francis' life and work.

People specifically interested in Francis and animals will find Franciscan themes developed in my *Animal Theology* (London: SCM Press and Chicago: University of Illinois Press, 1994). Franciscan spirituality is explored in my and Dan Cohn Sherbok's *After Noah: Animals and the Liberation of Theology* (London: Mowbray and Continuum Publishing, 1997). I also offer an attempt to develop Franciscan-style liturgies in my *Animal Rites: Liturgies of Animal Care* (London: SCM Press, and Cleveland, OH: The Pilgrim Press, 1999). Some of the ideas presented here are developed further in my and Ara Barsam's article on St Francis in *Fifty Key Thinkers on the Environment*, edited by Joy Palmer (London and New York: Routledge, 2001).

The will of St Francis
The Editors

Before he died, Francis, who had embraced a life with the Lady Poverty, wrote a will which is known as his Testament. Obviously he had no earthly property to bequeath, but therein lies a treasury of perceptions which point to contemporary issues which we inherit and also struggle with today.

Faith in churches

In a time when the institutional Church in Europe is slowly losing both authority and support, it may be noted that Francis showed a loyal, if critical, attitude to the Church of his day. He would have sensed much frustration in how it chose to conduct its affairs, and he broke away from a passive attendance at the regular worship where he found it hollow or proud. Yet he obviously loved to visit and pray in churches and was disturbed by the sight of church buildings in disrepair. He approached renewal, as it were, from within the structures. Many today find it difficult to relate to the Church as they have been introduced to it, managing only to support the local gathered Christian community for occasions such as the Midnight Mass or a friend's funeral. Francis did not start a new denomination or divide congregations. His is a movement from within, and provides a safe model of how the existing body of Christ can be regenerated and renewed without causing it to fracture further.

Franciscan prayer

Periods of silence and stillness, offering both a preparation for prayer and recovery of peace of mind and heart, are perhaps more essential today than for any previous generation. The lives of so many have become frantically busy, driving them to achieve more and more, at a perilous pace. The result can only be that the mind picks up a similar pace, and heart and soul cease to connect. It is a fast track to a dysfunctional lifestyle. While there is no particular way that Francis taught his people to pray, the elements are clear: he included the regular round of offices of the Church or the reciting of the Lord's Prayer; he placed the Eucharist at the centre of his spirituality; and he spent time in stillness and silence, often alone, in contemplation and acts of penitence.

One of the identifiable roots of his prayer was an attitude of penance, through which he recognized his need of God, his sinfulness before God (a perception which grew during his life as he became ever closer to God's reality), and the extent of God's love for a wayward humanity.

The Eucharist lay at the heart of his prayer, as there he was intimately united in bread and wine, the elements of creation and the work of human hands, with the Lord whose life and sacrifice brought healing, refreshment and life.

Use of Scripture

If we recognize in St Francis a respect for all that surrounded him, it isn't surprising to discover his reverence for even a stray discarded page on which was written the Word of God. He picked it up and put it in a safe place to be venerated. We would find it hard to emulate the practice in these days of photocopiers and hard copies at an instant command to the printer! However, he makes a valid point, not simply that the Word of God should be treasured, but also that it is to be received with earnest care, and responded to without unnecessary interpretation or watering down. When he trustingly opened the Book of the Gospels, it confirmed that he was to be itinerant, was not to own a second coat, and was called into the way of the cross. He accepted those directions as his way of life for the rest of his days. In fact he positively enthused that he had been directed by God's Word.

A Franciscan vocation

Francis did not set out to found a religious Order! His mind was set, rather, on living the Gospel. He attracted his followers because in looking to Francis they were significantly helped in their own pilgrimage of faith, and were encouraged to respond to the call of Jesus, 'Come, follow me', and in so doing 'to take up their cross daily'. Within his lifetime Francis was surrounded by three vibrant Orders who, according to their availability, took upon themselves this particular witness to Christ.

The brothers lived a mendicant life, inspired and directed by the saint. They lived as 'lesser brothers' under a Gospel rule and the evangelical counsels. Humility, poverty, simplicity of life and prayer were the four foundation stones. There was no special standard of education in this First Order, but rather the lifestyle was based on dedication and devotion to Christ. It became urgent, however, that the Order should create some structure to survive the vast numbers that came to join him, though this was developed more deliberately after Francis' death. When he died in 1226 there were probably around eight to nine thousand friars minor. Today there are tens of thousands, but numbers are falling and the average age is increasing. Whatever God has in store, it is hoped that there will remain a witness of friars dedicated to sharing the mission of the Church.

Clare was the first sister of a Second Order: Francis had no valid option in his day other than to direct her towards a life of enclosure and prayer. Clare was an inspiration for the friars, and her Order provided an equal witness to poverty and to Gospel living. While followers of the Clare tradition can be found today in both apostolic and enclosed congregations, they are consecrated to contemplative living, and provide that essential undergirding of prayer for the world just as the current provides for the ocean.

The Third Order came about as a result of Francis' local preaching, when a whole village, moved by his preaching and appeal to penitence, asked that they might also be brothers and sisters. With duties and responsibilities to maintain, they were not free to join Francis or Clare in community. The solution was to create an Order that would live out the spirit of the Franciscan rule, to which they pledged themselves with equal sincerity. The Secular Franciscan Order (SFO) and the Anglican equivalent are providing today an expression of Gospel living alongside the secular pressures of modern life with its responsibilities to maintain financial, parental or other needs. We rejoice at the growth in this part of the Franciscan family in present times.

Sharing the life of the Trinity

The mission of the Church has always been to join in the mission of Christ, whose life, death and resurrection are bringing about the Kingdom of God 'on earth as it is in heaven'. Through the action of the Holy Spirit, all things are being made new, to the glory of the Father. Just as Francis saw the life of the Holy Trinity as itself a community, so he reflected on the unity of creation under one Father in heaven. His broad vision comes down to our contemporary world with a refreshing and challenging call to change our attitudes, and the mindset of our time. That would regenerate within the churches an 'order of penitents' which, pray God, he will provide, both visibly and invisibly.

7

The Prayers of Francis and Clare

Austin Davis SSF

For Francis and for Clare, prayer undergirded, enriched and enlivened their whole being. Sometimes in caves on the side of mountains, in abandoned chapels or simply on the road, Francis could be found rapt in silent contemplation or praying the Daily Offices. For almost forty years Clare spent many hours of each day in the little chapel of San Damiano in devotion.

It is easy to think of Francis as the 'active' one and Clare as the 'contemplative' one but this would be unfair to both. Francis spent many of the hours of each day in prayer, and often had several long retreats in prayer each year. Clare in her monastery might have been centred on the life of prayer but it was balanced with work as well. Of course most of these hours of prayer have not resulted in prayers that we now have, but this time spent with God so ordered and empowered their lives that all that they did and said was in the light of prayer.

It is not possible to give full justice to this subject in a short introductory essay for two main reasons. First, Francis wrote and used so many prayers, and Clare, although recorded as using formal prayers, wrote none herself! Second, and perhaps more important, to read these prayers without reference to when they were written and for what reason will detract from their 'value'. For this reason I would urge the reader to read a biography of each of our two saints. Several are to be found in the bibliography section, and if you familiarize yourself with the lives and the times of Francis and Clare then the content of the prayers and character of the pray-ers will have much more impact.

Many of the texts in this chapter are taken from a very valuable translation of the Franciscan writings: *Francis of Assisi: Early Documents* (three volumes, London: New City, 1999–2001).

Francis

Thomas of Celano, Francis' earliest biographer, records that when his attention was directed to the Lord 'Francis was not so much praying as becoming a prayer himself'. This is an attractive image but it gives us problems. Francis could be so caught up in his communication with God that we who are onlookers can find it difficult to see what constitutes a prayer. Where does a prayer become a conversation with God or an exhortation to his brothers? At one point even Thomas records some words of Francis and notes that he is not sure if it is a prayer or an imprecation! We must also remember that Francis was not a theologian (and not highly educated) and never intended to produce a systematic body of prayers – he prayed wherever and whenever in a free, vibrant, and spontaneous manner. His prayers are from throughout his life, from the beginning of his conversion to the point of his death.

He was so steeped in Scripture that a number of his prayers are virtually collages made from lines from the Psalms or verses from Old and New Testaments. Something rather clumsy might have resulted but what he has left us is thought-provoking and often has considerable vitality and beauty.

As a number of the prayers cannot be dated at all, and others can be dated only with various degrees of accuracy, I have tried to be roughly chronological, and inserted undated material as seems appropriate. In a study such as this I feel it would be a mistake to include only the written prayers that have survived, so I have also added the prayers we have that his contemporaries recorded. Sometimes these throw a different light and help to give a clearer view of 'the little poor man of Assisi'.

~

In the early stages of his conversion, in 1205/6, when Francis was still uncertain of what God was calling him to do or to be, he knelt before the crucifix in the little church of San Damiano and offered this prayer:

The prayer before the crucifix

Most High glorious God,
enlighten the darkness of my heart
and give me true faith, certain hope,
and perfect charity, sense and knowledge, Lord
that I may carry out
Your holy and true command.

~

When Bernard, Francis' first follower, was pretending to sleep he witnessed Francis in prayer through the night as *The Little Flowers* records:

When he thought Bernard was fast asleep, he got out of bed and began to pray. Looking up to Heaven and raising his hands he prayed with intense fervour and devotion, saying '*My God and my all.*' And he sobbed out these words with so many tears and kept repeating them with such devout persistence that until matins he said nothing but '*My God and my all.*' (Fior, 2)

Francis often seems to have used short repeated prayers. Thomas of Celano records that in the early days when there were few brothers: 'he wished the Lord would show him the course of life for him and his brothers, and he went to a place of prayer. He remained there a long time with fear and trembling . . . frequently repeating this phrase '*Lord be merciful to me a sinner*' (1Cel, 11.26).

St Bonaventure writes of Francis telling his brothers that 'if a religious is visited by God in his prayer he should say "Lord you have sent this comfort from Heaven even though I am a sinner and unworthy, and I entrust it to your keeping because I know that I only steal your treasures"' (LM, 10.4).

~

As the Order grew, brothers joined who wanted to bring in their own ideas and modify the life as Francis envisaged it. Thomas of Celano records one episode (2Cel, 156) when two brothers grew long beards 'under the pretext of greater self-contempt'. Francis was less than approving, and we certainly see another aspect of him: 'he stretched out his hands to heaven, his face streaming with tears, broke out into words of prayer, or rather a curse:'

Lord Jesus Christ,
You chose twelve Apostles,
though one fell, the rest clung to You,
and filled with one spirit, preached the Holy Gospel.
You, Lord, in this last hour,
remembering Your ancient mercies,
have planted the religion of the brothers
as a support for Your faith,
and that the mystery of Your Gospel through them
    might be fulfilled.
Who, then, will make satisfaction for them before You,
if they not only fail to show examples of Light to all,
but, rather, display works of Darkness?
By You, most holy Lord, and by the whole court of
    Heaven,
and by me, Your little one,

may they be cursed who break up and destroy by their
bad example
what You earlier built up, and do not cease to build up,
through holy brothers of this religion!

~

One of the treasures that Francis left is perhaps the only
example of his teaching on how to pray, the lovely

Prayer inspired by the 'Our Father'

O *Our Father* most holy:
Our Creator, Redeemer, Consoler, and Saviour:

Who are in heaven:
In the angels and in the saints, enlightening them to know,
for You, Lord, are light; inflaming them to love, for You,
Lord, are love; dwelling in them and filling them with
happiness, for You, Lord, are Supreme Good, the Eternal
Good, from whom all good comes, without whom there
is no good.

Holy be Your Name:
May knowledge of You become clearer in us, that we
may know the breadth of Your blessings, the length of
Your promises, the height of Your majesty, the depth of
Your judgements.

Your kingdom come:
That You may rule in us through Your grace, and enable
us to come to Your kingdom, where there is clear vision
of You, perfect love of You, blessed companionship with
You, eternal enjoyment of You.

Your will be done on earth as in heaven:
That we may love You with our whole heart by always
thinking of You, with our whole soul by always desiring
You, with our whole mind by always directing all our

intentions to You, and by seeking Your glory in everything, with all our whole strength by exerting all our
energies and affection of body and soul in the service of
Your love and of nothing else; and may we love our neighbour as ourselves, by drawing them all to Your love with
our whole strength, by rejoicing in the good of others as
in our own, by suffering with others at their misfortunes,
and by giving offence to no one.

Give us this day:
In remembrance, understanding, and reverence of that
love which our Lord Jesus Christ had for us, and of those
things that he said and did and suffered for us.

Our daily Bread:
Your own beloved Son, our Lord Jesus Christ.

Forgive us our trespasses:
Through Your ineffable mercy, through the power of the
passion of Your beloved Son, and through the merits and
intercessions of the ever-blessed Virgin and all Your elect.

As we forgive those who trespass against us:
And what we do not completely forgive, make us, Lord,
forgive completely, that we may truly love our enemies
because of You, and may we fervently intercede for them
before You, returning no one evil for evil, and may we
strive to help everyone in You.

And lead us not into temptation:
Hidden or obvious, sudden or persistent.

But deliver us from evil:
Past, present and to come.

Glory to the Father, and to the Son, and to the Holy Spirit.
As it was in the beginning, is now, and will be for ever.
Amen.

~

The following prayer was found written on a wooden panel of the altar in the hermitage of St Mary of the Angels of Cesi di Terni in the Spoleto Valley. The prayer survives, though unfortunately the panel has now been lost. It is composed mostly of lines from the Psalms, and shows Francis in his enthusiasm to promote the praise of God. What results may seem unsophisticated, but it has considerable range and depth. It is known as the

Exhortation to the praise of God

Fear the Lord and give him honour.
Worthy is the Lord to receive praise and honour.
All you who fear the Lord praise him.
Hail Mary, full of grace, the Lord is with you.
Heaven and earth, praise him.
All you rivers, praise the Lord.
All you children of God, praise the Lord.
This is the day that the Lord has made, let us rejoice and
    be glad in it!
Alleluia, alleluia, alleluia! The King of Israel!
Let every spirit praise the Lord.
Praise the Lord because he is good;
All you who read this, bless the Lord.
All you creatures, bless the Lord.
All you birds of heaven, praise the Lord.
All you children, praise the Lord.
Young men and virgins, praise the Lord.
Worthy is the Lamb who was slain to receive praise,
    glory, and honour.
Blessed be the Holy Trinity and Undivided Unity.
St Michael the Archangel, defend us in battle.

~

A shorter exhortation is found in the second version of one of Francis' letters, his 'Letter to the Faithful' (2Lt F61). It comes

at the end of a long and moving piece on the necessity and
value of penance.

Exhortation from the 'Letter to the Faithful'

Let every creature
in heaven, on earth, in the sea and in the depths,
give praise, glory, honour and blessing
to Him Who suffered so much,
Who has given and will give in the future every good,
for He is our power and strength,
Who alone is good,
Who alone is almighty,
Who alone is omnipotent, wonderful, glorious,
and Who alone is Holy,
worthy of praise and blessing
through endless ages.
Amen.

∾

Francis had a great devotion to the Blessed Virgin Mary. She is
cited in several of his writings, and through them can be seen
the centrality of the incarnation within his spirituality.

A salutation of the Blessed Virgin Mary

Hail, O Lady,
Holy Queen,
Mary, holy Mother of God,
Who are the Virgin made Church,
chosen by the most Holy Father in heaven,
whom he consecrated with His most holy beloved Son,
and with the Holy Spirit the Paraclete,
in whom there was and is
all fullness of grace and every good.
Hail His Palace!

Hail His Tabernacle!
Hail His Dwelling!
Hail His Robe!
Hail His Servant!
Hail His Mother!
And hail all You holy virtues
which are poured into the hearts of the faithful
through the grace and enlightenment of the Holy Spirit,
that from being unbelievers,
You may make them faithful to God.

∾

In the last piece Francis cites the Holy Virtues, and in the following, he takes up the theme in a similar, but more elaborate manner. Here Francis *can* be considered a theologian – of the workings of the Spirit.

The salutation of the virtues

Hail Queen Wisdom!
May the Lord protect You, with Your sister, holy pure
    Simplicity!
Lady holy Poverty, may the Lord protect You,
with Your Sister, holy Humility!
Lady holy Charity, may the Lord protect you,
with Your Sister, holy Obedience.
Most holy Virtues, may the Lord protect all of You
from Whom You come and proceed.
There is surely no one in the whole world
who can possess any one of You without dying first.
Whoever possesses one and does not offend the others
    possesses all.
Whoever offends one does not possess any and offends
    all.
And each one confounds vice and sin.
Holy Wisdom confounds Satan and all his cunning.

Pure holy Simplicity confounds
all the wisdom of this world and the wisdom of the
  body.
Holy Poverty confounds the desire for riches,
greed, and the cares of this world.
Holy Humility confounds pride,
all the people who are in the world and all that is in the
  world.
Holy Charity confounds
every diabolical and carnal temptation and every carnal
  fear.
Holy Obedience confounds every corporal and carnal
  wish,
binds its mortified body to obedience of the Spirit
and obedience to one's brother, so that it is subject and
  submissive
to everyone in the world, not only to people,
but to every beast and wild animal as well,
that they may do whatever they want with it
in so far as it has been given to them from above
by the Lord.

~

Francis wrote several Rules to govern his Order, and the
earlier ones have a degree of spontaneity that was edited out
of the final one that was given Papal approval. One would
hardly expect a writer of a legal document to burst into praise
and prayer in the middle of it, but Francis could! Two prayers
come to us from the Earlier Rule, finalized in 1221 (chapters
18 and 23):

First prayer from the Earlier Rule

Let us refer all good to the Lord God Almighty and
  Most High,
acknowledge that every good is His, and thank Him,

from Whom all good comes, for everything.
May He, the Almighty and Most High, the only true
    God,
have, be given, and receive all honour and respect,
all praise and blessing, all thanks and glory,
to Whom all good belongs,
He who alone is good.
When we see or hear evil spoken or done
or God blasphemed,
let us speak and do well and praise God
Who is blessed forever.

~

The second of the two prayers must be one of the most all-
encompassing prayers ever written.

Second prayer from the Earlier Rule

All-powerful, most holy, Almighty and supreme God,
Holy and just Father,
Lord King of heaven and earth,
we thank You for Yourself
for through Your holy will and through Your only Son
with the Holy Spirit
You have created everything spiritual and corporal,
and, after making us in Your own image and likeness,
You placed us in paradise.
Through our own fault we fell.

We thank You for, as through Your Son You created
    us,
so through Your holy love with which You loved us
You brought about His birth as true God and true man
by the glorious, ever-virgin, most blessed, holy Mary
and You willed to redeem us captives
through His cross and blood and death.

We thank You for Your Son himself will come again
in the glory of His majesty,
to send to the eternal fire the wicked ones
who have not done penance and have not known You
and to say to all those who have known You,
adored You, and served You in penance:
'Come, you blessed of my Father,
receive the kingdom prepared for you
from the beginning of the world.'

Because all of us, wretches and sinners,
are not worthy to pronounce Your name,
we humbly ask our Lord Jesus Christ, Your beloved Son,
in whom You were well pleased,
together with the Holy Spirit, the Paraclete,
to give You thanks for everything
as it pleases You and Him,
Who always satisfies You in everything,
through Whom You have done so much for us.
Alleluia!

Because of Your love, we humbly beg the glorious
    Mother,
the most blessed, ever-virgin Mary,
Blessed Michael, Gabriel, and Raphael,
all the choirs of the blessed seraphim, cherubim,
thrones, dominations, principalities,
powers, virtues, angels, archangels,
Blessed John the Baptist,
John the Evangelist, Peter, Paul,
the blessed patriarchs and prophets, the innocents,
apostles, evangelists, disciples,
the martyrs, confessors and virgins,
the blessed Elijah and Henoch,
all the saints who were, who will be, and who are:
to give You thanks for these things, as it pleases You,
God true and supreme, eternal and living,
with Your most beloved Son, our Lord Jesus Christ,

and the Holy Spirit, the Paraclete,
world without end.
Amen.
Alleluia!

All of us lesser brothers, useless servants,
humbly ask and beg those who wish to serve the Lord God
within the holy Catholic and Apostolic Church,
and all the following orders:
priests, deacons, subdeacons, acolytes,
exorcists, lectors, porters, and all clerics,
all religious men and women,
all penitents and youths,
the poor and needy, kings and princes,
workers and farmers, servants and masters,
all virgins, continent and married women,
all lay people, men and women,
all children, adolescents, young and old,
the healthy and the sick,
all the small and the great,
all people, races, tribes, and tongues,
all nations and all peoples everywhere on earth,
who are and who will be,
to persevere in the true faith and in penance,
for otherwise no one will be saved.

With our whole heart, our whole soul, our whole mind,
with our whole strength and fortitude, with our whole
    understanding,
with all our powers, with every effort, every affection,
every feeling, every desire and wish,
let us all love the Lord God,
Who has given and gives to each one of us
our whole body, our whole soul and our whole life,
Who has created, redeemed and will save us by His
    mercy alone,
Who did and does everything good for us,
miserable and wretched, rotten and foul,

ungrateful and evil ones.
Therefore, let us desire nothing else, let us want nothing else,
let nothing else please us and cause us delight
except our Creator, Redeemer and Saviour,
the only true God, Who is the fullness of good,
all good, every good, the true and supreme good,
Who alone is good, merciful, gentle, delightful, and sweet,
Who alone is holy, just, true, holy and upright,
Who alone is kind, innocent, clean,
from Whom, through Whom, and in Whom,
is all pardon, all grace, all glory of all penitents and just ones,
of all the blessed rejoicing together in heaven.

Therefore, let nothing hinder us,
nothing separate us,
nothing come between us.

Wherever we are, in every place,
at every hour, at every time of day,
every day and continually,
let us all truly and humbly believe,
hold in our heart and love, honour, adore, serve,
praise and bless, glorify and exalt, magnify and give thanks
to the Most High and Supreme Eternal God, Trinity and
    Unity,
Father, Son and Holy Spirit,
Creator of all,
Saviour of all who believe and hope in Him, and love Him,
Who, without beginning and end, is unchangeable,
invisible, indescribable, ineffable, incomprehensible,
    unfathomable,
blessed, praiseworthy, glorious, exalted, sublime, most high,
gentle, loveable, delightful,
and totally desirable above all else
for ever.
Amen.

~

The order had grown so rapidly that a few years before his death Francis realized that new leadership was needed. Thomas of Celano records (2Cel, 143) that: 'some brothers saw themselves orphaned of such a father. But Francis rising and with his hands joined and his eyes raised to heaven said:'

Lord, I commend to You the family that You heretofore have entrusted to me. But now, because of my infirmities, as You know, most sweet Lord, I am unable to care for it, so I entrust it to the ministers. Let them be obliged to render an account before You, Lord, on judgement day, if any brother of them perishes because of their negligence, or example, or harsh correction.

〜

One prayer that was thought at one time to have been written by Francis is the 'Absorbeat'. Francis certainly used it, but it is reckoned to be of earlier medieval origin. It encapsulates Francis' spirituality, and makes the events on Mount La Verna more understandable.

The Absorbeat

I beg You, Lord,
let the glowing and honey-sweet force of Your love
draw my mind away from all things that are under
    heaven,
that I may die for love of the love of You,
who thought it a worthy thing to die for the love of me.

〜

In 1224 Francis went to Mount La Verna for a long retreat accompanied by Brother Leo as his aide. *The Little Flowers* records that one night early in his retreat, when he was praying, he was assailed by 'a great number of the fiercest devils'.

The Prayers on Mount La Verna

After being persecuted for some time, Francis cried out and said:

My Lord Jesus Christ,
I thank You for the great love and charity which You are
   showing me,
because it is a sign of great love
when the Lord punishes His servant well for all his faults
   in this world,
so that he may not be punished for them in the next world.
And I am prepared to endure with joy every pain and every
   adversity
which You, my God, wish to send me for my sins.

Then the devils, defeated by his endurance and patience, went away.

Not only was Francis troubled by devils, he was concerned over the future of his Order, for he was in poor health.

One day while he was thinking about his death and the state of his Order when he was no longer alive, and he was saying: 'Lord God, after my death what will happen to Your poor little family which in Your kindness You entrusted to this sinner? Who will console them? Who will correct them? Who will pray to You for them?' An angel sent by God appeared and consoled him.

Not long before Holy Cross day, 14 September, Brother Leo was listening to Francis praying in the moonlight, 'with his face lifted to the sky and his hands held out to God, saying these words in fervour of spirit: "Who are You, my dearest God? And what am I, Your vilest worm and useless little servant?"'

Leo then witnessed a heavenly light descend upon Francis. When he asked Francis what had happened he was told that

God had spoken to him in that fire. Francis continued: 'And among other things which He said to me then, He asked me to give Him three gifts. And I replied:'

> My Lord, I am entirely Yours.
> You know that I have nothing but a habit and cord and
>   breeches,
> and those three things are likewise Yours.
> So what can I give Your majesty?
> For heaven and earth, fire and water,
> and everything in them, are Yours, Lord.
> Who indeed has anything that is not Yours?
> Therefore when we offer You anything, we give You
>   back what is Yours.
> So what can I offer to You, the Lord God,
> King of Heaven and earth and all creation?
> For what do I have that is not Yours?

Before dawn on Holy Cross day itself, Francis prayed:

> My Lord Jesus Christ, I pray You to grant me two graces before I die: the first is that during my life I may feel in my body, as much as possible, that pain which You, dear Jesus, sustained in the hour of Your most bitter passion. The second is that I may feel in my heart, as much as possible, that excessive love with which You, O Son of God, were inflamed in willingly enduring such suffering for us sinners.

And then Francis was granted that most mysterious miracle, the imprinting of the Wounds of Christ, the stigmata.

∾

Before they left La Verna, Leo was 'yearning with a great desire to have something encouraging from the words of our Lord, commented on and written by Francis' own hand'. And so we have the 'Praises of God' and the 'Blessing of Brother

Leo', which were kept by Leo, are still extant, and are now kept in the Basilica in Assisi.

The praises of God

You are the holy Lord God Who does wonderful things.

You are strong. You are great. You are the Most High.
You are the almighty king. You holy Father,
King of heaven and earth.

You are three and one, the Lord God of gods;
You are the good, all good, the highest good,
Lord God living and true.

You are love, charity; You are wisdom, You are
    humility.
You are patience, You are beauty, You are meekness.
You are security, You are rest.
You are gladness and joy, You are our hope, You are
    justice.
You are moderation, You are all our riches to
    sufficiency.

You are beauty, You are meekness.
You are the protector, You are our custodian and
    defender.
You are strength, You are refreshment, You are our
    hope.
You are our faith, You are our charity.
You are all our sweetness, You are our eternal life:
Great and wonderful Lord, Almighty God, Merciful
    Saviour.

∽

The Blessing for Leo

May the Lord bless you and keep you.
May He show his face to you and be merciful to you.

May He turn his countenance to you and give you peace.
May the Lord bless you, Brother Leo.

~

In the last two years of his life, Francis was ill most of the
time, and incapacitated, virtually blind, and in constant pain.
A brother suggested that he prayed to God 'that he might treat
you more mildly'. As his biographer St Bonaventure records:
'Even though he was completely worn out by his prolonged
and serious illness, he threw himself on the ground bruising
his weakened knees . . . kissed the ground and said:'

> I thank You Lord God for all these sufferings of mine; and
> I ask You, my Lord, if it pleases You, to increase them a
> hundredfold. Because it will be most acceptable to me, that
> You do not spare me, afflicting me with suffering, since the
> fulfilment of Your will is an overflowing consolation for
> me.

One night in this period, his hut was plagued by mice, such
that together with his illnesses he 'could neither pray nor rest'
as *The Mirror of Perfection* tells us.

> So tormented by so many troubles and feeling sorry for him-
> self he prayed inwardly: 'Lord look on me and help me in
> my troubles, and give me strength to bear them patiently,'
> and at once he heard a voice within his soul saying, 'Tell me
> brother; if in recompense for these infirmities and tribula-
> tions you were to be given so vast and precious treasure
> that, were the whole world pure gold, its stones jewels, and
> all its waters balsam, you would regard them as nothing
> in comparison to this vast treasure, would you not be very
> happy?' And blessed Francis replied, 'Lord, such a treasure
> would be vast and precious, very lovely and desirable.' And
> he heard the voice speak to him once more, 'Then be glad,
> brother, and rejoice in your troubles and infirmities. As for

the rest, trust in Me, as though you were already in My Kingdom.'

∿

The *Canticle of the Creatures* is perhaps the best-known writing of Francis and very many studies have been made of it. G. K. Chesterton said of it: 'It is a supremely characteristic work and much of Saint Francis could be reconstructed from that work alone.'

The mystical vision of Francis can be found here, and it provides many insights into his life of faith. He became so intimate with God's creation that he could, quite simply, call all things Brother and Sister, members of one family.

We know from the 'Assisi Compilation' (an early source) that the Canticle was composed in three parts. It was probably begun in 1225 when he was suffering considerably from his physical infirmities. We are told that Francis said:

I want to write a new Praise of the Lord for his creatures, which we use every day, and without which we cannot live. Through them the human race greatly offends the Creator, and every day we are ungrateful for such graces, because we do not praise, as we should, our Creator and the Giver of all good.

The second part was written in a peacemaking attempt to bring together the Mayor and Bishop of Assisi, who were at odds. The last stanza was written on his deathbed.

Canticle of the Creatures

Most High, all-powerful, good Lord,
    Yours are the praises, the glory, and the honour, and
    all blessing.
To You alone, Most High, do they belong,
    and no human is worthy to mention Your name.

Praised be You, my Lord, with all Your creatures,
　　especially Sir Brother Sun,
　　　Who is the day and through whom You give us light.
And he is beautiful and radiant with great splendour;
　　and bears a likeness of You, Most High One.
Praised be You, my Lord, through Sister Moon and the
　　stars,
　　　in heaven You formed them clear and precious and
　　　　beautiful.
Praised be You, my Lord, through Brother Wind,
　　and through the air, cloudy and serene, and every
　　　　kind of weather,
　　　through whom You give sustenance to your
　　　　creatures.
Praised be You, my Lord, through Sister Water,
　　who is very useful and humble and precious and
　　　　chaste.
Praised be You, my Lord, through Brother Fire,
　　through whom You light the night,
　　and he is beautiful and playful and robust and strong.
Praised be You, my Lord, through our Sister Mother Earth,
　　who sustains and governs us,
　　and who produces various fruit with coloured flowers
　　　　and herbs.

Praised be You, my Lord, through those who give pardon
　　　for Your love,
　　and bear infirmity and tribulation.
　　Blessed are those who endure in peace
　　　for by You, Most High, shall they be crowned.

Praised be You, my Lord, through our Sister Bodily
　　　Death,
　　from whom no one living can escape.
　　Woe to those who die in mortal sin.
　　Blessed are those whom death will find in Your most
　　　holy will,
　　　　for the second death shall do them no harm.

Praise and bless my Lord and give Him thanks
and serve Him with great humility.

∽

Although in 1225 Francis was nearing the end of his earthly
life, and he was no longer Minister General of the Order, his
concern for his brothers had not lessened. He wrote a letter exhorting his brothers to reverence Jesus, particularly in
the Eucharist. It ends with a prayer which shows the balance
Francis achieved in his spiritual life.

Prayer concluding 'A Letter to the Entire Order'

Almighty, eternal, just and merciful God,
give us miserable ones
the grace to do for You alone
what we know You want us to do,
and always desire what pleases You.
Inwardly cleansed,
interiorly enlightened,
and inflamed by the fire of the Holy Spirit,
may we be able to follow
in the footprints of Your beloved Son,
our Lord Jesus Christ,
and, by Your grace alone,
may we make our way to You,
Most High,
Who live and rule
in perfect Trinity and simple Unity,
and are glorified
God almighty,
for ever and ever.
Amen.

∽

While he was staying with the Bishop in Assisi so that he could be cared for, Thomas of Celano records (1Cel, 108) that he called the Minister General, Elias, and the brothers to him so that he could bless them. In his blindness he had to ask whom he was blessing. 'Brother Elias,' they replied. 'And this is what I want to do,' Francis replied:

> I bless you, my son, in all and through all, and just as the Most High has increased my brothers and sons in your hands, so too, upon you and in you, I bless them all. May the King of all bless you in heaven and on earth. I bless you as I can, and more than I can, and what I cannot do may the One who can do all things do in you. May God remember your work and labours, and may a place be reserved for you among the rewards of the just. May you receive every blessing you desire and may your every worthy request be fulfilled.
>
> Goodbye all my sons. Live in the fear of God and remain in Him always, for a great test will come upon you and tribulation is drawing near! Happy are those who will persevere in what they have begun: many will be separated from them by the scandals that are to come. But now I am hurrying to the Lord and I am confident that I am going to my God whom I have served in my spirit.

~

From the Bishop's palace, Francis was taken in a litter to the chapel of St Mary of the Angels in the plain below Assisi. Halfway there they stopped, and *The Mirror of Perfection* sets the scene: 'although almost deprived of sight, he had the litter turned to face the city, saying:'

The blessing of Assisi

Lord, it is said that in former days this city was the haunt of wicked men. But now it is clear that of Your infinite mercy, and in Your own time, You have been pleased to shower especial and abundant favours upon it. Of Your goodness alone have You chosen it for Yourself, that it may become the home and dwelling of those who know You in truth and glorify Your Holy Name, and spread abroad the fragrance of a good report, of holy life, of true doctrine, and of evangelical perfection to all Christian people.

I therefore ask You, O Lord Jesus Christ, Father of mercies, that You will not remember our ingratitude, but ever be mindful of Your abundant compassion which You have showed towards it, that it may ever be the home and dwelling place of those who know You in truth and glorify Your blessed and most glorious Name for ever and ever. Amen.

∽

As Francis lay dying near the chapel of St Mary of the Angels, he dictated his Testament, which is full of care and concern for the brothers who would follow him. It has remained a document of considerable importance to all Franciscans. Amongst guidance and exhortation he left a prayer, which was not new but had been on his lips many times before:

Prayer on entering a church

We adore You Lord Jesus Christ, in all Your churches throughout the whole world, and we bless You because by Your holy cross You have redeemed the world.

∽

The Praises to be said at All the Hours, and the Office of the Passion, together form a large work. Although written by Francis, both he and Clare used the Office daily until their deaths. The Hours are the cycle of services or Offices that make up the formal cycle of prayers through the day. By adding to them the Praises and the psalms he composed for the Office of the Passion, Francis added considerably to the formal prayers of his brothers.

In the introduction to the Office is written, 'these are the psalms which our most Holy Father Francis composed in reverence, memory, and praise of the passion of the Lord. They should be said during each of the Hours of the day and the one Hour of the night'. Their content is partly specific to the time of day, particularly with the drama of Christ's Passion and the supposed time that each element of it took place.

They begin with the Compline of Holy (Maundy) Thursday, 'For on that night our Lord Jesus Christ was betrayed and taken captive'. This psalm reflects the prayers of Jesus in Gethsemane. This office has been set out, in a form that can be used devotionally, at the commencement of the next chapter.

Both of these works are virtually 'collages' of biblical texts. The Praises are taken mainly from Revelation. The Office of the Passion includes some fifteen psalms selected mostly from verses of the biblical Psalms, set out under various Hours.

The verses composed for Matins contain echoes of the capture and trials of Jesus during that night, with his complete confidence in God even during the dark uncertainties of waiting. Prime was understood in the Middle Ages to be the time of the trial before Pilate, but interestingly this psalm also looks forward to the discovery of the resurrection of Jesus 'as the first day of the week was dawning'. The psalm at Terce reflects the prayers of Jesus during the scourging, the crowning with thorns, and the mockery of the soldiers and the crowd. Sext was the Hour of the Crucifixion, at noon. The Office of None was the time of the death of Jesus, and the psalm contains both that despair and the hope of the resurrection. The psalm for Vespers expresses the joy of the resurrection, traditionally celebrated at this time of day. It also carries a reminder that all are called to follow in the way of Jesus and 'carry his holy cross'.

After the Antiphon 'Holy Virgin Mary' there would have been biblical psalms in honour of Our Lady, and others chosen for the particular Office.

The psalms were written with the church seasons in mind and are divided into five sections:

1) For the Sacred Triduum of Holy Week (Maundy Thursday to Easter Day). These were also used on ordinary weekdays throughout the year.
2) For the Easter season.
3) For Sundays and Principal Feasts.
4) For the season of Advent.
5) For Christmas and the Octave of Epiphany.

The full text of the Office of the Passion, with the psalms, as composed and selected by Francis, are to be found in Andre Cirino's book, *The Geste of the Great King*, published by Laurent Gallant, 2001.

Clare

We have a different situation with Clare, for she left no formal prayers. That she was a very prayerful sister there is no doubt. She followed the regular cycle of the Daily Offices, and we know that she also used the Office of the Passion that Francis had written. We also have the witness of her sisters in the monastery of St Damian. In the records of the canonization process there is constant mention of her at prayer: 'the witness also said that mother Saint Clare was very assiduous, day and night, in prayer' (Canonization Process 2, 9).

Her biographer is more florid but well worth quoting (*Legend of Clare*, 20):

The usual signs prove how much strength she received in her furnace of ardent prayer, how sweet the divine goodness was to her in that enjoyment. For when she returned with joy from holy prayer she brought from the altar of the Lord burning words that also inflamed the hearts of her sisters.

But alas no written prayers – indeed, we have very little from Clare: just five letters, four to Agnes of Prague and one to Ermentrude of Bruges, together with her Testament, Rule of Life and a Blessing to her sisters. The Blessing is probably the closest to a prayer we have from Clare's hand.

~

Although the Letters are not prayers, anyone receiving them would surely be spurred on to greater endeavour in their own life of prayer. In her first letter to Agnes, Clare writes:

> What a great and praiseworthy exchange:
> to leave the things of time for those of eternity,
> to choose the things of heaven for the goods of earth,
> to receive the hundredfold in place of one,
> and to possess a blessed eternal life.

In the fourth letter to Agnes there is a wonderful passage on the 'Mirror of Eternity' that has earned Clare the title of 'Mirror mystic', where she exhorts Agnes to contemplate herself and the Christ in this mirror. This letter certainly offers us some insights into Clare's life of contemplative prayer. A long and beautiful passage reaches its climax:

> From this moment, then, O Queen of our heavenly King, let yourself be inflamed more strongly with the fervour of charity. As you further contemplate His ineffable delights, eternal riches and honours, and sigh for them in the great desire and love of your heart, may you cry out:

> Draw me after You, we will run in the fragrance of Your perfumes,

O heavenly Spouse!
I will run and not tire, until You bring me into the wine
cellar,
until Your left hand is under my head,
and Your right hand will embrace me happily,
and You will kiss me with the happiest kiss of Your
mouth.

Quoting scripture Clare may have been, but what wonderfully
emotive language.

~

As she was coming to the end of her life in the summer of
1253, as well as her Testament, Clare left her sisters her blessing. In some ways it echoes the blessing given by Francis to
Leo on Mount La Verna.

The blessing of Clare

In the name of the Father and of the Son and of the Holy
Spirit,
May the Lord bless you and keep you.
May He show His face to you and be merciful to you.
May He turn his countenance to you, my sisters and
daughters, and give peace to you, and to all others who
come and remain in your company, as well as to others
now and in the future, who have persevered in every other
monastery of the Poor Ladies.

I, Clare, a servant of Christ, a little plant of our most holy
Father Francis, a sister and mother of you and the other
poor sisters, although unworthy, beg our Lord Jesus Christ
through His mercy, and the intercession of His most holy
Mother Mary and blessed Michael the Archangel and all
the holy angels of God, of our blessed Father Francis, and
all the men and women saints, that the heavenly Father give

you and confirm for you this most holy blessing in heaven and on earth. On earth may He multiply you in His grace and His virtues among His servants and handmaids in His Church Militant. In heaven, may He exalt you and glorify you among His men and women saints in His Church Triumphant.

I bless you during my life and after my death, as I am able, out of all the blessings with which the Father of mercies has and does bless His sons and daughters in heaven and on earth and a spiritual father and mother have blessed and bless their spiritual sons and daughters. Amen.

Always be lovers of your souls and those of all your sisters. And may you always be eager to observe what you have promised the Lord.

May the Lord always be with you, and may you always be with Him.

Amen.

~

There is always a possibility that in some dusty sacristy cupboard in a Poor Clare convent there may be found one day a bundle of parchments that will turn out to be more of Clare's writings. Let us hope so, for they may contain further gems that will enrich our lives.

~

If you have carefully gone through this work on the prayers of Francis and Clare and are thinking, 'what about that prayer of Francis that goes, "Lord make me an instrument of your peace"' – well, you haven't found it yet because it was not written, or used, by Francis. It was researched by the Franciscan scholar and Anglican bishop, the late John Moorman. He concluded that the author is unknown, but the prayer was first noted in France about 1913, and shortly after issued on a card as a 'Prayer for Peace' with a picture of Francis on the back. In 1936 Francis' name was mistakenly connected with the prayer by a publisher, and the two have been linked since then.

As Bishop Moorman says, 'although the prayer has no connection with S. Francis having been written nearly seven hundred years after his death, it may be said, in some ways to express his thoughts as known from his authentic writings'. For this reason this modern 'Prayer of St Francis' has been included.

Lord, make me an instrument of your peace.
Where there is hatred, let me sow love;
   where there is injury, pardon;
   where there is doubt, faith;
   where there is despair, hope;
   where there is darkness, light;
   where there is sadness, joy.
O Divine Master, grant that I may not so much
   seek to be consoled as to console,
   to be understood as to understand,
   to be loved as to love.
For it is in giving that we receive,
   it is in pardoning that we are pardoned,
   and it is in dying that we are born to eternal life.
Amen.

8

Settings of the Office

A Franciscan Office

The following form of prayer may be used in full or in part
at any Franciscan gathering. Suitable psalms, hymns or songs
may be interspersed where appropriate.

The Invocation

We adore you,
**most holy Lord Jesus Christ,
here and in all your churches throughout the world;**
and we bless you
**because by your holy cross
you have redeemed the world.**

Come, Holy Spirit, and fill the hearts of your faithful
    people,
And kindle in us the fire of your love.

Blessed be God: Father, Son and Holy Spirit;
And blessed be his kingdom now and for ever.

Then may be said or sung one of the following canticles:

The Praises Of God

You are the holy Lord God; who does wonderful things.
You are strong; you are great; you are the Most High.

You are the almighty King.
You, holy Father, King of heaven and earth.

You are three and one, the Lord God of gods;
you are the good, all good, the highest good, Lord God,
    living and true.

You are love, charity; you are wisdom, you are humility,
you are patience, you are beauty, you are meekness, you
    are security, you are rest.

You are gladness and joy, you are our hope, you are justice,
you are moderation, you are all our riches to sufficiency.

You are beauty, you are meekness,
you are the protector, you are our custodian and defender.

You are strength, you are refreshment. You are our hope,
you are our faith, you are our charity.

You are all our sweetness, you are our eternal life:
Great and wonderful Lord, Almighty God, Merciful
    Saviour.

or:

The Canticle Of The Creatures

Most High, all-powerful, good Lord,
yours are the praises, the glory and the honour and all
    blessing,

to you alone, Most High, do they belong
and no human is worthy to mention your name.

Praised be you, my Lord, with all your creatures,
especially Brother Sun, who is the day and through whom
    you give us light.

And he is beautiful and radiant with great splendour;
and bears a likeness of you, Most High One.

Praised be you, my Lord, through Sister Moon and the
     stars,
in heaven you formed them clear and precious and
     beautiful.

Praised be you, my Lord, through Brother Wind,
and through the air, cloudy and serene, and every kind of
     weather,
through whom you give sustenance to your creatures.

Praised be you, my Lord, through Sister Water,
who is very useful and humble and precious and chaste.

Praised be you, my Lord, through Brother Fire,
through whom you light the night,
and he is beautiful and playful and robust and strong.

Praised be you, my Lord, through our Sister, Mother Earth,
who sustains and governs us,
and who produces various fruit with coloured flowers and
     herbs.

Praised be you, my Lord, through those who give pardon
     for your love,
and bear infirmity and tribulation.

Blessed are those who endure in peace,
for by you, Most High, they shall be crowned.

Praised be you, my Lord, through our Sister Bodily Death,
from whom no one living can escape.
Woe to those who die in mortal sin.

Blessed are those whom death will find in your most holy
     will,
for the second death shall do them no harm.

Praise and bless my Lord and give him thanks,
And serve him with great humility.

or:

The Praises to be Said at All Hours

Holy, holy, holy Lord God Almighty,
who is, and who was, and who is to come.
And let us praise and glorify him for ever.

O Lord our God, you are worthy to receive
praise, glory and honour and blessing.
And let us praise and glorify him for ever.

The Lamb who was slain is worthy to receive
power and divinity, wisdom and strength, honour and
   glory and blessing.
And let us praise and glorify him for ever.

Let us bless the Father and the Son with the Holy Spirit.
And let us praise and glorify him for ever.

Bless the Lord, all you works of the Lord.
And let us praise and glorify him for ever.

Sing praise to our God, all you his servants
and you who fear God, the small and the great.
And let us praise and glorify him for ever.

Let heaven and earth praise him who is glorious.
And let us praise and glorify him for ever.

Every creature in heaven, on earth and under the earth;
and in the sea and those which are in it.
And let us praise and glorify him for ever.

Glory to the Father and to the Son and to the Holy Spirit.
And let us praise and glorify him for ever.

As it was in the beginning, is now, and shall be for ever.
And let us praise and glorify him for ever.

At the end of the canticle, this prayer is said:

All-powerful, Most Holy, Most High, supreme God:
all good, supreme good, totally good, you who alone are good,
may we give you all praise, all glory, all thanks,
all honour, all blessing, and all good.
So be it! So be it!
Amen.

*A reading follows, depicting the Franciscan Life. The reading
may be selected from the Writings of St Francis or St Clare or
one of the early authors or any other suitable reading.*

Silence.

The Cross Prayers

Having in mind St Francis' devotion to the passion of Christ,
and looking upon the figure of the Crucified,
(with arms outstretched) let us pray to the Lord.

A short silence may be observed.

You have sealed, O Lord, your servant Francis,
With the sign of our redemption.

Lord Jesus Christ,
who, when the world was growing cold
to the inflaming of our hearts by the fire of your love,
raised up blessed Francis,
bearing in his body the marks of your passion:
mercifully grant to us, your people,
true penitence
and grace to bear the cross for love of you;
who live and reign with the Father and the Holy Spirit,
one God, now and for ever.
Amen.

*Prayers and intercession and thanksgiving may be offered
here, interspersed with Kyries or another suitable response.*

Lord, have mercy. **Lord, have mercy.**
Christ, have mercy. **Christ, have mercy.**

Lord, hear us. **Lord, graciously hear us.**

Lord, in your mercy, **Hear our prayer.**

The intercessions conclude with:

May the power of your love, Lord Christ,
fiery and sweet as honey,
so absorb our hearts
as to withdraw them from all that is under heaven.
Grant that we may be ready
to die for love of your love,
as you died for love of our love.
Amen.

The Lord's Prayer

Our Father . . .

The Blessing

May God kindle in us the fire of love.
Amen.

**Or the Aaronic blessing (as used by Francis when he
blessed Leo):**

The Lord bless you and keep you:
the Lord make his face to shine upon you and be gracious
to you;
the Lord lift up the light of his countenance
upon you and give you his peace.
My brothers and sisters, the Lord bless you.
Amen.

∾

The Office of the Passion

The following is a version of the Office of the Passion, originally written by St Francis for Compline on Holy (Maundy) Thursday. This is just one sample of the additional prayer material used by the saint and his brothers.

The Lord's Prayer

The Praises to be Said at All Hours

Holy, holy, holy Lord God Almighty,
who is, and who was, and who is to come.
And let us praise and glorify him for ever.

O Lord our God, you are worthy to receive
praise, glory and honour and blessing.
And let us praise and glorify him for ever.

The Lamb who was slain is worthy to receive
power and divinity, wisdom and strength, honour and
    glory and blessing.
And let us praise and glorify him for ever.

Let us bless the Father and the Son with the Holy Spirit.
And let us praise and glorify him for ever.

Bless the Lord, all you works of the Lord.
And let us praise and glorify him for ever.

Sing praise to our God, all you his servants
and you who fear God, the small and the great.
And let us praise and glorify him for ever.

Let heaven and earth praise him who is glorious.
And let us praise and glorify him for ever.

Every creature in heaven, on earth and under the earth;
and in the sea and those which are in it.
And let us praise and glorify him for ever.

Glory to the Father and to the Son and to the Holy Spirit.
And let us praise and glorify him for ever.

As it was in the beginning, is now, and will be for ever.
And let us praise and glorify him for ever.

All-powerful, most holy, most high, supreme God:
all good, supreme good, totally good, you who alone are
   good,
may we give you all praise, all glory, all thanks,
all honour, all blessing, and all good.
So be it! So be it!
Amen.

Antiphon: Holy Virgin Mary

Holy Virgin Mary,
among the women born into the world,
there is none like you.
Daughter and servant
of the most high and supreme King
and of the Father in heaven,
Mother of our most holy Lord Jesus Christ,
Spouse of the Holy Spirit,
pray for us
with St Michael the Archangel,
all the powers of heaven,
and all the saints,
at the side of your most holy beloved Son,
our Lord and Teacher.
Glory to the Father, and to the Son, and to the Holy Spirit.
As it was in the beginning, is now, and will be for ever.
Amen.

A Biblical Psalm for Our Lady (Psalm 113)

1 O sing praises you that are his servants:
    O praise the name of the Lord.
2 Let the name of the Lord be blessed:
    From this time forward and for ever.
3 From the rising of the sun to its going down:
    Let the name of the Lord be praised.
4 The Lord is exalted over all the nations:
    And his glory is above the heavens.
5 Who can be likened to the Lord our God:
    In heaven or upon the earth,
6 Who has his dwelling so high:
    Yet condescends to look on things beneath?
7 He raises the lowly from the dust:
    And lifts up the poor from their misery;
8 He gives them a place among the princes:
    Even among the princes of his people.
9 He causes the barren woman to keep house:
    And makes her a joyful mother of children.

Glory to the Father, and to the Son, and to the Holy
    Spirit.
    As it was in the beginning, is now, and will be for
    ever.
Amen.

Psalm of the Office

1 God I have told you of my life:*
    You have placed all my tears in your sight.
2 All my enemies were plotting evil against me:*
    They took counsel together.
3 They repaid me evil for good*
    And hatred for my love.
4 They slandered me in return for my love,*
    But I continued to pray.

5 My holy Father, King of heaven and earth, do not
       leave me*
           For trouble is near and there is no one to help.
6 Let my enemies be turned back
       on whatever day I shall call upon you;*
           For now I know that you are my God.
7 My friends and my neighbours have drawn near
       and have stood against me;*
           Those who were close to me have stayed far
           away.
8 You have driven my acquaintances far from me;*
           They have made me an abomination to them.
           I have been handed over and did not escape.
9 Holy Father, do not remove your help from me;*
           My God, look to my aid.
10 Come to my help,*
           Lord, God of my salvation.

    Glory to the Father, and to the Son, and to the Holy
       Spirit.
       As it was in the beginning, is now, and will be for
       ever.
    Amen.

Antiphon: Holy Virgin Mary

The Antiphon is repeated here (see p. 133).

Closing Prayer

Let us bless
the Lord God living and true!
Let us always render him
praise, glory, honour, blessing and every good.
Amen. Amen.
So be it. So be it.

9

Other Franciscan Devotions

Sheelagh O'Flynn FMDM

The prayer of Francis is Trinitarian. He prays to God the Father, he follows in the footsteps of Jesus, and he reminds his brothers that the Holy Spirit is the Minister General of the Order. His love for Jesus – especially for the crucified Christ – led Francis to want to live the Gospel literally, and to love the Scriptures, particularly the Psalms, which Jesus himself would have recited, and the Gospels, which recount the actions and teachings of Jesus. He held the Eucharist in great respect as the abiding presence of Christ in our midst; and he honoured Mary because it was she who made the Most High our Brother. Central to Franciscan Spirituality is the mystery of the Incarnation.

∼

Over the years Franciscan devotions have evolved which express devotion to the person of Jesus, seeking to make this available through practices and prayers that are accessible to all.

Devotions in honour of Our Lord Jesus Christ

The crib

No doubt there were many representations of the Nativity scene in art before the time of Francis. However, when in

1223 Francis invited the people of Greccio to help him create a live crib, this brought the reality of the Christmas scene to life for those present. This was the fruit of Francis' pondering of the incarnation, and it continues to invite us to keep our minds and hearts focused on the real meaning of Christmas. The custom of recreating the scene in churches and homes spread throughout Christendom.

The representation of the first Christmas may consist only of the Child and his Mother, but is often extended to include St Joseph, the shepherds, the angels, an ox and an ass, and, at Epiphany, the arrival of the three Wise Men.

The Way of the Cross

Tradition asserts that the Blessed Virgin used to visit daily the scenes of Christ's passion. St Jerome speaks of the crowds of people who used to visit the Holy Places. In time, representations were made in other lands.

Since 1342, when the Franciscans were given custody of the Holy Places in Jerusalem, the Stations, or Way of the Cross, have been closely associated with the Order. In the eighteenth century, St Leonard of Port Maurice did much to propagate this devotion.

Traditionally there are fourteen stations, though of late the resurrection has often been incorporated as a fifteenth station. There are many versions of the Way of the Cross; one is offered below. Each station consists of a refrain, a Scripture reading, and a prayer. As it is a journey accompanying Jesus to Calvary, it is appropriate where possible to move physically from one station to the next; a verse of a hymn might be sung between stations.

The First Station – Pilate condemns Jesus to death

We adore you, O Christ, and we bless you:
Because by your holy cross you have redeemed the world.

It was Preparation Day for Passover, and the hour was about noon. Pilate said to the Jews, 'Look at your king!' At this they shouted, 'Away with him! Crucify him!' 'What!' Pilate exclaimed. 'Shall I crucify your king?' The chief priests replied, 'We have no king but Caesar.' In the end, Pilate handed Jesus over to be crucified. (Jn 19.14–16)

Lord Jesus,
We are one with the enemy whenever we choose that which separates us from you and your Gospel. Help us choose to act out of love.

The Second Station – Jesus takes up his cross

We adore you, O Christ, and we bless you:
Because by your holy cross you have redeemed the world.

When they had finished mocking him, they stripped him of the purple robe, dressed him in his own clothes, and led him out to crucify him. (Mk 15.20)

Lord Jesus,
You invite us to take up our cross each day.
Do not let our lives be a mockery by conveniently separating our life from our faith.

The Third Station – Jesus falls the first time

We adore you, O Christ, and we bless you:
Because by your holy cross you have redeemed the world.

He advanced a little and fell to the ground, praying that this hour might pass him by if it were possible. He kept saying, 'Abba (Father), you have the power to do all things. Take this cup away from me. But let it be as you will, not as I will.' (Mk 14.35–36)

Lord Jesus,
You sought the Father and his Reign alone.

Our lives are often fractured by our selfishness with little regard for our spiritual needs and the needs of others. Give us a generous spirit.

The Fourth Station – Jesus meets his mother

We adore you, O Christ, and we bless you:
Because by your holy cross you have redeemed the world.

Come, all you who pass by the way, look and see whether there is any suffering like my suffering. (Lam 1.12)
Simeon said to Mary his mother . . . 'And a sword shall pierce your own soul too.' (Lk 2.34–35)

Lord Jesus,
Your mother's heart was broken by our sins.
Even in this hour of darkness she stood by you.
May her prayers and example give us the courage to be faithful in times of darkness and distress.

The Fifth Station – Simon of Cyrene helps Jesus

We adore you, O Christ, and we bless you:
Because by your holy cross you have redeemed the world.

As they led him away, they laid hold of one Simon of Cyrene who was coming in from the fields. They laid the cross on his shoulder, to carry behind Jesus. (Lk 23.26)
'As often as you did it for one of these the least of my brothers, you did it for me.' (Mt 25.40)

Lord Jesus,
Grant us the vision to see you in all of our brothers and sisters, and the generosity to respond to their needs.

The Sixth Station – Veronica wipes the face of Jesus

We adore you, O Christ, and we bless you:
Because by your holy cross you have redeemed the world.

There was in him no stately bearing to make us look at him, nor appearance that would attract us to him. (Is 53.2)
'Whoever has seen me has seen the Father.' (Jn 14.9)

Lord Jesus,
We were made in your image but have marred the likeness. Grant us, like Veronica, to reflect your true image to the world by a life of compassion.

The Seventh Station – Jesus falls the second time

We adore you, O Christ, and bless you:
Because by your holy cross you have redeemed the world.

'Come to me, all you who are weary and find life burdensome, and I will refresh you.' (Mt 11.28)
'Be on guard and pray that you may not be put to the test. The spirit is willing but nature is weak.' (Mk 14.38)

Lord Jesus,
We are so caught up in our own comfort that we frequently neglect the life of the spirit. Teach us the value of self-denial, sacrifice and prayer.

The Eighth Station – Jesus speaks to the women of Jerusalem

We adore you, O Christ, and we bless you:
Because by your holy cross you have redeemed the world.

A great crowd of people followed him, including women who beat their breasts and lamented over him. Jesus turned to them and said: 'Daughters of Jerusalem, do not weep for me. Weep rather, for yourselves and for your children.' (Lk 23.27–28)

Lord Jesus,
Even in your final hours, your thought was for others. Give

us hearts that care for others even in the midst of our own disappointments and grief.

The Ninth Station – Jesus falls the third time

We adore you, O Christ, and we bless you:
Because by your holy cross you have redeemed the world.

Jesus said: 'The hour has come for the Son of Man to be glorified. I solemnly assure you, unless the grain of wheat falls to the earth and dies, it remains just a grain of wheat. But if it dies, it produces much fruit.' (Jn 12.23–24)

Lord Jesus,
When we are weighed down by sin, weakness or depression, raise us up and give us the energy we need for a new beginning.

The Tenth Station – Jesus is stripped of his clothes

We adore you, O Christ, and we bless you:
Because by your holy cross you have redeemed the world.

Then they crucified him and divided up his garments by rolling dice to see what each should take. (Mk 15.24)
'You cannot be my disciples unless you renounce all your possessions.' (Lk 14.33)

Lord Jesus,
We find it difficult to love with gentleness, to give our shirt when someone takes our coat, to walk the extra mile. Clothe us with your humility and meekness.

The Eleventh Station – Jesus is nailed to the cross

We adore you, O Christ, and we bless you:
Because by your holy cross you have redeemed the world.

When they came to the Place of the Skull they crucified him

there and the criminals as well, one on his right and the other on his left. Jesus said, 'Father, forgive them; they do not know what they are doing.' (Lk 23.33–34)

Lord Jesus,
You forgave those who nailed you to the cross, give us the largeness of heart to forgive those who hurt and wrong us.

The Twelfth Station – Jesus dies on the cross

We adore you, O Christ, and we bless you:
Because by your holy cross you have redeemed the world.

It was now around midday, and the darkness came over the whole land until mid-afternoon with an eclipse of the sun. The curtain in the sanctuary was torn in two. Jesus uttered a loud cry and said, 'Father, into your hands I commend my spirit.' After he said this, he expired. (Lk 23.44–46)

Lord Jesus,
You laid down your life so that there might be one shepherd and one fold. Help us to work for unity among your people.

The Thirteenth Station – Jesus is taken down from the cross and laid in his mother's arms

We adore you, O Christ, and we bless you:
Because by your holy cross you have redeemed the world.

Near the cross of Jesus there stood his mother, his mother's sister, Mary the wife of Cleopas, and Mary Magdalen . . . Jesus had said to his mother, 'Woman, there is your son.' Then he turned to the disciple and said, 'There is your mother.' (Jn 19.25, 27)

Lord Jesus,
With your dying breath you gave us Mary as our mother, now you are returned to her to hold and cherish once again. May we learn from her to receive tenderly all who are weak, hurt,

and deprived of the fullness of life. Imitating her faithfulness, may we stand by others in their pain, and welcome with an open heart and open arms all the members of your broken body.

The Fourteenth Station – Jesus is laid in the tomb

We adore you, O Christ, and we bless you:
Because by your holy cross you have redeemed the world.

They took Jesus' body, and in accordance with Jewish burial custom bound it up in wrappings of cloth with perfumed oils. In the place where he had been crucified there was a garden, and in the garden a new tomb in which no one had ever been buried. Because of the Jewish Preparation day they buried Jesus there, for the tomb was close at hand. (Jn 19.40–42)

Lord Jesus,
In our baptism we were buried with you so that we might be raised to life. Grant that we may so follow you that in life and in death we may never be separated from you.

The stations erected may include the resurrection. More commonly, when the Way of the Cross is made in, or close to a church, time is spent before the Blessed Sacrament, to give thanks for the abiding presence of the Risen Christ in our midst.

～

Other devotions fostered within the Franciscan Tradition to honour Our Lord include Devotion to and Exposition of the Blessed Sacrament, and Devotion to the Holy Name.

～

Marian devotions

The Franciscan crown

This Rosary, which is also known as the Rosary of the Seven Joys of the Blessed Virgin Mary, consists of seven decades. Tradition dates this Rosary back to 1422. Along with other forms of the Rosary, it was approved by Leo X in 1517.

Beads may be used as an aid in the recitation of the Rosary but are not essential.

It begins with the Sign of the Cross. Each decade consists of one Our Father, ten Hail Marys, and the Glory be to the Father.

The verse 'All praise and all thanksgiving be to the Most Blessed Trinity for all the graces bestowed upon Mary' may be recited together after each decade.

At the conclusion of the seven decades add an Our Father, Hail Mary, and Glory be to the Father; and two additional Hail Marys. According to tradition, the Hail Marys represent the 72 years of Mary's earthly life.

A prayer in honour of Our Lady is generally added to conclude the Crown.

1 – The Annunciation

The virgin is with child and shall bear a son, and she will call him Emmanuel. (Is 7.14; also Lk 1.26–33)

Let us thank God for his presence to us in his Word.

2 – The Visitation

All generations will call me blessed, for the Almighty has done great things for me. Holy is his name. (Lk 1.48–49; also Lk 1.39–47)

Let us thank God for his presence to us through others.

3 – The Nativity

Daughter of Zion, exult; shout aloud, daughter of Jerusalem! Your King is coming, the Holy One, the Saviour of the world. (Zech 9.9; also Lk 2.4–7)

Let us thank God for his presence to us in Jesus.

4 – The Adoration of the Magi

The Lord and Ruler is coming; kingship is his, and government and power. (Mic 5.1; Ps 96; also Mt 2.9–11)

Let us thank God for his presence in the wonder of Creation.

5 – The Finding in the Temple

He went down with them and came to Nazareth, and was obedient to them. His mother meanwhile treasured all these things in her heart. (Lk 2.51)

Let us thank God for his presence when we gather together in his name.

6 – The Resurrection

Christ has become our paschal sacrifice; let us feast with the unleavened bread of sincerity and truth. (1 Cor 5.7–8; also Lk 24.1–6)

Let us thank God for the presence of the Risen Lord.

7 – The Assumption and Crowning of Mary as Queen of Heaven

A great sign appeared in heaven: a woman clothed with the sun, the moon beneath her feet, and a crown of twelve stars on her head. (Rev 12.1; also Ps 45.14–15)

Let us thank God for the gift of eternal life.

Concluding prayer

The Memorare (or other prayer)

Remember, most loving Virgin Mary, never was it heard that anyone who turned to you for help was left unaided. Inspired by this confidence, though burdened by my sins, I run to your protection for you are my mother. Mother of the Word of God, do not despise my words of pleading but be merciful and hear my prayer. Amen.

∾

Three other significant Franciscan devotions must be mentioned.

The custom of Renewal of Vows on 16 April

This was the day on which Francis made his profession into the hands of Innocent III. On this day it is customary for communities of professed members to gather and renew their own commitment to the life they have vowed. This is a devotional renewal for those who have made life commitment. It takes place either during the celebration of the Eucharist (after the Gospel and the homily), or at Evening Prayer – possibly solemn Evening Prayer with Exposition of the Blessed Sacrament.

If the Blessed Sacrament is not exposed, the Paschal Candle may be lit as a reminder of the Risen Christ to whom we make our commitment. Symbols of profession may be displayed.

Below follows a possible form of words which may be adapted to the situation.

The Officiant – priest or leader – begins:

Let us recall the words of Saint Francis:
'Most beloved brothers and sisters, blessed children, hear me. We have promised great things, still greater things are promised to us.
Let us keep our promises and strive to attain what has been promised to us.'

All the brothers and sisters in profession then say together:

Most High and everlasting God,
Accept us now as we come to renew our love and service.
Gathered in your name and by your grace we affirm once again our promise and vow to you, in the sight of the holy angels, and of all the company of heaven, and dedicate ourselves to the service of our Lord Jesus Christ in the way of the blessed Francis by living in obedience, without property, and in chastity, according to the Rule of our Community and the life of the Gospel, with the help of God.

The Officiant then gives the blessing:

In the words of the blessed Francis, I bless you.
'May whoever observes all these things be filled in heaven with the blessings of the Most High, and on earth with the blessing of Jesus Christ, in union with the blessing of the Holy Spirit, the Comforter, and all the powers of heaven and all the saints. And I, your poor servant, as much as I am able, confirm for you + this most holy blessing.'
Amen.

A Sign of Peace may be exchanged.

Celebration of the Great Pardon

This indulgence, which is granted on the feast of Our Lady of the Angels of the Portiuncula, was first limited to the Portiuncula. But it has over the years been extended, first to all Franciscan churches, and then, in 1967 under Pope Paul VI, to cathedrals and to parish churches:

> The Catholic faithful may gain a plenary indulgence on 2 August, under the usual conditions (Sacramental confession, Holy Communion and prayers for the Supreme Pontiff), by devoutly visiting the parish church and there reciting the Lord's Prayer and the Creed. To gain this indulgence the faithful must be free from any attachment to sin.

Memorial of the passing of St Francis

At twilight on 3 October, the eve of his feast, the followers of Francis gather to celebrate his passing from this life to everlasting life. The ceremony varies but generally the elements below will form part of the 'Transitus', as it is also known.

- The death of Francis in the context of praise: the singing of the Canticle of the Creatures (see pp. 115–16).
- A motif of 'leave taking' – Francis has the Gospel of Jesus washing the apostles' feet read (Jn 13.1–20) and shares bread.
- The singing of Psalm 142.
- Readings on the passing of Francis might be selected from Celano, Bonaventure and *The Legend of Perugia*.
- The exhortation and blessing:

> Let the sisters and brothers always be mindful that they should desire one thing alone, namely, the Spirit of God at work within them. Always obedient to the Church and firmly established in the Catholic faith, let them live according to the poverty, the humility and the holy Gospel of our Lord Jesus Christ which they have solemnly promised to observe. Whoever will observe these things shall be filled with the blessings of the Most High Father in heaven, and on earth with the blessing of his beloved Son, with the Holy Spirit, and with all virtues and with all the saints.

And I, Brother Francis, your little one and servant, in so far as I am able, confirm to you within and without this most Holy Blessing.

The final blessing may be said or sung (below is the blessing Francis wrote for Brother Leo).

May the Lord bless you and keep you.
May he show his face to you and be merciful to you.
May he turn his countenance to you and give you peace.

Following Francis and Clare

Damian Kirkpatrick SSF

A Franciscan calendar

4 January	Bl. Angela of Foligno
7 February	St Colette
2 March	Bl. Agnes of Prague
24 April	St Fidelis of Sigmaringen
12 May	Leopold of Castelnuovo
18 May	St Felix of Cantalice
20 May	St Bernardine of Siena
13 June	St Anthony of Padua
1 July	Bl. Junipero Serra
5 July	St Bonaventure
21 July	St Laurence of Brindisi
2 August	St Mary of the Angels of the Portiuncula
8 August	St Dominic
11 August	St Clare
14 August	St Maximilian Kolbe
25 August	St Louis IX of France
10 September	Bl. Agnellus of Pisa
17 September	Stigmata of St Francis
23 September	St Pio of Pietrelcina (Padre Pio)
4 October	St Francis
19 October	St Peter of Alcantara
30 October	Dedication of Franciscan Churches
8 November	Bl. John Duns Scotus

17 November	St Elizabeth of Hungary
19 November	St Agnes of Assisi
24 November	Commemoration of all deceased Franciscans and benefactors
29 November	All Saints of the Seraphic Order
8 December	Immaculate Conception of the Blessed Virgin Mary

Some Franciscan saints

Among the vast company of Franciscan saints, these have been selected as those most commonly observed within the whole Franciscan family, and their stories are briefly told in the following pages. There are many others.

Bl. Agnellus of Pisa – 10 September

Born around 1195 in Pisa, Agnellus joined Francis as a young man and was present at the first Chapter of Mats in 1221. After being given responsibility for the Custody of France, Francis sent him on to found the English Province in 1224. He established the first House at Greyfriars in Canterbury, and then at Oxford, where he died in 1236, and where his remains were venerated until the time of the Reformation. While he was not recognized particularly as a scholar, he gained influence in matters of state under Henry III. He was beatified in 1892.

St Agnes of Assisi – 19 November

Agnes, born Catherine di Offreduccio, was from the same noble family of Assisi as St Clare. She joined her elder sister in the Benedictine Convent where Francis had temporarily placed Clare only sixteen days earlier. Thus began the Second Order, which came to be known as the Poor Clares. When her irate father, Favarone, demanded she return home, it is said that her body became so heavily rooted into the ground that she could not be lifted. Later she governed the Convent in Florence before returning to Assisi – as one extant letter to Clare suggests, she agonized over their being separated. Agnes died only weeks after her sister in 1253.

Bl. Agnes of Prague – 2 March

The daughter of Premislaus, king of Bohemia, Agnes was born around the year 1205. She avoided marriage to the emperor and others, with her mind set on establishing a monastery of Poor Clares in Prague in 1236. She entered this monastery herself and later became the Abbess for many years. She enjoyed a special friendship with St Clare, and the letters addressed to her by Clare on questions of 'seraphic perfection' remain extant, in which Clare admonishes Agnes to 'look into that mirror without spot daily . . . In that mirror are reflected poverty, humility and ineffable charity, as, with the grace of God, you may perceive.' There are, unfortunately, no records of Agnes' replies. She died some time between 1280 and 1283.

Bl. Angela of Foligno – 4 January

Angela was born in Umbria in 1248. She renounced a rather indulgent way of life and was instrumental in drawing other women to join her in the Third Order of St Francis. She developed an ardent spirit of poverty, patience and humility, being exemplary in her charity and concern for the poor. Enriched by great spiritual graces, she was particularly devoted to the mysteries of the life of Jesus. She has left a valuable legacy of mystical doctrine in her *Book of the Experiences of the True Faithful*, and she has been described as a teacher of theologians. She died in Foligno in 1309.

St Anthony of Padua – 13 June

Born of a noble family in Lisbon in 1195, Anthony first followed the vocation of a canon regular (Augustinian) at Holy Cross in Coimbra, and was present in 1220 when the remains of the first five Franciscan martyrs were returned from Morocco to be buried in his priory. After an abortive visit to Morocco he was forced by sickness to return home to Portugal but his ship was caught in a storm, and docked in Sicily. Here he learnt of a General Chapter of Franciscans being held in Assisi, where he asked to become a friar. His earlier training stood him in good stead with St Francis who permitted him to teach theology within the Order. His preaching was with extraordinary power and conviction, and his ministry grew throughout Italy and back in Portugal. He earnestly challenged heresy and filled his homilies with biblical teaching which earned him the title of 'arca testamenti' (storehouse of the holy Scriptures). He also lived for a while in France. Without doubt Anthony won massive popularity in these parts of Europe, and his short but energetic life ended in his final home at Padua on 13 June 1231. He was named a Doctor of the Church in 1946.

Though the origin of the cult is uncertain, Anthony is often referred to as 'the Patron Saint of Lost Things', though the local Italian tradition narrows this down to 'lost children', based on his vision of the Infant Jesus. He is depicted in statuary holding a child in his arms. The cult grew in popularity with mothers who feared their sons were straying from the faith.

St Bernardine of Siena – 20 May

One of the great preachers of the Italian Renaissance, Bernardine, born at Massa di Carrera in 1380, studied at Siena and became a Franciscan at the age of 22. After some years in solitude, he began a prodigious ministry of preaching and crowds came to listen to him for hours at a time. This brought a rich harvest of miracles, the reconciling of factions, and established a devotion to the Holy Name of Jesus. In 1438 he became the Provincial of the Observant Franciscans in Italy, and their numbers multiplied dramatically around this time. He returned to a preaching ministry for the last two years of his life and died 'on the road' on 20 May 1444.

Bernardine, along with John of Capistrano, was the inspiration towards the establishing of a Feast Day to commemorate the Name of Jesus, which from the sixteenth century has appeared in the Church's calendar in January. His symbol 'IHS' – the first letters of the name of Jesus in the Greek language – surrounded by the flames of the sun, has been widely taken up by different Churches.

St Bonaventure – 15 July

Certainly among the greatest and most celebrated philosophers and theologians of the Middle Ages, Bonaventure, born in 1221 near Viturbo in Italy, entered the Order of Friars Minor at the age of 20. He studied in Paris, where he later taught theology and Holy Scripture, until he was elected Minister General of the Order in 1257. Bonaventure has been described as the second founder of the Franciscan Order, since his reforms helped to bring about a harmony among the friars after the turbulent period following the death of St Francis. He conceded the establishment of chapels and libraries and friaries. At the same time that he demanded that any friar who took a fee should deliver half to the secular clergy, he curbed begging by itinerant friars, which was becoming a social menace (Bonaventure's comment was that people would rather meet a robber than a wandering friar!). He established a uniform habit, and he required that letters of credence be carried to distinguish them from bogus imitators. In the wider Church, having turned down the See of York in 1265, he was prevailed upon to become Cardinal Bishop of Albano in 1273 and was then entrusted with the task of helping to bring about a reunion of the Eastern and Western Church, which was temporarily achieved at the Council of Lyons in July 1274. He died eight days later on 15 July.

Many early lives and stories surrounding St Francis had emerged, some incredible and beyond belief, and so Bonaventure was asked by the Order's Chapter to write the official life of St Francis using all available sources. His considerable learning followed the tradition derived from St Augustine and St Anselm. Yet he humbly followed in the way of St Francis, so aptly illustrated by the legend that is told of the occasion when the papal delegates arrived at the friary in Florence bearing his Cardinal's hat: Bonaventure insisted on completing the task of washing the dishes, and suggested they hang it on a tree outside until he had finished.

St Clare of Assisi – 11 August

See Chapters 2 and 4.

St Colette – 7 February

St Colette was born in France in the year 1381. After the death of her parents she distributed her wealth to the poor and took the habit of the Franciscan Third Order, living for some time as a recluse. She later entered the Poor Clares, and with papal approval was responsible for the renewal of many of the communities of the First and Second Orders through her commitment to prayer and poverty. She founded seventeen houses of the reform in France and Flanders. Though untrained and unprepared for any such work, she achieved much by the simple application of faith and holiness with a determination that no opposition could discourage. She died at Ghent on 6 March 1447.

St Dominic – 8 August

Born in Castile in Spain in the year 1170, St Dominic was a contemporary and friend of St Francis, and founded the Order of Preachers, a congregation that also broke from the principles of the monastic life by becoming mendicant in lifestyle and missionary in its primary aims. His Order grew rapidly as Dominic identified the need to preach a Christian Gospel that declared the innate goodness of God's creation, and that things spiritual and temporal were both of God. With the Franciscans, Dominic's innovative style of zeal and simplicity gave rise to the great spiritual tide that swept over western Europe; and no further developments of significance within the religious life arose for the next three hundred years, until the period of the Reformation.

Dominic was proclaimed 'Standard-bearer of the city of Bologna', whose scholarship at that time was a beacon of learning for the civilized world, where he died in 1221. Traditionally, since then, all Archbishops of Bologna have received the habit of the Dominican tertiary.

St Elizabeth of Hungary – 17 November

Elizabeth's life was short, tragic, full and fruitful. Of royal birth, she lived from 1207 until 1231. She was given in marriage to Louis IV, Landgrave of Thuringa, to whom she bore three children. Louis died of the plague, leaving Elizabeth an early widow. She settled in Marburg, became a member of the Franciscan Third Order, and practised a life of austerity, contemplation, and devoted outpouring of herself to those most in need. Founding a hospital at Marburg, she spent her energies tending the sick and disabled, attending the more wretched and degraded at her own table. Soon her own body gave way under this punishing programme and her own severe religious disciplines. She is a patroness of the Franciscan Third Order.

St Felix of Cantalice – 18 May

Born in 1515, Felix Porri entered the Capuchin Order of friars in 1543. Through his holy life and marked Franciscan witness, he gained a reputation for simplicity of life and fraternal charity. He exemplified the teaching of St Francis that humility, patience, perfect simplicity and true peace of heart become our chief aim, but above everything else the heart desires the fear of God, the divine wisdom and the divine love of the Father, Son and Holy Spirit. He served in Rome exercising the office of questor for forty years until his death in 1587.

St Fidelis of Sigmaringen – 24 April

Fidelis, born in Germany in 1578, became a Capuchin friar marked with a deep spirit of devotion, intellectual gifts in philosophy and law, and a strong zeal for preaching. He was directed to preach among the Zwinglians of the Grisons area in Switzerland, but was killed by enraged peasants at Seewis in 1622 in his attempts to bring about a reconciliation with Rome, an early martyr of the Capuchin Order.

St Francis of Assisi – 4 October

See Chapter 2.

Stigmata of St Francis – 17 September

Francis held in special regard the phrase, 'For the Love of God', which surely would have led him in his devotions to the mystery of Christ's cross, and to his preaching of Christ crucified. Following his conversion, this contemplation of God's love deepened within his whole being. In the year 1224 he embarked on a long period of withdrawal at Mount La Verna in Tuscany, which he accepted as a gift from Count Orlando, for uninterrupted communion with

God. Only Brother Leo, his companion, was allowed even in the vicinity of this retreat. Three days after Holy Cross Day, there appeared to Francis a Seraph of Christ Crucified, which reproduced in Francis' own flesh the five wounds of Jesus in hands, feet and side.

This is the first recorded account of a stigmata, marking the human body with the wounds of the Crucified. While Francis tried to hide the marks of the stigmata, the wounds never in fact healed during the remaining two years of his life, and were covered with bandages. Pope Benedict XI gave authority for the recalling of this event annually by the Brothers.

Dedication of Franciscan churches – 30 October

The anniversary of dedication in consecrated churches of the various Franciscan Orders is celebrated on this day, unless some other festival is appropriate to mark the occasion. It may also be observed on 2 August in honour of the first church of St Francis, St Mary of the Angels in Assisi (see below).

Commemoration of all deceased Franciscans and benefactors – 24 November

A day, really a continuation of All Souls Day (2 November), which is set aside to remember with thanksgiving and prayer the souls of all who have lived and died within the family and the inspiration of Francis and Clare of Assisi, and those who have given generously of themselves for the benefit of the Franciscan movement within the Churches.

Bl. John Duns Scotus – 8 November

John Duns Scotus was born in 1264, at Duns in Berwickshire, Scotland. He received the Franciscan habit while at Oxford, and continued his studies at Paris and Cologne, where he established a reputation as a thinker and theologian, and where he died suddenly in 1308. His theology is complex and difficult to define, but in the simplest terms the beginning and end of his theological endeavour was love. He understood God as love, and so, in line with Franciscan thought, he emphasized the practical aspect of theology, God is love, rather than its abstractions and speculations. For Scotus the purpose of theology is to love God above all things and there is only one subject of theology – the God who is love – and God creates not out of necessity but out of love.

Scotus is often referred to as 'the Marian Doctor' because of his development of the doctrine of the Immaculate Conception. He also provided the speculative framework of what has become known as Franciscan Christology: in Scotus' thought, the incarnation of the Son of God is itself a manifestation of God's infinite love, and is willed by God from all eternity, quite apart from God knowing that human beings would sin. The primary action of God was the incarnation, and redemption was a secondary purpose made necessary by the need for an act of salvation.

The disagreement between Duns Scotus and the Dominicans, particularly Thomas Aquinas, led to his vilification over several centuries, the term *dunce* having become a popular form of disparagement throughout the world. Only in recent years has the true worth of his thought been acknowledged, and he was beatified by Pope John Paul II as a man of holiness in 1992.

Bl. Junipero Serra – 1 July

While California awaits the full beatification of the Spanish friar who founded the Californian Missions in the eighteenth century, Juniper is honoured for his pioneering work which stretched down the Pacific coastline of America and into Mexico. Already aged 56, Juniper set foot in what is now California on 1 July 1769 and a total of twenty-one missions were established from San Diego in the south up to Sonoma in the north. He died in 1784 at Mission San Carlos Borromeo

(Carmel), one hundred miles south of San Francisco, the city which took its name finally from St Francis.

Laurence of Brindisi – 21 July

Laurence was born to a wealthy Venetian family in 1559 and was received into the Franciscan Order at the age of 16. He developed an extraordinary gift for learning languages, both ancient and modern, and for the study of biblical texts. He was commissioned by Pope Clement VIII to work in Rome for the conversion of the Jewish people, and later sent to establish the Capuchin Franciscan reform in Germany. He held various offices within the Order and acquired some political and even military importance. After withdrawing for a while in contemplative devotion, he was sent to Spain and Portugal on political business and died in Lisbon on 21 July 1618. Laurence is remembered for his writings, and Pope John XXIII declared him a Doctor of the Church.

St Leopold of Castelnuova – 12 May

Bogdan John was born the twelfth and last child of Peter and Carlotta Mandich in Herceg Novi (in Italian, Castelnuova) in 1866. The family lost its fortune and its place in society in the political upheavals of the time, and Bogdan joined a Capuchin seminary as a late teenager, being professed in Padua in 1888. Suffering from both his Dalmatian nationality and also his minimal height (he was only 4'5" tall) he found himself exiled during the First World War in Southern Italy. He then returned to Padua where he remained for the rest of his life, earning a high reputation as a confessor. When accused of being too lenient in his ministry in the confessional, he replied, 'If the Lord wants to accuse me of showing too much leniency towards sinners, I will tell him that it was he who gave me the example.' He died on 30 July 1942, and was canonized in 1983 when he was declared patron of the Sacrament of Reconciliation.

St Louis IX of France – 25 August

Born in 1214 in Poissy, Louis was crowned king of France aged 21. Married and a father of eleven, he dutifully brought up his children and ruled his nation with equal devoutness and devotion. He was known as a peacemaker, and nursed many a sick person with his own hands. He overflowed with charity and respect for his neighbour and upheld a spiritual life of penance and prayer. He is revered as a patron of the Franciscan Third Order. He was engaged in the Crusades, particularly to the Holy Land and for the deliverance of the Holy Places, but in the year 1270, along with many of his army, he fell victim to typhus and died in the ancient city lying under what is now Tunis.

St Mary of the Angels of the Portiuncula – 2 August

St Francis held the Church of the Portiuncula (Little Portion) close to his heart for several good reasons: it was the context for the beginning and early growth of the Order; there he received Clare and gave her the habit; and it was there that he chose to die. Dedicated to the Virgin Mary, to whom he bore a particular devotion, it became his favourite place, and represented in its smallness and simplicity a model of the Lesser Brothers' vocation to the highest poverty and humility. 'Wherefore, my sons,' he wrote, 'consider this dwelling place of God to be worthy of all honour, and with all your heart, with the voice of joy and praise, give glory to God in this place.' Indeed the place of Mary is central in the Franciscan tradition as she was in the faith of Francis.

The Portiuncula is now housed within the large Basilica of St Mary of the Angels in the valley below the town of Assisi, which also preserves the place of Francis' death.

The Celebration of the Great Pardon is described in Chapter 9 (p. 147f.).

Immaculate Conception of the Blessed Virgin Mary – 8 December

This doctrine of faith was defined within the Roman Catholic Church in 1854. Mary, from the very beginning of her existence as a human person in her mother's womb, was preserved free from all stain of original sin by a singular grace and privilege of God, granted in view of the merits of Jesus Christ. This 'singular grace' means that Mary is the only person who has been immaculately conceived. This privilege, granted 'in view of the merits of Jesus Christ', means that Mary, like all of us, needed redemption. But in her case redemption was 'preservative'. She was preserved from contracting original sin through the foreseen merits of Christ. Scotus developed the notion of preservative redemption and so prepared the way for the definition of this dogma in 1854 which established the feast.

The Immaculate Conception was a preparation for the divine motherhood of Mary. She had to be a worthy mother of Jesus, the Eternal Son of God, not only biologically but spiritually. In a word, she had to be sinless from the first moment of her existence as a human person.

This sinlessness of Mary has been celebrated in both East and West since the seventh century, though the Eastern Church does not use the expression 'Immaculate Conception'. Mary thus receives the titles Godbearer, and Mother of God, as mother of Jesus, Son of God.

St Maximilian Kolbe – 14 August

Raymond Kolbe was born in Zdunska-Vola in Poland in 1894. As a boy he had a vision of Our Lady in which she offered him either a life of purity or one of martyrdom. He asked for both! With his brother he began training as a priest at the Franciscan Seminary in Luow in 1907, and in 1910 tested his vocation as a Conventual, continuing his studies in Rome. There he established the 'Knights of Mary Immaculate', a movement that sought to bring personal and social renewal through Christian conversion. Returning to Poland, this led, in 1927, to his 'Niepokalanov' or 'City of the Immaculate' which grew into a Franciscan friary of 738 friars, whose work was the promotion of Christian journalism. A similar friary was established in Japan, near the city of Nagasaki.

During the Second World War he was arrested by the Nazis as an intellectual and for hiding Jews in his city. He was sent to Auschwitz in May 1941, and as Prisoner 16670 he was especially vilified because he was a Catholic priest. This severe treatment did not stop him secretly celebrating Mass and caring for others. On 30 July that year another prisoner escaped, and the Camp officers retaliated by randomly selecting ten men to be starved to death. A married sergeant, Francis Gajowniczek, had been chosen but Maximilian immediately offered to take his place; and so he with the other nine were marched to the starvation cell. Characteristically he filled the cell with singing the praises of God. He died slowly on the eve of the Feast of the Assumption, 14 August, 1941.

Maximilian's canonization in 1982 took place before a crowd in St Peter's Square, Rome of 150,000, which included the man whose place at Auschwitz he took, together with his family. He had died as he had lived, a fool for Christ, recklessly in love with God and humanity. His devotion to Mary Immaculate was a central part of his faith, which he applied in huge measure in devotion to his neighbour. He is included in the array of twentieth-century martyrs unveiled over the west door of Westminster Abbey in London in December 1997.

St Pio of Pietrelcina (Padre Pio) – 23 September

Born into a Christian family who lived in Pietrelcina in Southern Italy in 1887, Francesco Forgione entered the Capuchin Order of Friars Minor in 1903. His health let him down, forcing him to live apart from the Community for a time.

However, he settled at the friary in San Giovanni Rotondo, where he spent the next fifty years of his life.

Some deemed him 'a friar of little use' because of his delicate health, but his holiness began to be recognized by those around him. From 1910 Padre Pio, as he became known, suffered from an invisible stigmata. However, when he was 31, on 20 September 1918, whilst in prayer in choir before the crucifix, he received a visible stigmata which he bore until his death. As news of this event spread, and his wisdom, humour and holiness were recognized, he was much sought after in the confessional from people all over the world, who also asked to attend his Masses. Church authorities felt it necessary to restrict his pastoral ministries over a nine-year period of enquiry, which he accepted with grace and humble obedience. In 1933 Pius XI restored his priestly freedom and it was estimated that he would hear 25,000 confessions a year until 1967.

Padre Pio's concern for people's holiness and wholeness took the form not only of a sacramental ministry but also of intercessory prayer and the practical setting up of a hospital near the friary. His mystical life, rooted in intimacy with Christ in the Gospel and in the Eucharist, was clearly seen erupting into his life, ministry and bodily flesh. He died in 1968 and was canonized in 2002.

St Peter of Alcantara – 19 October

Peter was born in Alcantara in Spain in 1499. After studying at Salamanca he entered the Order of Friars Minor. Ordained in 1524, he was sent as a preacher both in Spain and Portugal, and undertook several offices in the Order. Later he developed a series of reforms, training the friars in penance, abstinence, prolonged prayer and strict poverty. He was noticed by Teresa of Avila whom he encouraged to reform the Carmelite Order. To her he wrote, 'I do not praise poverty as such, but only that which we endure patiently out of love for our Crucified Redeemer, and that, still more to be desired, which we freely undertake out of love for him.' On missions he often planted a raised cross before he left to remind all within sight of the new life to which they were called, a custom that was taken up at the close of many a Franciscan mission in the years that followed.

All Saints of the Seraphic Order – 29 November

On the eve of St Andrew's Day, this festival is observed for us to give thanks for and commemorate the vast number of sisters and brothers who have lived a Franciscan vocation with the outstanding measure of humility, love and joy that so marked the lives of Francis and Clare of Assisi throughout the world. Also we should recall those whose lives were taken in the course of their living out of this vocation, particularly in the last century, when more Christians were killed than in all the previous centuries of Christianity put together. For the named and un-named saints whose path to glory was with Francis, we give thanks!

∼

Everlasting God, you have adorned your Church with the splendour of the saintly followers of our holy father, Francis: grant that as we commemorate their holiness, we may come at last with all the pure in heart to share the vision of your glory; through Jesus Christ our Lord.

Some Franciscan tertiaries

The Franciscan vision and vocation has touched the lives of several people, also made famous by the events of history, and a sample selection is listed below from among those called to a secular Franciscan life.

Robert the Bruce (1274–1329)

He lived in the tempestuous times of medieval Scottish history with its constant battles both against the English and also over rival claims to the Scottish throne. His remarkable military victory at the Battle of Bannockburn over the English forces of Edward II, who outnumbered Bruce's men by three to one, secured the final independence of his kingdom in 1314.

Christopher Columbus (1451–1506)

An Italian weaver from Genoa, deeply concerned to journey into the unknown West, Christopher Columbus finally called at the Observant friary at La Rabida in Spain to talk with the Guardian, John Perez. This friar had knowledge of navigation and also astronomy. So Perez assisted Columbus in preparing for his expedition which set sail in 1492. Columbus left his son in the care of the Spanish friars. On a second voyage, Perez accompanied Columbus as his astronomer, and other friars joined the fleet with the purpose of evangelizing the New World. However, there they met with heavy opposition until more Observants arrived and new convents were established at San Domingo. In the year 1500 several indigenous people were baptized, but for some time to come it remained tough going. In 1504 the first Bishop at Hispaniola was a Friar Minor, Garsia of Pavilla.

St Jean-Baptiste Vianney, Curé d'Ars (1786–1859)

He was slow to achieve the required academic standard to be ordained, though finally he was made priest at the age of 29. After three years, he was sent to the remote French village of Ars where his humble attitudes won him a growing ministry. His wise counsel attracted people from neighbouring villages, but soon this expanded as he received penitents from across France and much further afield. It is said that he heard 20,000 confessions a year and was confined to the confessional for up to eighteen hours a day. He is Patron Saint of parish priests.

Dante Alighieri (1265–1321)

An Italian poet and philosopher, Dante fell under the influence of the friars, both Dominican and Franciscan. He is remembered for his *Divine Comedy* which established him as one of the world's outstanding poets and spiritual writers. The Canticle of the Creatures is said to have inspired Dante to write the *Divine Comedy* in Italian rather than in Latin. He devoted eighty lines of this work to Francis and mentions Bernard, Giles and Sylvester in the text. Dante Alighieri may have been a Franciscan Tertiary and may even have for a short time been a friar, drawn from the reference to taking off the cord wherewith he was girt (*Inferno*, canto 16). He undoubtedly had a high respect for Francis to whom he made reference with devotion in the *Paradiso*, cantos 11, 21. 90, 32. 35.

Joan of Arc (1412–1431)

The Maid of Orleans, the second Patron of France, in her short life influenced the army of the House of Orleans in the war against the House of Burgundy. Her pious upbringing, her 'voices', and her visions inspired Charles VII to permit her to lead an expedition to Orleans which led to his being crowned King of France at Reims. In her next assault she was defeated by the Burgundian troops, and finally she was condemned as a relapsed heretic, her dreams being declared false. As a result she was burnt at the stake at Rouen. Twenty-five years later she was reinstated as a heroine, and was canonized in 1920.

John XXIII (1881–1963)

He was born Angelo Roncalli, of a peasant family at Sotto il Monte in Northern Italy. The bells from the Convent of the Friars Minor in neighbouring Baccanello would have been a childhood memory, creating a first link with the Franciscans of which he became a tertiary. 'Where is my spirit of penitence and humility, my modesty and prayerfulness and true wisdom?' he wrote in his journal during his ordination retreat in 1904. He became a great priest, and as bishop, cardinal and finally Pope in 1958, he was affectionately described as 'everybody's priest'. He astonished the world with his warm concern for all people, was deeply moved by the poor, showed a simplicity of heart and a missionary and pastoral spirit. He was profoundly ecumenical; in 1960 he established the Secretariat for Promoting Christian Unity and in the same year he invited Archbishop Geoffrey Fisher to meet him in the Vatican – the first encounter between a Pope and an Archbishop of Canterbury since the Reformation. He will always be remembered for calling the Second Vatican Council in Rome (1962–66), but he died on 3 June 1963 with only the first Session completed.

Bl. Ramon Lull (1236–1315)

Ramon was born of a noble family at Palma in Majorca. Hearing a sermon on St Francis Day about poverty and love, he was converted to a holy life which he devoted to study, to teaching and also to contemplation and prayer. After the death of his wife, and when his children had grown up, he joined the Franciscan Third Order, taking upon himself the task of providing Christian books for the use of Muslim people, travelling widely through Europe, Palestine and North Africa and preaching the love of Christ. He was imprisoned several times, eventually being stoned and left for dead in the Algerian port of Bugia. Merchants tried to revive him, and took him on board their ship, but he died before reaching the shores of his homeland. He was a mystic, evangelist and missionary of exceptional quality, and he was made patron of Majorca.

Michelangelo Buonarroti (1475–1564)

Michelangelo was a sculptor, painter and poet of the Italian Renaissance, whose Pietà in St Peter's, Rome, and the frescoes representing the 'Creation of Light' and the 'Creation of Man' in the Sistine Chapel, leave the visitors of succeeding generations in awe and wonder. The sculpture of David from a colossal block of marble also expresses the genius of one who combined solemnity and grandeur and human energy into his creative design. He was also recognized for his talent as an architect and as a military engineer. In his latter years, Michelangelo made several visits to one of the Franciscan hermitages near Spoleto.

Raphael Sanzio (1483–1520)

Raphael became the most well-known of the Renaissance painters. He began his career in Perugia, before moving to Florence where he came under the influence of Michelangelo and Leonardo da Vinci. He was ordered to Rome to decorate the Vatican 'Stanze' with its beautiful paintings on walls and ceilings, including many biblical subjects. Later he was appointed chief architect of St Peter's Basilica.

Desmond Tutu (1931–)

He was born in Soweto in South Africa and trained as a priest in the Anglican Church. He became a leader in the struggle against apartheid, calling for economic sanctions against the all-white government but insisting on non-violent means in the fight for justice for all in his country. He was awarded the Nobel Peace Prize in 1984, and as Archbishop of Cape Town was in a strong position to assist the overthrow of apartheid under Nelson Mandela. He was also deeply influenced by Bishop Trevor Huddleston who had once respectfully raised his hat to Desmond's mother in the open street of the black township of his childhood.

Lech Walesa (1943–)

He rose from humble origins in Poland to lead the Solidarity movement, campaigning for the rights of workers to form independent unions. He was awarded the Nobel Peace Prize in 1983 and won a substantial victory in the Polish presidential elections of 1990.

Galvani (1737–1798), Ampère (1775–1836), Volta (1745–1827)

The eighteenth century brought a time when three physicists in Europe, two Italians, Luige Galvani and Count Alessandro Volta, and the mathematician Andre Ampère – all members of the Franciscan Third Order – discovered various aspects of modern electricity. By investigating the natural world, they believed they would learn more about the Creator; and they pursued their experiments as part of their spiritual devotion. In so doing they also contributed towards the reconciling of natural science and traditional Church doctrine (after the disaster with Galileo). As Galvani studied anatomy, he noticed the natural electricity present in the leg of a frog, which could be detected by a movement of the leg when a small electric voltage, producing an electric field, was applied to it. The movement had been caused by the interaction between this electric field and the very small electric impulses within the living creature. The device known as a galvanometer carries his name, as also the unit of electric current, the amp, comes from Ampère. The measure of electric pressure known as a volt was developed by Volta, who invented the electric battery.

The Franciscan Family

A Family History
The Editors

On the death of Francis

Francis died in 1226. By then the Order had grown to some thousands. Already some organization into separate provinces had been established, the first of which were created in 1217 when 11 provinces were designated in Italy, France, Germany, Spain and the Near East. A new Province was formed in the British Isles in 1224 after the Brothers landed in Canterbury.

At the time of Francis' death there was no Minister General, though Francis himself had virtually resigned from the leadership of the Order some years before. Br Elias took immediate charge as Vicar of the Order and he wrote a general letter to the friars and more publicly to announce the occasion of the Saint's death and also to disclose his stigmata which until then had been kept secret.

A chapter in Assisi was called at Pentecost 1227 to choose a Minister General. John Parenti was elected, a friar who had been under the direct influence of Francis and who was known and loved as a devout and conscientious man, whose simplicity and poverty were clearly seen as he visited around the Order 'with bare feet', according to the Rule of 1221.

Meanwhile Br Elias was busy in Assisi, aware that probably since the days of the early Church there had not appeared a follower of the gospel as eminent as the Poverello. Elias planned and built the Basilica (of St Francis) on the rock known as the 'Collis infernos' as a permanent shrine for his body. The foundation stone was laid by Cardinal Hugolino, who had just been elected Pope Gregory IX in 1228. This also became the occasion for the formal canonization of St Francis. In 1232 Elias replaced John as Minister General.

Elias had been utterly trusted by Francis in his lifetime and was now elected by his brothers to lead the Order forward. It was perhaps surprising to observe the means by which he proposed stability in this rapidly growing congregation. He desired to make Assisi a centre of pilgrimage for the whole world and to increase the standing of the Order of Friars Minor. He took away some of the powers of the ministers by increasing the number of provinces. His aim was to establish 72 provinces in honour of the disciples sent out by Jesus. Elias didn't achieve this, but by 1239 there were 32, half being outside the States of Italy. His ambitious and persuasive energies, however, got the better of him and he became headstrong and acted way beyond his authority. He turned to seek the approval of Emperor Frederick II and by thus doing he put himself under a general excommunication which had been pronounced against all who consorted with the Emperor. His office was taken over by the gentle John of Palma in 1247, a brother known as a peacemaker.

Further growth brings Bonaventure

Of the friar movement of the thirteenth century the Dominicans were ahead in the work within the developing universities in Europe, and in some places were seen as a direct threat because they virtually monopolized the faculties of theology, notably in Paris and Oxford. The Franciscans were also treated with some suspicion, being resented for taking the place of secular teachers who were reliant on the universities for their personal income. With varying degrees of success the Franciscans established their influence over the major cities, universities and cathedrals across Europe.

Bonaventure joined the friars in the early 1240s. By 1253 he had been appointed master in the Franciscan school in Paris and in 1257 was elected Minister General – at the age of 36. His influence on the Order was enormous, bringing spiritual and intellectual leadership, together with clear reforms of discipline, and regaining an internal unity within the Brotherhood. Chapter 10 gives a short account of Bonaventure's life.

Tensions persist

Agreement as to what were the essential priorities of the Franciscan witness was hard to identify and perhaps inevitably there developed a split between the friars, which was later formally recognized in 1517. Some concessions had been authorized by appeal to the Pope, John XXII, concerning the interpretation of the vow of poverty. The group known as the Spirituals upheld, and were themselves dedicated to, the absolute poverty of Christ, fearing any desire for possessions as a road to sin. The brothers known as the Conventuals were more prepared to accept the modifications prescribed by Pope John, and perhaps grew in popularity because they did not appear to be condemning the interpretations of the Western Church at large.

The Pope, grappling with the continuous attempts to persuade dissidents and to hold the friars together, wrote to them on the theme 'Great is poverty; greater is chastity but the greatest good of all is obedience if it is strictly kept'. Such was the clash of principles that four friars in Marseilles were burnt to death. This caused huge shock-waves throughout the Brotherhood, Spirituals and Conventuals alike, for obedience was certainly Francis' clear witness to the gospel life. Pope John then felt he needed to crush the Spirituals altogether.

The friars of the Observant Reform arose around 1368, being encouraged by Pope Gregory XI to both live separately and to recruit. Their separate witness was lived out in Spain and across to Italy. They set out the standard for all future relations between the Conventuals and the Spirituals for the next hundred years. However, the divisions deepened seriously so that the official clarifications offered in 1517 came as a relief, a new start and from separate premises.

The defining of the two Orders in 1517 marks something of a historical watershed. Europe in this period was passing through the turmoil of the Protestant Reformation. Luther had posted his protest (regarding the sale of indulgences) to the door of the church in Wittenberg in the same year. The Catholic Church was slowly undergoing its own reforms, which were enhanced in the Counter Reformation Movement, in which the Franciscans had a considerable role.

St Clare's Poor Ladies

Around the year 1206 Francis was engaged in his first task for God, to rebuild the church. One day, according to the Testament of Clare, Francis pleaded in his rather typical spontaneous manner, 'Come and help me with this monastery of San Damiano, for here there will be an order of ladies whose fame and holy life will glorify the heavenly Father in his whole Church.'

Clare's personal story is told in Chapter 2, along with the establishment of the Second Order. Her Rule (see Chapter 4), which in radical terms safeguarded the sisters' commitment to the poverty of Christ and the gospel life lived by the brothers, was only formally approved a few days before her death in 1253.

The immediate response from a number of women who shared the vision of Francis and Clare meant that outside the town of Assisi several convents of Poor Ladies were already established in Italy and beyond. The expansion of the friars will have brought opportunities for the growth of the Clares. And at the same time the difficulties experienced by the brothers, particularly over the interpretation of the life of poverty, affected their own witness also. By the early fifteenth century various endowments had accumulated with signs of wealth visible. Records show that some houses, under the leadership of sisters who had come from noble families, became extremely well off. Others were very poor and vulnerable to both plague and persecution.

It was largely due to the zeal of the Observant friars that the Poor Clare reforms came. Colette (d. 1447) became one of the noted reformers in France and Flanders at this time, both within the Poor Ladies and also through her recruiting of friar chaplains to the Clares, who later became known as the Colettans. (These brothers were influenced by the Observant friars though they expressed allegiance to the Minister General of the Friars Minor as they emerged in the settlement of 1517.) Others like Felicia Meda and Catherine of Bologna lived such self-effacing lives of poverty and devotion as to bring about the re-flowering of the Order.

The Capuchins

Caught by various secular and political pressures and events in northern Italy in the early sixteenth century the Observant friars were unable to contain some individual reformers who wished to maintain the stricter Franciscan life. Further influences from the Spanish mystical tradition of the Carmelites, John of the Cross and Teresa of Avila brought about a new Franciscan witness and Friars of the Eremitical Life, as they became known, opened a number of new hermitages and held their first independent chapter in 1529. They later became known as the Order of Friars Minor Capuchin and were formally accepted as autonomous within the Franciscan family in 1617. Their distinct habit with extended hood or 'capuce' expressed their identity with the purest ideals of the Franciscan life, and are now one of the three major communities of friars serving in the Church.

Third Order Regular

'The range of different manners of living the Franciscan life that emerged in the sixteenth century is itself a testament to the vitality of the charism and the wealth of expressions that could authentically represent the Franciscan spirit.' Thus writes Philippe Yates OFM, the current Principal of the Franciscan International Study Centre in Canterbury.

The Third Order Regular for men came into being in the fifteenth century as local congregations of people chose to live out the Franciscan charism in different ways with a commitment under vows. Pope Sixtus IV sought to regularize them, and a later Pope, Leo X, in 1521 promulgated a Rule for both male and female tertiaries who felt called to live in community. Insisting on full autonomy they were recognized as an independent Franciscan Order in 1586.

Similarly Pope Leo's provision for women to live as active religious prompted considerable expansion of Franciscan sisterhoods living together in a variety of contexts, all under the umbrella of the Third Order Regular for women. The reforms of this time encouraged many women to adopt new and often stricter forms of Franciscan life. The Ursulines were founded as a congregation of tertiaries following the Third Order Rule, though their significant growth only occurred in the twentieth century, particularly in India. The Grey Sisters were largely influenced by the Observant friars in France and the Low Countries, many of whom were engaged in hospital service. Others, notably the Annunciades, shared the enclosed life but with the Third Order Rule. The decisions of the Council of Trent in 1563 required all women religious to adopt the enclosure. This took some time fully to take effect, as some obstinate resistance was expressed for a time. By the end of the seventeenth century most women's communities were bound by the cloister.

Third Order Secular

Francis founded three orders, the third for those unable to commit themselves to a life in community or make religious vows because of family or other commitments. It all came about when Francis was journeying through the Lower

Spoleto Valley and was preaching to villagers in Cannara. He was interrupted by the cries of a flock of swallows. Distracted, Francis bade them keep silent, which they respectfully did. The villagers were so moved by his persuasive preaching that they asked to join him. Francis felt compelled to give them a Rule, probably similar in tone to the 'Letter to all the Faithful' which he wrote in 1215. They were officially known at first as the Order of Penance.

Lay followers and others who were members of the secular clergy were known as Brothers and Sisters of Penance, and later as the Third Order of St Francis. Hence the opportunity was given to live out the spirit of the Franciscan vocation within people's own personal circumstances. It has of course over the centuries produced saintly kings, hermits, artists, scientists, priests and many other holy men and women. The Rule has been revised from time to time, the latest revision being the one approved by Paul VI in 1978 when the Order became known as the Secular Franciscan Order (SFO). Numbers fluctuate: in the last century the total number had risen to over four million tertiaries, though numbers dropped after the Second World War. A renewal of the Rule brought new vocations. History reflects an interesting trend that when the Church is itself strong the Franciscan element is smaller; when the Church is not so strong, there is a complementary rise in the Franciscan contribution!

Modern times

Such a brief summary of our history can trace only the trends of the Franciscan movement. Throughout it has remained a loyal servant within and to the Church at large. It is set on the direct following of basic Christian gospel imperatives. It rejoices in the popularity of the founders, emulating the lives of Francis and Clare before them, who shone like bright stars in the way of poverty, prayer and obedience, extolling the merits of living simply, in proclaiming the gospel message of God's love and calling people to penitence.

The nineteenth century brought new opportunities as the Catholic Church responded to the social needs of people in post-revolutionary Europe and new congregations began to spring up with an active apostolate. The Sisters of the Holy Cross (HC) were founded in Switzerland in 1844 to teach children, a foundation that quickly spread through Europe, India, South Africa and South America. The Institute of Franciscan Missionaries of Mary (FMM) were founded in 1877 in South India with a worldwide apostolate in 84 foundations during the lifetime of their foundress. Others sprang up as secular Third Order members formed themselves into religious congregations. The Franciscan Missionaries of the Divine Motherhood (FMDM) came into being in 1896 at Hampstead in London, with sisters now spread all over the world engaged principally in health care. The Sisters of St Clare (OSC), as a contemplative order, felt compelled to provide schools, beginning in 1831 in Ireland. Later their work of providing a Catholic education spread to the UK, the United States and Central America. The establishment of these religious institutes within the Catholic Church gave opportunity for literally hundreds of congregations to appear across the Christian world, though not all have survived to the present day. In Britain the traditional Orders were only slowly welcomed back to establish themselves and to work freely, restricting their activities to running parishes or to found a school or a hospital. Now, in days when all institutions are having a difficult time, along with other religious orders, the need for change and adaptability in the context of the Western Church is proving a difficult challenge. The provinces of other countries where vocations are flourishing are providing needful resources where local vocations are less.

Anglican/Episcopalian Franciscans

The appearing of the religious life in the Anglican Communion brought a similar flowering in the twentieth century, though numbers are relatively small. The first in 1894 was a group of both priests and laymen, known as the Society of the Divine Compassion in Plaistow in East London. They, together with other small communities, were formed together in 1937 as the Society of St Francis (SSF). In 1905 the women's Community of St Francis (CSF) was also founded in that area. In America the Franciscan life in the Episcopal Church emerged in 1919 serving the church in the City and State of New York.

The Anglican 'Clares' brought an added witness to the contemplative life both in America between 1922–2000, and in Oxford, England, from 1950. Again, they are small in number, but, pioneering within the Anglican Church, the sisters have sought to discover how to live as modern-day followers of St Clare. Their Rule has been written and revised by its existing members.

The first professions in the Third Order of St Francis in America was in 1926. In Britain the tertiary movement was formed in 1936 and grew out of the life of the brothers who were operating from a farmhouse in Dorset. More recently, with ever-increasing numbers, the Anglican Tertiaries share with the Secular Franciscan Order in the Roman Catholic Church the opportunity for ordinary people to take on the spirit of the Franciscan life in their own settings and with their own secular commitments. Those with a sense of the Franciscan vocation and who are helped by the precepts of Franciscan spirituality are thereby able to use their particular missionary opportunities and also have a basis upon which to witness to a disciplined Christian way of life. The marks of this vocation in their lives are described in their Rule as humility, love and joy – the strains which were so obviously present in Francis and Clare.

Ecumenical links

There are many signs of a unity that has been built up within the Franciscan family in recent generations. This may be seen not only in the working together of the major Franciscan congregations through their ministers general and reverend mothers but extends to many opportunities for co-operation that exist between congregations and communions. Assisi has become an inter-faith symbol for prayers for world peace following the occasion in 1986 when Pope John Paul called the world faith leaders to pray with him. The Franciscan Institute at St Bonaventure, New York, and the International Study Centre in Canterbury draw their staff and students from a wide spectrum within the Franciscan family. The Week of Prayer for Christian Unity was promoted by the brothers known as the Franciscan Friars of the Atonement (SA) in 1908 in conjunction with an Anglican priest. The Order was founded in 1898 at Graymoor in New York as an Episcopal congregation, but their brothers and sisters converted to the Roman Catholic Church, making unity one of their primary objects. The Franciscan Herald Press and the St Anthony Messenger Press have each offered a wide selection of material that has appealed to all sections of the Church. Franciscans International operates at the United Nations as an NGO with a major branch working in Geneva. Accommodation has been made available by the host church in Assisi to provide non-Catholics with a place to celebrate a Sunday Eucharist and also to establish an Anglican chaplaincy. The Anglican Clares have been invited to take the Poor Clare acronym 'OSC' as a symbol of their belonging to the same family, and they pray for each other daily. The Franciscan Hermitage at Shepherds Law in Northumberland, UK, twinned with a hermitage in France, is registered with the Secretariat for Promoting Christian Unity at the Vatican and the Anglican Diocese of Newcastle. There is so much more to tell! Then add the countless friendships across the globe which have been made through a shared appreciation of the little poor man of Assisi, his call to peace and to prayer, his embracing of all who fall outside society's acceptance, his care of the environment, his venturing towards people of other faiths, his insistence on the basic call to create brotherhood and sisterhood in a world that is so ready to settle into divisions. The Franciscan family is above all else inclusive.

The Franciscans in Ireland
Pat Conlan OFM

Early foundations

When the Franciscans met with the Celts in Ireland they recognized kindred spirits. Both stressed the poetic rather than the rigorous, valued the individual above the group, and put the goodness of creation before human achievement. There is a tradition that the friars came to Ireland before the saint's death in 1226. Richard of Ingworth became the first Irish minister provincial in 1230. The first houses were on the east and south coasts, from Cork through Waterford to Dublin and Carrickfergus. Inland sites such as Athlone and Armagh followed, and local rulers invited the friars to the west and south. Finally there was an effort to pick up on places that had been missed, so that there were thirty-three Irish friaries by the end of the thirteenth century.

The first friars lived in outhouses while praying in parish churches. Proper friaries were built in such places as Nenagh and Waterford as early as 1240. These had a large long narrow church running east to west with a cloister area to the north. The friars preached among the people in their own language and were extremely popular. Thomas Quin was the first of many to be elected bishop. Two Irish friars went to the Holy Land in 1322, while another went to China in 1316.

Irishmen soon joined the order, and tension arose between the Irish and Anglo-Irish before the turn of the century. A royal commission reported that the friars made too much use of the Irish language. A prelate claimed that it was not a sin to kill an Irishman and he would not hesitate to say Mass afterwards. A compromise was reached after a tumultuous chapter at Cork in 1291. The province was split into custodies, of which one was Irish, the others Anglo-Irish, and the minister provincial was appointed with the consent of the English monarch.

The fourteenth and fifteenth centuries

The fourteenth century was a time of stasis. There were few new foundations, an exception being that at Ballybeg on the Isle of Man. A dispute with the archbishop of Armagh about the rights of the friars to preach and hear confessions rumbled on for decades. At stake were the generous gifts given by benefactors for burial rights. The Black Death decimated communities in 1348/49. Twenty-five friars died in Drogheda alone.

The fifteenth century opened on a brighter note. There was a cultural revitalization in Ireland. The Observant reform was recognized in new constitutions in 1430. With its stress on penance and prayer in quiet places, it suited the Irish spirit. The first Observant foundation was at Quin in 1433, followed by Muckross in 1445. Soon there were ten Observant houses, mainly in country areas in the west and north. At the same time, small houses for brothers of the Franciscan Third Order Regular emerged as quasi-hermitages in remote areas. They numbered about forty before vanishing at the Reformation. The Conventual or non-reform friars made five foundations in the same areas. The royal right to confirm the provincial was ignored so that native Irishmen could take office. From 1460, the Conventual provincial operated alongside an Observant vicar provincial.

Surviving the Reformation

The province, along with the order, was split in two in 1517. There were fifty-eight friaries in Ireland on the eve of the Reformation, of which about twenty-two were Conventual and thirty-six Observant. The Irish Parliament passed the bill suppressing the monasteries in 1537. The first friaries, Dublin and Kilcullen, were seized in 1539. Houses in towns in the east and south were soon suppressed. Those in the west and north survived well into the reign of Elizabeth. The Conventuals, who were concentrated in cities and towns, suffered grievously. A commissary general was appointed in 1564 and their last house, probably Roscrea, was seized in 1579. Individual friars lived on, for example around Buttevant, into the seventeenth century; but the province had vanished as an entity. The Conventuals returned to Ireland in 1986, when they took over a parish in Dublin.

The Observants held on, often forced into hiding by persecution. Pressure grew after the excommunication of Elizabeth I in 1570. At this stage the friars became associated with Irish nationalism, particularly through efforts to get Spanish military aid. The list of beatified Irish Franciscan martyrs begins in this period: Blessed Patrick O'Healy and Conn O'Rourke (Killmallock, 1579); Conor O'Devaney (Dublin, 1612); John Kearney (Clonmel, 1653); Charles Meehan (Wales, 1679). There were still a good number of friars scattered around the country at the end of Elizabeth's reign. The recent wars had made life difficult – for example, Donagh Mooney, who joined the friars in Donegal, had to flee to finish his noviciate in the Midlands, and made his profession in gaol before arranging the escape of both himself and the provincial!

Florence Conry was appointed provincial at the general chapter of 1606. He realized the need for proper formation in the spirit of the Counter-Reform and opened the first Irish Franciscan Continental College at Leuven in 1607. Others followed in Rome (1625), Prague (1630), Capranica (1656) and Boulay (1700); St Anthony's College, Leuven, specialized in Irish studies, producing a major history of Ireland, the first Irish grammar, the first book printed in that language and a series of pastoral works in Irish. The friars there also opened a mission to the Gaelic-speaking areas of Scotland. Directed by Luke Wadding, the community at St Isidore's in Rome worked on Franciscan studies. They produced the first edition of the writings of St Francis, a history of the first centuries of the Order (*Annales minorum*), a catalogue of Franciscan authors and the first edition of the works of Blessed John Duns Scotus. This, and the effect that the returning friars had in Ireland, led to the period 1610–50 being labelled the Golden Age of the Irish friars.

The remaining Irish friars were gathered into eight communities in 1612 and a process initiated of returning to abandoned sites. By 1629 there were thirty-four friaries, rising to sixty-two in 1646. An Irish Capuchin mission was established in 1608. The first friars arrived home in 1615 and there were fifty-one in six houses by 1642. The Poor Clares arrived in Ireland in 1629, having established a base in the Lowlands in 1625. Driven out of Dublin by the authorities, they finally settled at Bethlehem, north of Athlone, in 1630.

Renewed historical pressures

War broke out in 1641. The country, including the friars, was split in two. The majority favoured the nationalist and Old Irish line, with a minority backing the royalists and Old English. The divisions led to bitter disputes. The arrival of Oliver Cromwell in Dublin in 1649 brought severe persecution, and confusion continued after the Restoration in 1660. The first normal chapter in decades took place in 1672, when there were fifty-six communities. The persecution during the Titus Oates plot was replaced by optimism following the coronation of James II in 1685.

Ireland was caught up in the Williamite war against the Stuarts. The end result was the Banishment of Religious Act of 1695. The 500 members of the Irish province could go into hiding, pretend to be diocesan clergy, or move to the continent. They went into hiding near cities and towns such as Dublin and Athlone. The friars ran parishes in large parts of the Midlands and north, such as the area around Trim from 1720 to 1826. They also took on parishes near their houses, such as Athlone from 1723 to 1766. Finally, a large number fled to the continent, where many became military chaplains or developed an academic career.

The friars could move more freely from 1725. But Rome, worried about the quality of religious life in Ireland, issued a decree in 1751 closing noviciates there. This led to a drastic fall in vocations. By 1766 there were only a hundred friars in Ireland trying to staff twenty-four houses, and about seventy-five in parishes. At the end of the century there were 120 friars at thirty-seven sites. In addition the province had opened its first foreign mission, looking after the Irish exiles in Newfoundland, where the first five bishops were Irish Franciscans.

Thousands of friars vanished in the maelstrom of the French Revolution and provinces shrank to a few men in a couple of houses. The Irish lost their colleges, but Rome had repealed the ban on noviciates in Ireland and it was possible to train friars at home. The new national seminary at Maynooth produced sufficient priests to replace the friars in parishes. This led to re-organization. By 1832, there were only fifty priests serving sixteen friaries. Initial optimism, with major rebuilding in many places, was offset by the anti-religious aspects of the Catholic Emancipation Act of 1829. This envisaged that friars in the country would register, formation centres would close and any who returned after training on the continent would be outlaws. It proved impossible to enforce the Act, but it did delay re-organization.

Reforming and rebuilding

The continental Franciscans rebuilt the order around the concepts of strict observance and community life. This involved a monastic existence, wearing the habit everywhere and living a strict life in community. The Irish had emerged from persecution living like priests in a presbytery. For most of the nineteenth century, continental friars tried to impose their ideas on the Irish. The first was Father Bernard van Loo during his attempts to revitalize Franciscan life in England. He arranged the opening of a strict noviciate in Drogheda in 1860, as well as a Belgian (later English) house in Killarney to show the Irish how religious life should be lived. By 1870, about eighty friars staffed a house of formation on the continent and thirteen houses in Ireland.

The last Irish Franciscan bishop in Newfoundland died in 1869. Irish friars were already working in Australian parishes, where the first friary opened in Sydney in 1879. Growth was slow, but the Province of the Holy Spirit, covering Australia and New Zealand, came into existence in 1939.

Father Gregor Janknecht of the Province of Saxony, visitor in 1879, was appalled by the lack of vision among the Irish friars. A crisis over the provision of lecturers at St Isidore's in Rome enabled him to slip in his man, Father Bernard Doebbing, and then send other Germans to help him. Next the Irish were persuaded to send the novices to Germany. Finally he was behind the publication of a reform decree in 1888. The old friars, known as the Black Friars because they wore clerical dress, would not be allowed to recruit and would die out. The new Brown Friars, who wore the habit in public, would be in charge of formation. They would staff the houses in Ireland as the old men died. The first house taken over was Multyfarnham in 1896, and the last was Waterford in 1927. A new provincial administration of five Brown and one Black friars was appointed in 1899. The reform envisaged a rise in educational standards. A seraphic college opened in Capranica in 1891, moving to Multyfarnham in 1899. The noviciate went to Ennis in 1899, moving to Killarney when it was taken over by the Irish friars in 1902. A special house of humanities for clerics opened in Cork in 1909 but had a chequered history until they went to University College, Galway, in 1932. The old college in Leuven was re-opened in 1925, while that in Rome became the centre for theology.

The Brown Friars re-introduced the brother, seen as a support for the priest. They developed their pastoral ministry around preaching, confession and special devotions. They also undertook parish missions and retreats. The province had 150 members in 1920, 250 by 1945, and peaked at about 435 in 1966. Numbers are now down to under two hundred, partially as a result of missions becoming an independent province and also because of a decline in vocations.

Some friars served as military chaplains during both World

Wars. The spirit of optimism led to expansion and rebuilding, including a new friary in Donegal. Great stress was laid on education, with several friars obtaining professorships at universities. A house of Irish Studies was started in Killiney in 1945. With Australia on the verge of independence, a new mission was established in China in 1935. It closed in 1951 after an unfortunate history due to war. New fields opened in South Africa, where the Irish friars took over the vicariate of Kokstad, the National Seminary in Pretoria and a large area to the south of Johannesburg. These are now part of the province of South Africa. The friars went to Southern Rhodesia (now Zimbabwe) in 1958, where the mission became the custody of the Good Shepherd in 1990. They answered the call of John XXIII for priests in Latin America. Initially a small group helped in Chile before a mission was started in El Salvador in 1968. This became part of the new province of Central America in 1987.

Today's opportunities

The core ministry of the Irish friars has remained the service church. Since Vatican II, reconciliation rooms have replaced confessionals and confessional bells replaced set times. Reconciliation has been supplemented by counselling. Some friars became involved in diocesan ministry, initially as chaplains (colleges, transport, hotels, and theatres), then as parish clergy, and finally one as a bishop! Education has remained a priority. The seraphic college was transformed into a secondary boarding school when it moved to Gormanston in 1956. Several friars have been successful in the print media and on radio.

Beginning with the provincial chapter of 1981, the Irish friars have tried to develop a vision for the third millennium. This has involved a more authentic lifestyle and the involvement of the laity in ministry. There is more freedom in prayer, now seen as a personal relationship with God. It is an experience rather than an exercise. Friaries have been designated as centres for prayer, justice and peace. Two of these function as retreat centres, and a permanent hermitage has opened in Carrick-on-Suir. Formation has been re-organized, partly in conjunction with the English province. With four Irishmen involved in the general curia of the order, the Irish province feels that it is making a worthwhile contribution towards bringing the spirit of Francis to people of the third millennium.

Franciscan Holy Places: A Pilgrim's Guide

Around Assisi
Martin Shaw

There's a delightful story concerning Bernard and Francis, which might at first seem to reveal an uncomfortable and mutual suspicion. Bernard was undoubtedly attracted to following Francis, but remained uncertain of the authenticity of Francis' spirituality. Such uncertainty may indeed be healthy. Bernard had heard of Francis' simplicity of prayer. For example, Francis used a simple acclamation to enter into a contemplative adoration of God: 'My God! My All!' He had also learnt that Francis would follow the Christ-like prayer life by praying in the middle of the night. Bernard was sceptical of this. While following Francis on one of his preaching pilgrimages, Bernard feigned sleep and snored loudly! When he thought Bernard was asleep, Francis then rose to pray: 'My God! My All!', repeated gently and with that attention that marks all those who are gifted with a contemplative heart. After some time, Francis returned to bed and slept soundly. Bernard needed no more convincing! He had seen and made pilgrimage with prayer and love at its depth. If you want to know what the spiritual life is about, watch and listen to someone who practises it. Then by practising it oneself, the spirituality becomes a present reality.

Following in the way of Francis is a present reality. It is about praying and living the Christ-like life now. Any pilgrimage to a holy shrine is pointless unless it is an awakening to that dynamic. If a pilgrimage to Assisi and its associated sanctuaries is to reach beyond nostalgia, history and art, then the prayer 'My God! My All!' prayed simply and constantly with St Francis will mean that there will be an immediacy, a presence which will bear with it its own awakening for the pilgrim.

The seven-day itinerary that I offer is designed, not primarily as a historical, artistic or even a hagiographical experience, but as an opportunity to deepen the Christ-like life. This journey does in one sense have a beginning and an end, but in another it is a cyclic experience. It is a matter of spiritual discipline for the pilgrim to let go of the attitude that a pilgrimage is an exercise completed, an achievement to be marked up. In particular, a Franciscan pilgrimage is about freedom from possession and allowing God to direct the details of life.

As T. S. Eliot wrote in *The Four Quartets* ('Little Gidding'):

What we call the beginning is often the end
And to make an end is to make a beginning.
The end is where we start from.

In order that this itinerary is useful, I am assuming that the pilgrim will be able to find the time to be alone for at least a short period of time each day. I recommend that in advance the pilgrim reads a good 'Life of St Francis'. Elsewhere in this handbook, reading suggestions are listed. However, there is an inclination in some to read too much and miss the point of pilgrimage. As a general approach, it is important to look, observe, attend deeply and note what you want to learn more about. This process may well stimulate the pilgrim's return!

Not all became friars, or contemplatives like his intimate friend, Clare. For Francis, all Christians were like him summoned to rebuild or bring refreshment to the Church, the Body of Christ, which he adored. It is to that rebuilding and refreshing that the pilgrim is summoned wherever the pilgrim returns after the Franciscan 'Cycle'.

This 'Cycle' lasts six days, making the assumption that most people will be travelling to Assisi and back within a week. Depending on the time of year, getting up early in the morning reveals not only Assisi, but all of Umbria at its best. The light is incomparable, giving an insight into the more 'outward' spirituality of the Franciscans. A cappuccino, an amaretto (a local almond liqueur) or a grappa at a reasonable time so that you can rest will enable you to stay with the experience during the day. Wasting energy worrying about what presents you wish to take back can be an addiction for some that is difficult to break. Keep it simple. Take something back that relates to the beautiful story of the Tau Cross which is told elsewhere in this handbook. Keep a daily journal. In that way, you will find that you take better photographs that relate to the pilgrimage. If you draw or paint, take basic materials with you. And remember that a lot of churches and sanctuaries are shut at lunch-time. Rest and go Italian!

The description of the six-day pilgrimage cycle does not follow the details of Francis' life. That can be read and studied at any time. It is designed to offer experience, challenge and reflection. In no way is it definitive. It comes from many visits to Assisi and other Franciscan shrines around that part of Italy. The days can be changed according to the pilgrim's own pattern and desires. There are several travel agents who specialize in pilgrimages to Assisi, which simplifies accommodation and travel facilities. Their experience shows that many pilgrims are also looking for a time to visit some of the art treasures of Italy. Although this cycle does not touch on such considerations, its purpose is primarily to help the pilgrim become clear about the spiritual opportunities of the journey.

For a detailed travelling companion to Assisi and other Franciscan pilgrim places, see Judith Dean's Every Pilgrim's Guide to Assisi, *Canterbury Press, 2002.*

Day 1

San Rufino

San Rufino is the cathedral of Assisi. With the space in front of it, there is a strange paradox. This is a huge building and yet gives off an atmosphere of delicacy and gentleness. In this building, Francis was baptized. The pilgrim can walk across the large space in front of the cathedral and imagine the embarrassing scene of Francis removing all of his clothes, and all the gestures of abandonment that he used to draw his listeners' attention to utter trust in God. When inside the cathedral, it is important to make your way to the little chapel on the left at the far end of the cathedral. In this chapel, there is a disturbingly stark 'Pietà': the abandonment of God in his dead Son.

San Damiano

You can walk from Assisi to San Damiano. It involves a pleasant walk downhill – just remember you have to come back. However, you can get there by taxi (see 'The Carceri'). The detail of this little gem of a sanctuary you will never grasp, no matter how many times you come to Assisi. Because of the smallness of the building, it is all too easy to walk through it and not notice – or indeed be ushered through it depending how busy it is. Here it was that Francis experienced his vocation. In the dark little church, take time to look at a replica of the famous Icon Crucifix, which is now displayed in the Basilica of Santa Chiara, back inside Assisi. Francis in contemplating the crucifix heard words addressed to him: 'Francis, rebuild my Church!' It doesn't seem at all fanciful to me to change the name Francis for one's own name! Christ is with you. Listen to him. Be with him, now.

In an even smaller chapel, the pilgrim will find the Crucifix of Brother Innocent. Go close to the crucifix and walk from one side to another and notice the three aspects of Christ's suffering: the agony, the last breath of life, and the succeeding calm.

What kind of relationship Francis had with Clare is a matter for speculation. Francis was and remained a passionate man and he undoubtedly loved her as a young man might. Simply because they both took on the vows of chastity does not mean that this love ceased. All relationships in Christ are used. To stand anywhere in San Damiano and recall their relationship is to allow the pilgrim the opportunity for his or her own relationships, not to be denied, but to be transfigured.

Santa Chiara

Back in Assisi, in the higher part of the town, beyond the main town piazza, lies Santa Chiara. The Poor Clares moved inside the walled city to protect them from the vulnerability of much of the ethnic violence of the Middle Ages. The Sisters live by a rule that has been changed less than any of the great women's orders of the Roman Catholic Church. It is an enclosed contemplative community, and one senses the depth of that, immediately on entry into the Basilica.

It is worth visiting the Tomb of St Clare. Such shrines put the pilgrim in touch with the contact everyone has with history, whether we realize it or not. We are surrounded at this very moment, not just with memories but with the tiny unseen particulars of our ancestors. To be reminded visually of some of the greatest of them attaches us not to the past, but to the importance of the response in the present.

It is worth the pilgrim spending at least half an hour in prayer with the painted twelfth-century crucifix which used to be in San Damiano. This has become one of the vital symbols of Franciscan spirituality. Stare, gaze, even gawp(!) at the cross. 'Take up your own cross and follow me.'

Day 2

The Basilica of St Francis

The best introduction to the Basilica is to go to Mass at the tomb of St Francis early. The pilgrim has a sense that through the word and sacrament there is here something particular about the dynamic of Francis. Wonder at the saint certainly, but there is the challenge also: to remain faithful to the immediacy and simplicity of Francis. After the Mass you can walk around the tomb and buy a candle and put it in a tray. It will be used on the altar, as the candles constantly burn there. There is an ordinariness to the experience which is appropriate for Franciscan spirituality, and which can easily be recollected long after the pilgrim has returned home.

One of the reasons for reading a life of St Francis is that the pilgrim's appreciation of the Giotto frescos in the Upper Basilica will be all the deeper. It is relatively easy to get hold of books of reproductions of them before coming to Assisi. It will mean that the pilgrim can pray with the frescos without having to be dependent on guides or books. It is vital to give this experience a good length of time. Struggling to understand and be informed about them will get in the way. If the educational process is important, the pilgrim can always come back later during the pilgrimage.

The frescos in the Lower Basilica are beautiful. Again, being informed about them in advance is helpful. It will take the pressure off the pilgrim. The relics chapel is important to visit. In a glass case, there is the beautiful blessing which Francis gave to Leo. The story goes that after Francis had experienced the stigmata on Monte La Verna, Leo felt depressed that Francis would be world famous and no longer a special friend of his. Francis' reply was that he would be even more special to Leo. So he wrote out the blessing and gave Leo strict instructions that he was to keep the prayer next to his heart all his days. At his death, when Leo's habit was removed, the blessing was found sown inside, next to his heart.

Day 3

Santa Maria degli Angeli

At the bottom of the hill beneath Assisi lies this small town which the pilgrim almost certainly passes through on the way to Assisi, or arrives at by train. Indeed many pilgrims stay in the town's hotels and other accommodation during their visit to Assisi. Transport to and from Assisi is simple either by bus or by coach.

No one can miss the huge basilica of St Mary of the Angels. There are a number of places within the Basilica's complex that are important to visit with the help of guide books and tour guides themselves. The challenge for the pilgrim is to focus on what lies at the heart of Franciscan spirituality here.

There is a large concourse outside the main entrance to the Basilica. It may seem strange to suggest to the pilgrim to walk around its edge, but it was here that Francis had one of his earliest communities of friars. They lived in a series of small huts in utter simplicity, and came together for prayer in the Portiuncula, which is a tiny church cherished and honoured by the Basilica. This 'little portion of heaven' seems so tiny and fragile, and appropriately so. The pilgrim can stand in the enormous space of the Basilica and just look at it. What is it that happens to religious experience that it inevitably becomes powerful and then in danger of being static?

Close by the Portiuncula is the Transitus Chapel. The pilgrim here has the chance to be still and be reminded of the importance of preparing for his or her own death. Francis' relationship with 'Sister bodily death' was such that, when he was dying, it was not what might be expected. Bernard asked him why he looked occasionally sad as death approached. 'You now have thousands of followers'. 'That is why I am sad,' Francis sighed. This astonished those listening. Francis felt anxious that he had created another organization that needed maintenance, which inevitably would be in danger of losing its dynamic. So the pilgrim is asked here to ponder the vital importance of simplicity and freedom in keeping small and flexible. Pilgrimage, after all, is an act of praise for provisionality!

The Carceri Hermitage

You can walk up to the Carceri, but the walk is only for the hardy. The word simply means 'The Cells' – or little places to allow oneself to die to attachments. The hermitage lies on the side of Monte Subasio at about 800 metres. The pilgrim can get there by taxi from Assisi itself. If possible, it is worth going to the Carceri with one or two others who have the intention of praying there. After all, this hermitage was built on the site of a place to which Francis and his companions came frequently to pray. The visitor will pass down narrow stairs and see recesses in rock where Francis prayed and slept. Then on the other side of the hermitage, the walk leads through the ilex trees to an outdoor altar that is decorated by a large Tau Cross. Around this area, the brothers would come to pray in the open.

Three Brothers used to take it in turns to take on different roles in helping each to pray. For two or three days one of the Brothers would pray while another would listen to him and help him reflect on what was happening in the prayer. Simple spiritual direction, in fact. The third Brother provided food for the other two and gently looked after them. Then for the next few days, they would change roles. If there are two or three pilgrims, the simplicity of Franciscan prayer can be retained in this beautiful area, by praying and listening to each other as a way of encouraging prayer.

Day 4

Greccio

A good coach drive away from Assisi is the little village of Greccio. Once again, the hermitage is built into the side of the hillside cliffs. Getting up to the hermitage involves climbing up a considerable number of steps. When the pilgrim arrives at the top, the view across towards Rieti and up to Spoleto is breathtaking. There is a bench on a little patio here where you can sit and be undisturbed. The little chapel of the crib is a powerful place to be still and pray. Francis' frequent preaching tours up and down Italy meant that he had favourite stopping places, which over the years became shrines and hermitages for the friars. One Christmas, Francis celebrated Christ's birth by setting up a tableau of the Nativity scene at Bethlehem. Live animals and characters from the village were used and, of course, a baby. After all, if pilgrims could not get to the holy shrines of the Holy Land through the ravages of war, re-enacting the Gospel locally became a matter of necessity. There is a larger church above the hermitage where, around the balcony, there is an extensive collection of cribs.

A key symbol of the Franciscan crib can easily be overlooked. In the church at the back, there is a crib which shows various scenes from the Nativity story. The Christ-child has his arms spread. This, of course, is an attitude of joy, but it is also a pre-figuring of the crucifixion. The marks of the cross are already within his very being. The pilgrimage to Greccio has the potential of deepening the pilgrim's love for Mary, of whom it was said that a sword would pierce her own soul. The passion of Mary as well as Christ is deeply rooted in Franciscan spirituality – the passion beginning not in Jerusalem, but in Bethlehem.

Day 5

In Assisi, the pilgrim will never be able to explore every corner. It is therefore important to take a day off from travelling and visiting shrines, if for no other reason than to rest, enjoy the excellent restaurants of Assisi and to buy gifts to take back. However, it is countless pilgrims' experience that there are always some special spots that call for a second visit. Go back!

Above the town is La Rocca, the remains of the old castle. From here there is a spectacular view of Assisi itself and the valley across to Perugia. Here you have a sense of what it must have been like to live here in the thirteenth century when city-states and towns were at war with each other. It becomes all the more amazing to realize the extravagant confidence of Francis to change his life in the way he did given the enormous anxiety that was endemic among the people. The best time to come up here is the early morning. The pilgrim can then sit and look and pray for those who are experiencing anxiety through being rejected or who are refugees from war. Perhaps with the prayer attributed to St Francis 'Make me an instrument of your peace', the pilgrim might be more awake to the critical importance of peacemaking.

Day 6

Monte La Verna

On the journey to La Verna, it is worthwhile stopping at the small town of San Sepulchro. It is not far off the main route. In the town hall, there is the famous fresco of Piero della Francesca: the Resurrection. Arguably this is the greatest painting of the resurrection. It is not easy to pray here. The pilgrim can, however, become aware of the vital importance of waking up. The soldiers sleep before Christ's tomb while he stands pale and strong but with the look of suffering still in his face, looking directly at you! If the pilgrim lets it, the painting can increase the awareness of the presence of God in all things, to which we are blind most of the time!

Monte La Verna is also a good distance from Assisi, into Tuscany. One of the difficulties about travelling to Franciscan shrines is that a huge area of Franciscan spirituality is left unexperienced. Francis walked vast distances; so there is a sense that his life was a constant pilgrimage. This is not surprising, as he longed to identify with Christ in every conceivable way.

Francis' love affair with Lady Poverty is renowned. However, he was offered and, indeed, accepted: a mountain! Mountains, for the prophets, and indeed for the great Christian mystics, were places of contemplative union with God. La Verna had significance for Francis as Carmel did for Elijah. His desire was to experience, as intimately as God willed, all that Christ experienced, including the marks of his death. This is a story of mystery if not incomprehensibility. The stigmata, the marks or the signs of Christ's crucifixion on his hands, feet and side, are baldly and powerfully displayed in Cimabue's portrait of Francis in the lower Basilica in Assisi.

What really matters at La Verna is for the pilgrim to go into the little chapel that marks the place of the stigmata and pray sincerely that the desire to follow Christ may be deepened.

~

And so this short cycle ends, or begins again by the return of the pilgrim to where he or she first started, home, wherever it is, to 'discover it for the first time'.

The Holy Land
Sheelagh O'Flynn FMDM

Franciscans have long been deeply involved and immersed in the land where Jesus lived and from which his message was first carried. The Custody of the Holy Land was founded by St Francis in 1217. In 1342 Pope Clement VI mandated the friars to be the official custodians of the Holy Land. On 21 November 1992, the 650th anniversary of the bull of Clement VI, Pope John Paul II exhorted the friars to persevere in accomplishing this mandate.

The Custody is active today in Israel and its occupied Territories, in Jordan, Syria, Lebanon, Egypt, Cyprus, and Rhodes. The Custody comprises 332 Franciscans from thirty-two countries, belonging to fifty-nine provinces, with many women religious co-workers. It takes care of seventy-four shrines commemorating biblical events. There are twenty-one sanctuaries in Galilee, fifty in Judea, two in Syria and one in Jordan.

Pastoral care is exercised in twenty-nine parishes, sixteen schools, two residences for the elderly, three homes for orphans, 250 work-places and four Casa Novas which provide hospitality for pilgrims (see below).

Other involvements within the Custody include scholarship assistance and housing, ecumenical, cultural and scholarly activity in the Franciscan Biblical School of Jerusalem, the Jerusalem Theological School, the Franciscan Printing Press, the Christian Information Centre and the Centre for Christian Eastern Studies. A central aspect of the ministry of the Custody is that of welcoming pilgrims to the places entrusted to the Custody.

In forty-four countries throughout the world there are eighty-two Commissariats which help to foster interest in the Holy Land Sanctuaries.

∿

For most Christians, the opportunity to make a pilgrimage to the Holy land is the fulfilment of the dream of a lifetime. For Francis of Assisi it was the hope of martyrdom that drew him there in 1219–1220. Amazingly, his encounter with the Sultan of Egypt led to an inter-faith dialogue, not death; it is a dialogue that continues today. This land has been torn by wars and soaked in blood for centuries. For Christians, the exodus of local Christians from the Holy Land is a source of great concern and sadness. If they disappear completely, the Holy Land will become a museum for tourists and pilgrims to visit. It is very important that we support our brothers and sisters living there, and indeed our pilgrimages can help prevent people of other traditions becoming cut off from the rest of the world. When we go as pilgrims and not merely tourists we, like Francis, can be messengers of peace.

Each pilgrim group will have a desire to visit their own places of special interest or devotion. A helpful basic approach is to plan one's itinerary around the life of Jesus.

The following may prove a useful guide. Ideally allow at least ten days for the pilgrimage – a week is really too short.

Bold print denotes sanctuaries in the care of Franciscans.

Day 1

Fly into Tel Aviv and transfer to Bethlehem.

Day 2

In Bethlehem you can visit **the Basilica of the Nativity, the Shepherds' Field** and **the Milk Grotto.** The Grotto is a tiny chapel close to the Basilica where, according to tradition, Mary breast-fed her child, a place very dear to mothers. It conveys a sense of what the original birthplace of Jesus may have been like, a cave used to house people and animals. On this first day you can come into contact with an expression of the Christian life of the Arab people in the area, by visiting the House of Hope where orphaned children are cared for and taught skills – it will lift your spirits.

Day 3

On the following day it is possible to step back in time to gain insights into the culture and history of the Jewish people of whom Jesus was a member. Travel to Masada, where in AD 73, 960 Jewish men, women and children chose death rather than submit to Roman conquest; and Qumran, monastery of the Essenes where the Dead Sea Scrolls were discovered in 1947. No doubt you will want to have a swim in the Dead Sea on the return route. Then travel on to Galilee, along the Jordan valley, stopping at Beth Shean where King Saul was killed, to visit the fascinating Tel and excavations. As pilgrims you may wish to stay in Nazareth rather than Tiberias, which is a more commercial area, though there is the **Franciscan Church of St Peter** by the sea in Tiberias, which is worth a visit.

Day 4

In Nazareth you will want to visit the **Church of the Annunciation** with its various shrines. You might also like to travel the few miles to Sephoris, where there is **a church dedicated to Sts Joachim and Anne,** close to the ancient Roman city which had a Jewish Quarter – a place where Joseph's skills and perhaps those of Jesus as carpenters/builders may well have been employed. You will also be able to visit **Cana**, the site of Jesus' first miracle. Here the members of the group might wish to renew their own life commitment, be it in marriage, priesthood, religious life or as single lay Christians.

Day 5

This day could be spent around the Jordan Valley. Visit Yardenit to renew baptismal promises. Tracing Jesus' adult life will bring you to the shores of the Sea of Galilee. A highlight of the pilgrimage may be the opportunity to celebrate Mass on board one of the boats on the sea. A site of special interest by the lake is Capernaum, where you can see **the excavations of Peter's house underneath the modern church**, alongside the remains of a very fine fourth-century synagogue.

Here Jesus called and taught and healed. Visit Tabgha, the site of the multiplication of the loaves, and **Mensa Christi or Peter's Primacy** (Jn 21).

Day 6

Start on **the Mount of Beatitudes**. It is well worth travelling north past Bethsaida, which, along with Chorazin, is left with not a stone upon a stone as Jesus foretold, up to Mt Hermon, to visit Caesarea Philippi and see the crystal-clear waters that flow at the source of the Jordan down to the Sea of Galilee. This journey, if time allows, brings one to the borders of Syria and to the far side of the Sea of Galilee, giving one a broader sense of the land and peoples that Jesus knew.

Day 7

Leave Nazareth and Galilee and, with Jesus, turn your face towards Jerusalem. Take the route that brings you to **Mt Tabor**, the traditional site of the Transfiguration, and if you have the energy at least walk down from the mountain – going up is quite a climb! Drive on through the Wilderness of Jerusalem, and as you draw close to Jerusalem visit **Bethany**, the home of Martha and Mary and the scene of the raising of Lazarus, which led into the events of Holy Week. As you approach Jerusalem you come to the Mount of Olives. One of the most beautiful views is to be had from the tiny church of **Dominus Flevit**, shaped like a tear-drop, where Jesus may have stood to look at Jerusalem and weep for her. It is an ideal place to pause for meditation.

You might decide to return to Bethlehem and visit Jerusalem from there, or stay in Jerusalem for the last few days of your pilgrimage.

Day 8

In the Holy City there is so much to see. Certainly visit the Temple Mount and the Western Wall – you may manage to see a Bar Mitzvah there. Visiting the Christian Places, you could start at the Cenacle – no longer in Christian hands, but the friars have a very nice **chapel** nearby, which you might arrange to visit, to celebrate the Last Supper. The Church of St Peter in Gallicantu is near here and gives one a profound sense of what it might have been like to be imprisoned. It is a place to pray for prisoners and all who are held in bondage in whatever way, a good site to celebrate Reconciliation. It is a modern church built on the reputed site of the house of Caiaphas.

Cross the Kidron Valley and visit **the Garden of Olives** and the sombrely beautiful **Basilica of the Agony.** Entering the city by St Stephen's Gate, you can walk the Way of the Cross, visiting along the way the **Chapels of the Flagellation and the Condemnation and the Lithostrotos** where Roman soldiers played dice for the clothing of the prisoner to be crucified. On then to the **Church of the Holy Sepulchre** which encompasses what is left of the traditional rock of Calvary and the site of the Lord's tomb – both at the very heart of the Christian faith. These are places to return to if you can in the very early morning, so that in silence you can enter into prayer; during the day they can be distractingly busy.

Day 9

There are many other places you may want to visit. Just to mention a few significant places: the beautiful church of St Anne beside the Pool of Bethesda; the Garden Tomb outside the city walls, in which one can contemplate the resurrection; **Ein Kerim** with all its associations with Mary, Elizabeth and John the Baptist; and Yad Vashem, lest we forget the horrors of the Holocaust. It is good to allow time on this day for pilgrims to return to places of special personal devotion. Undoubtedly people will want to buy some little gifts to bring home, and the final afternoon might be left free for that, so it is not a distraction throughout the pilgrimage.

Day 10

If your flight leaves in the afternoon you would have time to visit Abu Gosh/Qiryat Yearim en route to Tel Aviv airport. Here the Ark of the Covenant was stranded for twenty years before King David transported it to his new capital in Jerusalem. There is a fine Benedictine church here which commemorates the Emmaus story (there is debate over the authenticity of the site). As one sets out like the disciples, post-resurrection, it is a good place to pause to share and to experience the Risen Christ who journeys with us.

~

As you travel through the Holy Land the Scriptures come alive – it is an experience to be lived, to which no itinerary on paper can do justice. Travelling as pilgrims, not tourists, is essential to reaping the benefit of this journey, which is one of faith, open to all the Lord wants to reveal to us in his own land. It is very helpful to have preparatory and follow up meetings at home and to gather each evening during the pilgrimage to reflect on the day and focus the following day.

Casa Novas

Franciscan House for Pilgrims
Casa Nova Street
P.O.B. 1321
91043
Jerusalem
Israel
Tel 02/628.27.91
Fax 27/626.43.70

Franciscan House of Pilgrims
P.O.B. 996
Bethlehem
Palestinian Authority
Tel 02/274.39.60-85 (6 lines)
Fax 02/274.35.40

Franciscan House for Pilgrims
Casa Nova Street
P.O.B. 198
16101
Nazareth
Israel
Tel 06/645.66.60
Fax 06/657.96.30

Basilica della Trasfigurazione
Convento di Terra Santa
P.O.B. 16
6100
Nazareth
Israel
Tel/Fax 06/673.22.83

Holy Land Commissariats

England, Scotland and Wales	Tel/Fax 020 8498 9994	
Washington, USA	Tel/Fax 202 526 6800	
Dublin, Ireland	Tel 1-6777651	Fax 1-6777293
NSW, Australia	Tel 02 9389 5955	Fax 02 9389 8597
Canada	Tel 613 737 6972	Fax 613 737 5479
Malaysia/Singapore	Tel 65 893 0926	Fax 65 764 3060
Malta	Tel 00356 242254	Fax 00356 332560
New Zealand	Tel 09 625 6651	Fax 09 625 7384
Philippines	Tel 063 2 373 2973	
South Africa	Tel 012 3461484	Fax 012 3461438
Taiwan	Tel 886 2 23312105	Fax 886 2 237 10971

Useful guide books

Richards, H. J., *Pilgrim to the Holy Land*, McCrimmon, 1985 – very comprehensive; includes material for worship.

Wareham, N. and Gill, J., *Every Pilgrim's Guide to the Holy Land*, Canterbury Press, 1996 – compact and very useful.

Jabusch, W., *Walk Where Jesus Walked*, Ave Maria Press, 1986 – the hymn selection may suit US pilgrims better.

Doyle, Stephen C., OFM, *The Pilgrim's New Guide to the Holy Land*, The Liturgical Press, Minnesota, 1984 – an excellent resource book with lots of interesting background information and clear maps.

The Franciscan missions of California
Guire Cleary SSF

California is a land founded on legend, and understanding its history is therefore a challenge. The very name of this state comes from a sixteenth-century Spanish novel about a fabulous island ruled over by an Amazon queen, Califa. The reality of the European discovery of California is far more prosaic, due to the military and economic factors. Somehow evangelization became part of that process. In the 1590s, Spain claimed California, wishing to build military bases to protect ships from Asia. The Manila galleons crossing the Western Pacific would make landfall in Northern California. But plans never materialized until the mid eighteenth century, when Russian ships hunting sea otters alarmed the Spanish who questioned their intentions, though there was no possibility of subjugating a huge country and its population. Instead the Spanish chose to Christianize and Hispanisize the Indians of California. Junipero Serra OFM was made President of the Missions, the first of which was founded in San Diego, California in 1769.

Serra wished to name a mission after St Francis, and requested the Inspector General, Galvez, to designate one of the missions. According to legend Galvez responded, 'If Francis wants a mission let me find a suitable port.' Although English and Spanish ships had been sailing along the California coast for 200 years, they had not sighted the small passage through the Coastal Mountains into San Francisco Bay, called the Golden Gate. An exploratory party coming by land discovered the passage on 31 October 1769, and to their stunned surprise they caught a glimpse of a strait through the mountains to one of the largest harbours of the world. St Francis was given his mission and city, San Francisco de Asis.

What later became known as San Francisco was settled by approximately 200 immigrants from Northern Mexico on 27 June 1776. This new settlement was so far from the established population centres in Mexico that the first colonists were the poorest of the poor with few other options. Padre Francisco Palau OFM, a former student of Junipero Serra and originally from Majorca, chose the new mission site to be close to a source of water and to be near the subjects of his missionary efforts, the Ohlone Indians of the village of Chutchui. The Ohlone and other native peoples made up the bulk of the parishioners of Mission San Francisco from its foundation in 1776 until about 1825. It was the Indians who

finished the existing church of St Francis in 1791, the oldest
intact building in the city and the oldest intact Christian
church in California. It remains today as a monument to their
efforts, creativity, labour and faith.

It must be understood that the twenty-one Franciscan missions of California were the property of the California Indians
who built them. At one time the holdings of the missions were
vast. Mission San Francisco alone had a circumference of 135
miles and stretched into three counties. The missions were the
birthplace of California's modern agricultural and industrial
enterprises. Until the secularization of the Franciscan missions
in 1835, they were the principal economic vehicle of the state,
exporting hides and tallow to places as far as Europe. Mission
San Francisco had twenty looms weaving into cloth the wool
gathered from its thousands of sheep. One historian has
identified fifty-two different crafts and technologies introduced into California by the Franciscan missions, the wealth
of which, together with the immense land holdings being
maintained in trust for the Indians, became a source of envy;
and ultimately the missions were secularized, and somehow
very little land found its way back into the possession of the
true owners and founders of California, the Indians.

The place of the Franciscan missions in California history is
thus assured, though somewhat controversial, and the issue of
European treatment of native peoples is still a flashpoint even
today. The twenty-one Franciscan missions of California are
visited by millions of tourists and schoolchildren every year.
Most are still active Roman Catholic parishes, and a handful
still have Franciscans on staff. The site of Blessed Junipero
Serra's tomb at Mission San Carlos Borrome (Carmel) is a goal
for many pilgrims, though his proposed sainthood guarantees
a lively discussion. The missions are still very much alive in
California and are places of beauty and history, while having
the ability to challenge both doubt and faith.

The Greyfriars, Canterbury
David Hayes

The House of the Grey Friars is situated in the centre of the
city of Canterbury, tucked behind the twelfth-century alms-
houses of Eastbridge Hospital. The trustees of the Hospital
now own the site, and their Master, also an Anglican brother,
is the administrator. The main access is from Stour Street and
it stands in open grounds after crossing the little bridge over
the River Stour.

Greyfriars was the first foundation in Britain of the
Franciscan friars who arrived on 10 September 1224, two
years before St Francis died. Agnellus of Pisa, along with eight
other Brothers, landed at Dover, and they were first enter-
tained by the monks of the cathedral priory. The local history
booklet explains:

> Four of the friars went off to London while five stayed behind
> under the care of Alexander of Gloucester who was Master
> of the Poor Priests Hospital in Stour Street. Alexander gave
> to the friars part of the Hospital's garden situated on a small
> island known as Binnewith formed by the forking of the
> river. Here they established their community, though all
> that remains today is the Greyfriars House itself.

The upper storey is set out as a chapel, and an Anglican
Eucharist is celebrated regularly on Wednesdays at 12.30 pm.
A new and exciting exhibition covering much of the history
and development of the Franciscan Orders is also housed in
the building. Links with the Franciscan International Study
Centre in Giles Lane, Canterbury are maintained. Greyfriars
House is open to the public from Easter Monday until the last
Saturday in September, between the hours of 2 pm and 4 pm.

13

Glossary of Franciscan Terms

Tristam Holland SSF

An asterisk (*) indicates that the word or phrase is further expanded elsewhere in this Glossary.

Aspirant
A person who hopes (aspires) to become a Religious* and has been in touch with a particular community, but has not yet begun to live with them.

Capuchins
From the Italian word *cappuccino*, meaning a pointed monastic hood, the group of friars* who became known as the Capuchin reform began in 1525 in the Italian Marches region. Rebelling against what they saw as a watering down of the Rule*, particularly with regard to the acceptance of monies, Friar Matteo di Bassi obtained a verbal authorization for the movement from Pope Clement VII to observe the Rule literally, particularly by a strict interpretation of the vow* of poverty and to wear the habit* with a pointed hood (which they regarded as *ab origine*). The Capuchins, as they became known, finally became formally detached from those known as the Observants* in 1536 and today form one of the three families of First Order* Franciscans in the Roman Catholic Church, and use the initials OFM Cap.

Celibacy
The commitment to remain unmarried and to refrain from sexual relationships. It is part of the vow* to chastity traditionally taken by Religious* and is one of the Evangelical

Counsels* of our Lord. Chastity is a commitment to sexual integrity, a term applicable to fidelity in marriage as well as to celibacy in Religious life.

Chapter
The council or meeting of Religious* to deliberate and make decisions about the community is known as a Chapter. In some orders, this may consist of all the professed members of the community; in others, the Chapter is a group of members elected by the community as a whole to be their representatives.

Clothing
The ceremony in which a postulant* of a community formally becomes a novice*, and begins the period of formation in the mind, work and spirit of the community is sometimes called the Clothing. It follows the initial stage of being a postulant when the prospective member first lives alongside the community. The clothing or novicing ceremony is characterized by the Religious* 'receiving' the habit* of the community.

Contemplative
All are called to contemplative prayer, whether living an active or monastic life. Sometimes the word 'contemplative' is also used to denote a Religious* whose life is concentrated on prayer inside the monastery or convent, rather than on social work or ministry outside the house. Some communities were founded with the specific intention of leading a contemplative lifestyle together. Others may have a single member or small group living such a vocation within a larger community oriented to outside work.

Conventuals
The Conventuals are one of the three branches of the First Order* Friars, taking their name from the large, usually urban, friaries or convents that were becoming more common in Franciscan life from the mid thirteenth century. As such, they began, from 1322, to accept papal privileges and dispensations permitting modifications to the original practice of strict

poverty. Until 1517, however, this title was not applied: it was only with the rise of the self-styled Observant* Friars* who were at that time given the right uniquely to use the style OFM that some distinguishing name was required. They became two independent congregations in 1517 and, since then, they have used the style OFM Conv.

Crown (of the Seven Joys of Mary) *see* **Franciscan Crown.**

Custos
The Custos has the care and charge of brothers and sisters in an incipient Province, sometimes directly under the Minister* General.

Damiano Crucifix
Thomas of Celano records that the young man Francis was praying in the dilapidated Church of San Damiano before the crucifix there. Whilst praying, he heard the words 'Francis, go, repair my house, which, as you see, is falling completely into ruin.' Through this directive, Francis received a decisive inspiration and, because of the significance of this event in Francis' life, the painted crucifix of San Damiano has been carefully preserved as an important and treasured Franciscan relic in the Basilica of St Clare in Assisi.

Enclosed
This term is applied to Religious* who stay within a particular convent or monastery – the 'enclosure' – to pursue more effectively a life of prayer. Such Religious would usually only leave the enclosure for medical treatment or for other exceptional reasons. This rule is intended to help the enclosed Religious be more easily protected from the distractions and attentions of the outside world.

Eremitic
The eremitic Religious* is one who lives the life of a hermit, that is, largely on his or her own. Hermits usually live singly, but may live in an eremitic community, where they meet

together for prayer on some occasions during each day. St Francis wrote a Rule* for hermitages* which seems to assume four hermits living together, having two as carers and the other two as the cared-for, the pairs changing roles after a period of time.

Evangelical Counsels
A collective name for the three vows* of poverty, chastity and obedience, as advocated by our Lord, are known as the Gospel or Evangelical Counsels.

Evangelical Life
The word 'evangelical' is used to describe the Franciscan Movement in contrast with the terms 'monastic' and 'apostolic', which were the traditional categories for Religious Orders in the Roman Catholic Church. Franciscan life fits into neither of these, yet embraces elements of each. Francis wanted only to live the Gospel by following in the footprints of Jesus Christ. In his desire to be true to the Lord, Francis would spend many months going apart with his brothers into 'hermitages' to commune more deeply with the Lord, and then he would return to 'the market place' to preach the Good News of God's love, calling people to respond to that love through repentance.

The term evangelical is also used in a specific context to speak of the Gospel Counsels of Poverty, Chastity and Obedience, which are the three vows made by professed members of the First, Second and Third Orders Regular. Those who live a life observing the Evangelical Counsels* are said to be living the Evangelical Life, in contrast to those living a community life, where some or all of such vows* are mitigated.

First Order
The first of the Orders to be created by Francis consisted of those men who followed Francis, taking the Evangelical Counsels* of poverty, chastity and obedience as vows*, and were received into the fellowship of the community. The

Roman Church recognizes that there are three branches of the First Order: the Order of Friars Minor (OFM), the Conventuals* (OFM Conv), and the Capuchins* (OFM Cap).

For Anglican Franciscans, the First Order also includes a women's community who follow the same Rule* as the First Order Brothers.

See also **Second Order** and **Third Order**.

Formulæ of Profession

The text required to be recited by all brothers and sisters at profession*, be it first or simple, life or solemn.

Franciscan Crown (of the Seven Joys of Mary)

The origins of this devotion are obscure, dating from the late fifteenth century, and relate to the legend of an apparition of the Blessed Virgin Mary to a Franciscan novice*. The young man, prior to admission, had daily crowned a statue of Mary with a wreath of roses, but was unable to maintain this as a novice and, because of this, was contemplating leaving the Order. One day, during his prayers, the blessed Virgin spoke to him, telling him not to grieve but instead to 'wreathe a crown of fervent prayer which will surpass the beauty of any crown of roses'. This 'crown' consisted of one Our Father and ten Hail Marys, in memory of the joys of Mary's Conception of Christ. These prayers would then be repeated in memory of the joys of the Visit of Mary to Elizabeth. The prayers would be said a third time to commemorate the joy of the Birth of the Saviour, without pain or the loss of virginity. Fourthly, the prayers would be repeated in honour of the joy of the visit of the Magi with their gifts. The prayers would be said a fifth time to remember the joy of the Finding of Christ in the Temple after anxious searching. Sixthly, the same prayers would be said to recall the joy of the Resurrection of our Lord. Finally, the prayers would be said a seventh time in honour of the Assumption of Mary into heaven. The story goes that Mary said to the young novice, 'In doing this faithfully every day, you will wreathe me a crown that will be more meritorious to you and much more pleasing to me.'

The devotion spread rapidly and widely among the Friars Minor*.

Friars Minor
From the Italian word for 'brother', the word 'Friar' became universally used for all those who joined the Order founded by Francis. But Francis gave his followers the particular designation of 'the Lesser Brothers', or 'Minores', to indicate that they should see themselves as having no rights or privileges, but only living a life of penury and extreme simplicity. It was also a noteworthy play on words when paralleled with the terminology used in the small city of Assisi, where those privileged to reside within the city walls were called the Majores, or Greater Ones, whilst those living outside the walls were termed the Minores, or Lesser Ones. Francis seems clearly to have aligned his community with the 'excluded' rather than the 'included'.

Friary
The designation of a place where the Friars lived and from which they went out. In the beginning, these were termed Convents, but as the followers of Francis began simply to be known as friars, or more particularly Franciscan friars, their places of residence became re-designated as Friaries.

Greyfriars
Francis and the first friars wore a habit* made from undyed cloth. In England this was from undyed sheep's wool, hence Greyfriars.

Guardian
Guardians are heads of houses or local communities and have the care and charge of brothers and sisters living in their friary* or convent. Francis deliberately chose the terms Minister* and Guardian in direct contrast to Superior, Abbot and Prior, indicating that those in positions of leadership in the Order should be seen as servants of the community.

Habit

The distinctive clothing of a community, common to all, is known as the habit. In some communities, the habit is worn at all times, in others only at certain times or for certain activities. In some communities, the habit is rarely worn, except perhaps for formal occasions. The white, three-knotted cord is a Franciscan symbol with the reminders of the three vows*.

Hermitages

Although opposed to his followers accepting buildings as places for them to reside, Francis himself felt able to accept a mountain! La Verna became for him a place of withdrawal from his arduous journeys and the conventual life of the Portiuncula*. At Alverna, he lived a hermit life and even wrote a Rule* for Hermits. Also, in the hills above Assisi, Francis would regularly meditate in a particular spot where rocks and forest created a natural enclave. A convent was built there in 1400 by St Bernardine. Hermitages began to be established in places hidden from the general populace, and in contrast to the normative conventual life.

Lady Poverty

Francis took the contemporary understanding of the chivalric attitude of reverence for women (always referred to as ladies), and re-interpreted it into a similar veneration for Poverty, attributing the title of Lady to the concept. Thus Lady Poverty was revered and had songs and poetry addressed to her, indicating that the only perfect state for a friar was when he could give himself completely to love of her.

Minister

Ministers have the care and charge of brothers and sisters in a Province (Minister Provincial) or of the whole Order (Minister General). Francis deliberately chose the terms Minister and Guardian* in direct contrast to Superior, Abbot and Prior, indicating that those in positions of leadership in the Order should be seen as servants of the community.

Novice / Noviciate

A member of a community who is in the formation stage of the Religious* Life, when he or she learns the mind, work and spirit of the particular community whilst living among its members, is normally known as a novice. The Noviciate is both the place where the novices live and are being trained, and also a name for the whole group of novices.

Observants

The Observant Reform in the First Order* began in the fourteenth century, as the Order began to accept modifications to the Rule* to conform with the gradual change to a more settled life based on the *convento* or friary*. Some felt that this was a betrayal of the spirit of the Rule, and fought for what they saw as the more perfect observance of the primitive tradition. In 1517, the papacy recognized this latter group, who had become known as the Observants, and granted them the title of OFM, thus causing the Conventuals* to modify their title.

Office / Daily Office / Divine Office

The round of liturgical services of prayer and worship, which mark the rhythm of the daily routine in the Religious* Life, is called the Office. Religious communities may use the services laid down by the Church or may have their own particular Office book. The Offices may be called Morning, Midday, Evening and Night Prayer, or may be referred to by their more traditional names, such as Matins, Lauds, Terce, Sext, None, Vespers and Compline. There might also be a separate Office of Readings.

Penance

It seems that Francis' first name for his Order was the Order of Penance, as he saw his friars as men of penance, whose life was one of prayer and work expressing sorrow for their own sins and the sins of the world. Only later did they become the Friars Minor* or Lesser Brothers.

Perfect Joy

In contrast to the normal understanding of what might be a perfect situation, Francis always seemed to see heavenly gifts, such as joy, in a new and different way. For him, 'perfect joy' was summed up in a friar's being rejected by the world, even by his own brothers, for it was only in being treated thus that the friar, and subsequently humanity, would come to have a proper understanding of the earthly and incarnate life of Christ, a life to be imitated such that it would act as a preparation for the life eternal.

Portiuncula

'The little piece' of land on the plain below Assisi where the Church of St Mary of the Angels was located, and where Francis and his followers went to live after leaving Rivo Torto, is called the Portiuncula. It is regarded as the mother house of the Order and indulgences are granted to those who make pilgrimage there on the feast of St Mary of the Angels, 2 August. This has more recently been extended to all churches.

Postulant

Someone who is in the first stage of living the Religious* Life. The postulancy usually begins when the aspirant* begins to live in community and ends when he or she becomes a novice* and 'receives the habit'*. Postulants sometimes wear a distinctive dress, or, more usually, wear secular clothes.

Poverello

The title Poverello, meaning the little poor one, was attributed to Francis by the early biographers and, within Franciscanism, is now a term uniquely used of him.

Profession

The ceremony at which a Religious* makes promises (or vows*) to live the Religious Life with integrity and fidelity to the Rule*. The profession of these vows may be for a limited period or for life. The usual pattern is to make a 'first' or simple profession in which the vows are made to the community. After three or more years a Life Profession may be made, which is to the Church, and so the vows are usually received by a bishop.

In the Roman Church, such vows can only be dispensed by the Apostolic See. In the Anglican Communion, Life Professed Religious can usually be secularized only by the Archbishop or Presiding Bishop of a Province.

Regular
The Latin word 'regular' simply means 'rule' and those who follow a rule of life* are often called Regulars.

See also **Third Order Regular.**

Religious
The general term for a person living the Religious Life, whether monk, nun, friar, brother, sister, etc.

Release / Dispensation / Secularization
The act of an individual withdrawing from community, and being properly released by due authority from any vow* or vows that have been taken.

Rule
The written text containing the principles and values by which the members of a community try to live. The Rule is not simply a set of regulations, although it may contain such; it is an attempt to capture the spirit and charism of a community in written form. Some communities follow traditional Rules, such as that of St Francis or St Clare; others have written their own in the spirit of Francis or Clare.

Rule of Life
A short rule adopted by an individual or a community laying out clearly the obligations and duties of the individual or each member of the community, such as prayer and attendance at Office* and Mass; confessional practice; study; work and leisure; retreats and quiet days, etc.

Second Order

The Order of the Poor Ladies of Assisi, who came to be known as the Order of St Clare or simply the Poor Clares, constitute the Second Order of the wider Franciscan Family.

See also **First Order** and **Third Order**.

Secular Franciscans *see* Tertiary.

Stigmata

The five wounds received by our Lord on the cross are traditionally known as the stigmata. They were made by the nails penetrating Christ's hands and feet when he was nailed to the cross, and by the lance of the soldier in the side of Christ (Jn 19.34).

The Stigmata of St Francis was the occasion in 1224 when St Francis received in his own body on Mount Alverna the stigmata of Christ, during a vigil following Holy Cross Day. This incident in the life of St Francis is usually celebrated on 17 September.

Tau

The Tau has its origin in biblical antiquity and is the last letter of the Hebrew alphabet. Francis' own devotion came out of a sermon preached by Pope Innocent III on St Martin's Day inaugurating the Fourth Lateran Council, where the Pope linked the Last Supper text with that of Ezekiel, likening himself to the young man dressed only in linen to whom the Lord said, 'Go through all the city . . . and mark the Tau on the foreheads of all.' Pope Innocent saw the Tau as a form of the cross of Christ, so that anyone who wore this sign appropriated the power of the cross and witnessed to it by word and deed. Francis was present at the sermon and took back the sign of the Tau to Assisi, 'signing it on all his letters and even painting it on the walls of his cell,' according to Thomas of Celano. Thus it has a special significance for Franciscans because Francis adopted it as a personal seal and encouraged his companions to do the same. St Bonaventure said that 'This Tau symbol had the saint's deep devotion and veneration.'

Tertiary / Third Order / Secular Franciscans

The term 'Tertiary' is usually associated with Franciscan communities, but is used by others too (such as the Dominican Third Order). The members of the Third Order are known as Tertiaries or Secular Franciscans: they are men and women who take vows* modified so that they are able to live in their own homes and have their own jobs. They may also marry and have children. They have a Rule of Life* and are linked to other Tertiaries through regular meetings. In the Franciscan family, the Third Order or Secular Franciscans complement both the First Order* of celibate friars and sisters and the Second Order* of contemplative* Religious.

See also **First Order** and **Second Order**.

Third Order *see* Tertiary.

Third Order Regular

Many Franciscan communities have developed and grown since the sixteenth century, and particularly from the eighteenth century for women living the active or apostolic Religious* Life. But with the defining of the three parts of the First Order* in 1517, all such Orders and communities following the way of St Francis founded since then, be they for men or women, are regarded by the Roman Church as Third Order Regular.

Transitus

St Francis died in the evening of 3 October 1226, after Vespers, and so his feast day is celebrated on 4 October, the 'day' having already started with Vespers. However, his 'passing over' or Transitus is observed by the followers of Francis re-enacting, in the early evening of 3 October, some of the events of that day. First this service, and then 3 October itself, came to be known as the Transitus.

Vow / Vows

The promise or promises made by a Religious* at profession*. Traditionally, they are vows of poverty, chastity and obedience.

14

A Franciscan Bibliography

Philippe Yates OFM

For a more complete bibliography on any subject, look at one of the 'serious' books and it will usually include a bibliography of older books. For this reason we present here usually only the more recent books in any area, with one or two notable exceptions.

Buying Franciscan books

Franciscan publishers' details and abbreviations

FIP – Franciscan Institute Publications, The Franciscan Institute, St Bonaventure University, St Bonaventure, NY 14778, USA. Website: www.sbu.edu

FP – Franciscan Press, Quincy University, 1800 College Avenue, Quincy, IL 62301-2699, USA.
Website: www.franciscanpress.com

FUP – Franciscan University Press, 1235 University Boulevard, Steubenville, OH 43952, USA.
Website: www.franuniv.edu/upress

SAM – St Anthony's Messenger Press, 1615 Republic St, Cincinnati, OH 45210, USA.
Website: www.americancatholic.org

Franciscan Bookshops

England

Franciscan International Study Centre Bookshop:
www.franciscans.ac.uk

Italy (Assisi)

Libreria Internazionale Francescana:
www.libreriafrancescana.com

USA

St Francis Online: www.stfrancisonline.com

FISC Bookstall

Franciscan books are available from the FISC Bookstall, Giles
Lane, Canterbury CT2 7NA, tel: 01227 769349, who produce a booklist of available books.

Life of St Francis

Academic

Bittle, B., *The Knight Errant of Assisi* (FIP 1982)
Boff, L., *St Francis: Model for Human Liberation* (Crossroad
1982)
Brooke, R., *The Image of St Francis: Responses to Sainthood
in the Thirteenth Century* (Cambridge University Press
2006)
Brunette, P., *Francis of Assisi and his Conversions* (FP 1997)
Cuthbert, *Life of St Francis of Assisi* (Longmans reprint
1960)
Dalarun, J., trans. P. Pearce, *Francis of Assisi and the Feminine*
(FIP 2006)

Dalarun, J., *The Misadventure of Francis of Assisi: Towards a Historical Use of the Francis Legends* (FIP 2002)

Dalarun, J., *The Stigmata of S. Francis: New Studies, New Perspectives* (FIP 2006)

Englebert, O., *St Francis of Assisi: A Biography* (Servant Publications 1982)

Fortini, A., *Francis of Assisi* (Crossroad 1981)

Frugoni, C., *Francis of Assisi: A Life* (Continuum 1998)

Hammond, J. M., *Francis of Assisi: History, Hagiography and Hermeneutics in the Early Documents* (New City Press 2004)

Haule, J. R., *The Ecstasies of St Francis: The Way of the Lady Poverty* (Lindisfarne 2004)

Leclerc, E., *Wisdom of the Poor One of Assisi* (Hope 1992)

Lortz, J., *Francis, the Incomparable Saint* (FIP 1986)

Manselli, R., *St Francis of Assisi* (FP 1988)

Matura, T., trans. P. Lachance, *Francis of Assisi: Writer and Spiritual Master* (SAM 2005)

McMichaels, S., *Journey Out of the Garden: St Francis and the Process of Individuation* (Paulist Press 1997)

Moorman, J., *St Francis of Assisi* (FP 1977)

Robson, M., *St Francis of Assisi: The Legend and the Life* (Geoffrey Chapman 2000)

Sabatier, P., *Life of St Francis of Assisi* (Charles Scribners 1928)

Schmucki, O., *The Stigmata of St Francis of Assisi* (FIP 1992)

Popular

Bodo, M., *Francis: The Journey and the Dream* (SAM 1988)

Chesterton, G., *St Francis of Assisi* (Image 1982)

Gasnick, R. and Noonan, H., *Francis of Assisi: The Song Goes On* (SAM 1987)

Green, J., *God's Fool: The Life and Times of Francis of Assisi* (Harper & Row 1997)

House, A., *Francis of Assisi* (Chatto and Windus 2000)

Hugo, W., *Studying the Life of Francis of Assisi: A Beginner's Workbook* (FP 1996)

Manning, Cardinal, tr., *Francis of Assisi* (Legenda maior) (Tan 1992)

Sweeny, J. M., *Light in the Dark Ages: The Friendship between Francis and Clare of Assisi* (SPCK 2007)

Historical fiction and poetic reflection

Bobin, C., trans. M. K. Kohn, *The Very Lowly: A Meditation on Francis of Assisi* (New Seeds 2006)

Bobin, C., *The Secret of St Francis of Assisi: A Meditation* (Shambhala 1997)

Corretto, C., *I, Francis* (Orbis 1982)

Gasnick, R., ed., *The Francis Book: 800 Years with the Saint from Assisi* (Macmillan 1980)

Kazantzakis, N., *God's Pauper* (Faber & Faber 1975)

Mueller, J., *Francis: The Saint of Assisi* (Thomas More 2000)

Petrie, R., *The Autumn of St Francis of Assisi* (SAM 1997)

Timmermans, F., *The Perfect Joy of St Francis* (Ignatius Press 1998)

Children's books

Bernthal, M. and Grayson, R., *Gifts of Christmas: A Heartwarming Francesco Story* (Lyric Studios 1997)

Billington, R., *St Francis of Assisi* (Hodder & Stoughton 1999)

Byrd, R., *Saint Francis and the Christmas Donkey* (Dutton Juvenile 2000)

DePaola, T., *Francis: The Poor Man of Assisi* (Holiday House 1982)

Joslin, M., *The Good Man of Assisi* (Lion 1997)

Mayo, M., *Brother Sun, Sister Moon* (Little Brown & Co. 2000)

Walsh, M., *Saint Francis Celebrates Christmas* (Loyola Press 1998)

Wildsmith, B., *St Francis* (Eerdmans 1996)

Life of St Clare

Bartoli, M., *Clare of Assisi* (FP 1993)
Bodo, M., *Clare: A Light in the Garden* (SAM 1992)
Carney, M., *The First Franciscan Woman: Clare of Assisi and Her Form of Life* (FP 1993)
Clare of Assisi: Investigations (FIP 1992)
Dhont, R.-C., *Clare Among Her Sisters* (FIP 1987)
Fonck, B., *To Cling With All Her Heart to Him: The Spirituality of St Clare of Assisi* (FP 1996)
Kirkham, J. P., *Clare of Assisi: A Light that Brightens the World* (Catholic Truth Society 2006)
Peterson, I., ed., *Clare of Assisi: A Medieval and Modern Woman: Clarefest Selected Papers* (FIP 1996)
Peterson, I., *Clare of Assisi: A Biographical Study* (FP 1993)

Franciscan sources and translations

St Anthony

Marcil, G., ed., *Anthony of Padua: Sermons for the Easter Cycle* (FIP 1994)
Life of St Anthony: Assidua (Messagero 1984)

St Clare

Armstrong, R., *Clare of Assisi 1194–1253: Early Documents* (New City Press 2005)
Armstrong, R. and Millane, P., eds, *Towards the Discovery of Clare of Assisi*, Vol. I: *Clare: Formed by Francis*; Vol. II: *Clare Discovers the Love of God in the Church*; Vol. III: *Clare's Form of the Gospel Life*; Vol. IV: *Fraternal Love* (FIP 1992)
Armstrong, R., ed., *Clare of Assisi: Early Documents* (FIP 1994)

Hone, M. F., *St Clare of Assisi and Her Order: A Bibliographic Guide* (Compendium of Sources for a Study of St Clare) (FIP 1995)

St Francis

Armstrong, R., Hellman, J. A. W. and Short, W., eds, *Francis of Assisi: Early Documents*, Vols I–III (New City Press 1999–2001)

Armstrong, R., *Francis of Assisi: Writings for a Gospel Life* (Crossroad 1994)

Armstrong, R. and Brady, I., *Praying with St Francis of Assisi* (Eerdmans 1997)

Brown, R., *The Little Flowers of St Francis* (Image Books 1971)

Habig, M., *St Francis of Assisi: Writing and Early Biographies: English Omnibus of the Sources for the Life of St Francis* (FP 1977)

Hardick, L., *Admonitions of St Francis of Assisi* (FP 1984)

Karris, R., *The Admonitions of St Francis: Sources and Meanings* (FIP 1999)

Thomas of Celano, *First Life of St Francis of Assisi* (SPCK 2000)

St Bonaventure

Bonaventure, *The Journey of the Mind to God* (Hackett 1993)

Cousins, E., *Bonaventure* (Classics of Western Spirituality) (Paulist Press 1994)

Doyle, E., ed., *The Disciple and the Master: St Bonaventure's 'Sermons on St Francis of Assisi'* (FP 1983)

The Works of Bonaventure (English translations), Vol. I: *Mystical Opuscula*; Vol. II: *Breviloquium*; Vol. III: *Opuscula, Second Series*; Vol. IV: *Defense of the Mendicants*; Vol. V: *Collations on the Six Days* (FP 1960–70)

Works of St Bonaventure (English translations), Vol. I: *De*

reductione artium; Vol. II: *Itinerarium mentis in Deum*;
Vol. III: *Disputed Questions on the Mystery of the Trinity*;
Vol. IV: *Disputed Questions of the Knowledge of Christ*;
Vol. V: *Writings Concerning the Franciscan Order*; Vol. VI:
Collations on the Ten Commandments; Vol. VII: *Selected
Works of Theology and Spirituality* (FIP 1955–2000)

Bl. John Duns Scotus

Etzkorn, G. and Wolter, A., *Questions on the Metaphysics of
Aristotle by John Duns Scotus*, 2 Vols (FIP 1997–98)
Wolter, A. and O'Neill, B., *John Duns Scotus: Mary's Architect*
(FP 1993)
Wolter, A., *John Duns Scotus: A Treatise on Potency and Act.
Questions on the Metaphysics of Aristotle Book IX* (FIP
2000)
John Duns Scotus: Political and Economic Philosophy (FIP
2000)
John Duns Scotus: Four Questions on Mary (FIP 2000)
Belle, R., *Roger Bacon: The Opus Majus*, Vols 1–2 (University
of Pennsylvania Press 2000–01)

William of Ockham

Davies, J., *A Compendium of Ockham's Teachings: A
Translation of 'Tractatus de Principiis Theologiae'* (FIP
1998)
*Ockham on Aristotle's Physics: A translation of Ockham's
'Brevis Summa Libri Physicorum'* (FIP 1989)
Freddosi, A. and Kelley, F., *William of Ockham Quodlibetal
Questions*, Vols I–II (Yale University Press 1991)
Kilcullen, J., trans., *William of Ockham: A Letter to the Friars
Minor and Other Writings*, Cambridge Texts in the History
of Political Thought (Cambridge University Press 1995)
Kilcullen, J., trans., *William of Ockham: A Short Discourse on
Tyrannical Government*, Cambridge Texts in the History of
Political Thought (Cambridge University Press 1992)

General

McElrath, D., *Franciscan Christology* (FIP 1980)
OFM Curia, *JPIC Texts: An Aid* (Office of JPIC, Rome 2006)

Popular collections

Bodo, M., *365 St Francis of Assisi: Meditations for Each Day of the Year* (HarperCollins 1997)
Through the Year with St Francis: Daily Meditations From His Words and Life (SAM 1993)
Daily Readings with St Francis of Assisi (Templegate 1992)
De la Warr, Countess, *The Writings of St Francis of Assisi* (Backhouse Halcyon 1994)
Howell, A., *Franciscan Days* (John Murphy 1951)
Palm Tree Pocket Prayer Books: Prayer of St Francis of Assisi (Kevin Mayhew 1995)

Franciscan spirituality

Cirino, A. and Raischl, J., eds, *A Pilgrimage Through the Franciscan Intellectual Tradition* (Franciscan International Study Centre 2008)

Eremitism and prayer

Cirino, A. and Raischl, J., eds, *Franciscan Solitude* (FIP 1995)
Costello, L. F., *Through the Veils of the Morning* (Veritas Publication 1999)
Crossley-Holland, N., *A Fifteenth Century Franciscan French Office* (Edwin Mellen 1990)
Delio, I., *Franciscan Prayer* (SAM 2004)
Frances Teresa, *Living the Incarnation: Praying with Francis and Clare of Assisi* (FP 1993)
Johnson, T., *Franciscans at Prayer* (Brill, Leiden 2007)

A Franciscan Bibliography

Jordan, P., *An Affair of the Heart: A Biblical and Franciscan Journey* (Gracewing Press 2008)

Lehmenn, L., *Francis Master of Prayer*, trans. Paulinus Van Halderen (Media House, Delhi 1999)

Mrozinski, R., *Franciscan Prayer Life: The Franciscan Active-Contemplative Synthesis and the Role of Centers of Prayer* (FP 1981)

Mission

Mission in the Franciscan Tradition (FIP 1994)

Moons, A. and Walsh, F., *Franciscan Missionary Charism* (FIP 1995)

Poverty and evangelical perfection

Hobday, J., *Simple Living* (Continuum 1998)

Lapsanski, D., *Evangelical Perfection: An Historical Examination of the Concept in the Early Franciscan Sources* (FIP 1977)

Lapsanski, D., *The First Franciscans and the Gospel* (FP 1976)

Lynch, C., ed., *A Poor Man's Legacy: An Anthology of Franciscan Poverty* (FIP 1988)

Short, W., *Poverty and Joy: The Franciscan Tradition* (Darton, Longman & Todd 1999)

Secular Franciscans

Fonck, B., ed., *Ritual of the Secular Franciscan Order* (SAM 1985)

SFO Resource Library, Vol. I: *Called to Follow Christ: Commentary on the Secular Franciscan Rule*; Vol. II: *Called to Rebuild the Church: A Spiritual Commentary on the General Constitutions of the SFO*; Vol. III: *Called to Live the Dynamic Power of the Gospel: Meditations on the Gospel Life for Secular Franciscans*; Vol. IV: *Called to*

Proclaim Christ: Commentaries on the Secular Franciscan Life; Vol. V: *Called to Make Present the Charism: The Meaning of the SFO Rule*; Vol. VI: *Called to Build a More Fraternal and Evangelical World: Concordance to the SFO Rule* (FP 1998–)

Marquand, P., *Formation of Lay Franciscans* (Franciscan Herald Press n.d.)

Mota, R., *The Rule of the Secular Franciscan Order: With a Catechism and Instructions* (FP 1980)
Secular Franciscan Companion (FP 1986)

St Anthony

Clasen, S., *St Anthony: Doctor of the Church* (FP 1973)

Hardick, L., *'He Came to You so that You Might Come to Him': The Life and Teaching of St Anthony of Padua* (FP 1989)

Spilsbury, P., *St Anthony of Padua 1195–1231* (Padua 2007)

St Bonaventure

Bowman, L., *A Retreat with St Bonaventure* (Element 1994)

Carpenter, C., *Theology as the Road to Holiness in St Bonaventure* (Paulist Press 1999)

Hayes, Z., *Bonaventure: Mystical Writings* (Crossroad 1999)

St Clare

Clare of Assisi: Model for Franciscan Women (FIP 1991)

Miller, R., *In the Footsteps of St Clare: A Pilgrim's Guide Book* (FIP 1993)

St Francis

Armstrong, A., *Saint Francis: Nature Mystic; The Derivation and Significance of the Nature Stories in the Franciscan Legend* (University of California Press 1973)

Boff, L. (trans. P. Berryman), *The Prayer of St Francis: A Message of Peace for the World Today* (Orbis 2001)

Boff, L., trans. T. Diercksmeier, *Francis of Assisi: Model for Human Liberation* (Orbis Books 2006)

Cook, W., *Francis of Assisi: The Way of Poverty and Humility* (Michael Glazier)

Doyle, E., *St Francis and the Song of Brotherhood and Sisterhood* (FIP 1996)

Esser, C., *The Rule and Testament of St Francis: Conferences to the Modern Followers of Francis* (FP 1977)

Gratian of Paris, *I Know Christ: The Personality and Spirituality of Saint Francis of Assisi* (FIP 1988)

Leclerc, E., *Francis of Assisi: Return to the Gospel* (FP 1983)

Matura, T., *A Dwelling Place for the Most High: Meditations with Francis of Assisi* (FP 1998)
Francis of Assisi: The Message of His Writings (FIP 1997)

Matura, T., Rotzetter, A. and Van Dijk, C., *Gospel Living: Francis of Assisi Yesterday and Today* (FIP 1994)

Rohr, R., *Hope against Darkness: The Transforming Vision of St Francis in an Age of Anxiety* (SAM 2001)

Trexler, R., *Naked before the Father: The Renunciation of Francis of Assisi* (Center for Medieval and Renaissance Studies 1989)

Vorreux, D., *First Encounter with Francis of Assisi* (FP 1979)

Other

Bodo, M., *Icarus in Assisi* (Editice Minerva 2002)

Carrozzo, A., Cushing, V. and Himes, K., eds, *Franciscan Leadership in Ministry: Foundations in History, Theology and Spirituality* (FIP 1997)
Franciscan Women: The Dynamics of Christian Fidelity (FP 1975)

Helen Julian, *Living the Gospel: The Spirituality of St Francis & St Clare* (BRF 2001)

Iriarte, L., *The Franciscan Calling* (FP 1974)

Jeffrey, D., *The Early English Lyric and Franciscan Spirituality*

(University of Nebraska Press 1975)

Lanchance, P., *Angela of Foligno: The Passionate Mystic of the Double Abyss* (New City Press 2006)

O'Mara, P., *Franciscan Leader* (FP 1997)

Sardello, J., *Making the Journey with Christ: The Way of the Cross* (FP)

Williams, R. C., *A Condition of Simplicity: Franciscan Wisdom for Today's World* (Canterbury Press 2003)

St Francis – popular

Allen, P. and Allen, J., *Francis of Assisi's Canticle of the Creatures* (Continuum 1999)

Anthony, E., *Canticle of Brother Sun* (SAM)

Bodo, M., *Tales of St Francis: Ancient Stories for Contemporary Living* (SAM)
The Way of St Francis: The Challenge of Franciscan Spirituality for Everyone (SAM 1995)

Bodo, M. and Sing, S., *Francis and Clare of Assisi: Following Our Pilgrim Hearts* (SAM 1996)

Haase, A., *Swimming in the Sun: Discovering the Lord's Prayer with Francis of Assisi and Thomas Merton* (SAM 1993)

Kirvan, J., *Peace of Heart: Based on the Life and Teaching of Francis of Assisi* (Ave Maria Press 1995)

Lupi, R., *The Identity Card of St Francis of Assisi* (Portiuncula Press 2003)

Nan, *The Message of St Francis: With Frescoes from the Basilica of St Francis at Assisi* (Frances Lincoln 1999)

Normile, P., *Following Francis of Assisi: A Spirituality for Daily Living* (SAM 1996)

Normile, P., Foley, L. and Wiegel, J., *To Live as Francis Lived: A Guide for Secular Franciscans* (SAM 2000)

Ramon, *Franciscan Spirituality: Following St Francis Today* (SPCK 1994)

Stoutzenburger, J. and Bohrer, J., *Praying with Francis of Assisi* (St Mary's Press 1989)

Talbot, J., *The Lessons of St Francis: How to Bring Simplicity and Spirituality into Your Daily Life* (E. P. Dutton 1997)

Talbot, J., *The Lover and the Beloved: A Way of Franciscan Prayer* (Crossroad 1985)

General – popular

Bernard, *Open to God: The Franciscan Life* (Collins 1986)

Ciampi, L., *Rebuild My Church: Meditations for Franciscan Laymen* (Franciscan Herald Press n.d.)

Elvins, M., *Gospel Chivalry: Franciscan Romanticism* (Gracewing 2006)

Elvins, M., *A Eucharistic Vision and the Spirituality of St Francis of Assisi* (Gracewing 2007)

Habig, M., *The Franciscan Book of Saints* (FP 1959)

McCloskey, P., *Franciscan Saint of the Day* (SAM 1991)

Padre Pio: The Wonder Worker (Park Press 1999)

Palmer, B., *Men of Habit: The Franciscan Ideal in Action* (Canterbury Press 1994)

Pearce, P., *Prayers From Franciscan Hearts: Contemporary Reflections from Women and Men* (SAM 2007)

Romb, A., *Maximilian Kolbe: Authentic Franciscan* (Prow Books 1990)

Schalück, H., *Stoking the Fire of Hope: Fioretti For Our Times* (FIP 1997)

SFO Catch Our Spirit (SAM)

St Anthony of Padua: Our Franciscan Friend (large print) (Catholic Book Publishing 1993)

St Anthony of Padua: The Story of His Life and Popular Devotions (SAM 1993)

Franciscan intellectual tradition

Bl. John Duns Scotus

Cross, R., *Duns Scotus on God* (Ashgate 2005)

Cross, R., *The Metaphysics of the Incarnation: Thomas Aquinas to Duns Scotus* (Oxford University Press 2003)

Hall, A. W., *Thomas Aquinas and Duns Scotus: Natural Theology in the High Middle Ages* (Continuum 2007)

Ingham, M., *The Harmony of Goodness: Mutuality and Moral Living According to John Duns Scotus* (FP 1996)

Ingham, M. B. and Dreyer, M., *The Philosophical Vision of John Duns Scotus* (Catholic University Press 2004)

Ingham, M. B., *Scotus for Dunces: An Introduction to the Subtle Doctor, St Bonaventure* (FIP 2003)

Shannon, T., *The Ethical Theory of John Duns Scotus: A Dialogue with Medieval and Modern Thought* (FP 1995)

Shannon, T. and Ingham, M., *Ethical Method of John Duns Scotus* (FIP 1993)

Vos, A., *Duns Scotus on Divine Love* (Ashgate 2003)

Vos, A., *The Philosophy of John Duns Scotus* (Edinburgh University Press 2006)

Williams, T., *The Cambridge Companion to Duns Scotus* (Cambridge University Press 2003)

St Bonaventure

Bettoni, E., *St Bonaventure* (Greenwood 1982)

Bougerol, J. G., *Introduction to the Works of St Bonaventure* (FP 1963)

Cullen, C., *Bonaventure* (Oxford University Press 2006)

Delio, I., *Burning Love of the Crucified* (FP 1998)

Gilson, E., *The Philosophy of St Bonaventure* (FP 1965)

Herbert, J., *The Road to Union: Johannine Dimensions of Bonaventure's Christology* (Fratri Editori di Quarracchi 2005; New City Press 2006)

Johnson, T., *Bonaventure: Mystic of God's Word* (New City Press 1999)

Johnson, T. J., *The Soul in Ascent: Bonaventure on Poverty, Prayer and Union with God* (FIP 2001)

Miller, P., *Marriage: the Sacrament of Divine–Human Communion: A Commentary on St Bonaventure's 'Breviloquium'* (FP 1996)

Ratzinger, J., *The Theology of History in St Bonaventure* (FP 1989)

Rout, P., *Francis and Bonaventure* (Triumph Christian Thinkers) (Liguori 1997)

Tavard, G., *The Forthbringer of God: St Bonaventure on the Virgin Mary* (FP 1989)

William of Ockham

Adams, M., *William Ockham*, Vols I–II (University of Notre Dame Press 1987)

Boehner, P. and Buytaert, E., *Collected Articles on Ockham* (FIP 1958)

Buescher, G., *The Eucharistic Teaching of William of Ockham* (FIP 1974)

Leff, G., *William of Ockham: The Metamorphosis of Scholastic Discourse* (Manchester University Press 1975)

Surveys

Cirino, A. and Raischl, J., eds, *A Pilgrimage through the Franciscan Intellectual Tradition* (Franciscan International Study Centre 2008)

Delio, I., *A Franciscan View of Creation: Learning to Live in a Sacramental World* (FIP 2003)

Delio, I., *The Humility of God: A Franciscan Perspective* (SAM 2005)

Northwehr, D., *The Franciscan View of the Human Person: Some Elements* (FIP 2005)

Osborne, K., *The Franciscan Intellectual Tradition* (FIP 2003)

Saggau, E., ed., *Franciscans and Creation: What Is Our Responsibility?* Washington Theological Union, Symposium Papers, CFIT/ESC-OFM Series 3 (FIP 2003)

Saggau, E., ed., *Franciscans and the Scriptures: Living in the Word of God*, CFIT/ESC-OFM Series 5 (FIP 2006)

Saggau, E., ed., *'Go Rebuild My House': Franciscans and the Church Today*. Washington Symposium Papers, CFIT/ESC-OFM (FIP 2004)

Saggau, E., ed., *The Franciscan Intellectual Tradition*, Washington Theological Union Symposium Papers, CFIT/ESC-OFM (FIP 2001)

Other

Burr, D., *Eucharistic Presence and Conversion in Late Thirteenth-Century Franciscan Thought* (American Philosophical Society 1984)

Carney, M. and Saggau, E., eds, *Franciscan Studies: The Difference Women are Making* (FIP 1999)

Carrozzo, A., ed., *In Solitude and Dialogue: Contemporary Franciscans Theologize* (FIP 2000)

Doyle, E., eds A. Cirino and J. Raischl, *My Heart's Quest: Collected Writings of Eric Doyle* (Franciscan International Study Centre 2005)

Dwyer, D. and Hines, H., eds, *Islam and Franciscanism* (FIP 2000)

Fleming, J., *An Introduction to Franciscan Literature of the Middle Ages* (FP 1977)

Gurley, M., *Franciscans Doing Theology: An Independent Study Program to Accompany the History of Franciscan Theology* (FIP 1999)

Hayes, Z., *The Hidden Centre* (FIP 2000)
A Window to the Divine: Creation Theology (FP 1997)

Hoeberichts, J., *Francis and Islam* (FP 1997)

Mulholland, S., *The Character of Eric Doyle's Theological Endeavour: Trinity, Christology, Ecclesiology, Franciscanology* (Franciscan International Study Centre 2005)

Nguyên-Van-Khanh, N., *The Teacher of His Heart* (FIP 1994)

Osborne, K., ed., *History of Franciscan Theology* (FIP 1994)

Raedts, P., *Richard Rufus of Cornwall and the Tradition of Oxford Theology* (Oxford University Press 1987)

Swanson, J., *John of Wales* (Cambridge University Press 1989)

Franciscan history

Overview

Carmody, M., *The Franciscan Story: St Francis of Assisi and His Influence Since the Thirteenth Century* (Athena Press 2008)

Holzapfel, H., *The History of the Franciscan Order* (St Joseph Seminary 1948)

Iriarte, L., *Franciscan History: The Three Orders of St Francis of Assisi* (FP 1983)

Monti, D., *Francis and His Brothers: A Popular History of the Franciscan Friars* (SAM 2009)

Short, W., *The Franciscans* (Michael Glazier 1994)

Vorreux, D., *A Short History of the Franciscan Family* (FP 1989)

Origins to 1517

Baird, J., Baglivi, G. and Kane, J., eds, *Chronicles of Adam of Salimbene* (FIP 1986)

Burr, D., *Olivi and Franciscan Poverty: The Origins of the Usus Pauper Controversy* (University of Pennsylvania Press 1999)

Burr, D., *et al.*, *Angelo Clareno: A Chronicle or History of the Seven Tribulations of the Order of Brothers Minor* (FIP 2005)

Cusato, M. and Warne, K., *True Followers of Justice: Identity,*

Insertion, and Itinerancy among the Early Franciscans (FIP 2000)

Desbonnets, T., *From Intuition to Institution: The Franciscans* (FP 1988)

Esser, C., *Origins of the Franciscan Order* (FP 1970)

Flood, D. and Matura, T., *The Birth of a Movement: A Study of the First Rule of St Francis* (FP 1975)

Lambert, M., *Franciscan Poverty* (FIP 1998)

MacVicar, T., *Franciscan Spirituals and the Capuchin Reform* (FIP 1987)

Moorman, J., *Medieval Franciscan Houses* (FIP 1983)
A History of the Franciscan Order, from the Origins to the Year 1517 (Oxford University Press reprints/Sandpiper Books 1997)

Nimmo, D., *Reform and Division in the Medieval Franciscan Order* (Capuchin Historical Institute 1987)

Robson, M., *Franciscans in the Middle Ages* (Boydell Press 2006)

Thomson, W., *Friars in the Cathedral: The First Franciscan Bishops 1226–1261* (Pont. Inst. of Mediaeval Hist. 1998)

Wood, J., *Women, Art and Spirituality: The Poor Clares of Early Modern Italy* (Cambridge University Press 1996)

1517 to present

Camps, A. and McCloskey, P., eds, *Friars Minor in China* (FIP 1996)

Carmody, M., *The Leonine Union of the Order of Friars Minor 1897* (FIP 1994)

Cuthbert, *The Capuchins*, 2 Vols (Sheed & Ward 1928)

Tedesco, M., *The Franciscan: Cardinal-Bishop Diomede Falconio 1842–1917* (Vantage 1972)

Williams, B., *The Franciscan Revival in the Anglican Communion* (Darton, Longman & Todd 1982)

Yates, P., *Recollect Franciscan Poverty: History and Legislation of a Stricter Observant Reform* (Fratri Editori di Quaracchi, Grottaferrata 2005)

Third Order/Secular Franciscans

Harline, C., *The Burdens of Sr Margaret: Inside a Seventeenth Century Convent* (Yale University Press 2001)

Pazzelli, R., *St Francis and the Third Order: The Franciscan and Pre-Franciscan Penitential Movement* (FP 1989)
The Franciscan Sisters: Outlines of History and Spirituality (FUP 1993)

Peano, P., *Franciscan Sisters: Origins, History and Outstanding Characteristics* (FUP 1996)

Stewart, R., *The Secular Rule* (FIP 1992)

Willmann, A., *Everywhere People Waiting: A Life of Helene de Chappotin de Neuville (Mother Mary of the Passion) 1839–1904, Foundress of the Franciscan Missionaries of Mary* (Christopher Publishing 1973)

Missions

Daniel, E. R., *The Franciscan Concept of Mission in the High Middle Ages* (FIP 1992)

Dawson, C., *The Mongol Mission: Narratives and Letters of the Franciscan Missionaries in Mongolia and China in the Thirteenth and Fourteenth Centuries* (AMS Press 1980)

Morales, F., *Franciscan Presence in the Americas* (Academy of American Franciscan History 1984)

British and Irish Franciscan history

Concannon, H., *The Poor Clares in Ireland* (Gill 1930)

Conlan, P., *Franciscan Ireland* (Lilliput 1999)
Missionary Work of the Irish Franciscans (Veritas 1996)

Cotter, F., *Friars Minor in Ireland from Their Arrival to 1400* (FIP 1994)

Devas, D., *et al.*, *Seventh Centenary of the Franciscan Order in England*: Vol. I: *The First Province (1224–1534)*; Vol. II: *The Martyrs*; Vol. III: *The Second Province*; Vol. IV: *The*

Third Province; Vol. V: *The Franciscans in Scotland*; Vol. VI: *The Poor Clares*; Vol. VII: *The Third Order Regular*; Vol. VIII: *The Third Order Secular* (St Antony's Press 1924)

Dockery, J., *Christopher Davenport: Friar and Diplomat* (Burns & Oates 1960)
Collingridge: A Franciscan Contribution to Catholic Emancipation (R. H. Johns 1954)

Dunstan, P., *This Poor Sort: A History of the European Province of the Society of St Francis* (Darton, Longman & Todd 1997)

Hunnybun, M., *Registers of the English Poor Clares at Gravelines, Including those Who Founded Filiations at Aire, Dunkirk, and Rouen, 1608–1837* in: Catholic Record Society, *Miscellanea IX* (Mercat Press 1914), pp. 25–173.

Jukes, J., *The English Province of the Order of Friars Minor Conventual* (1967)

McDonough, H., *Paul Atkinson: Prisoner of Hurst Castle Hampshire (1700–1729)* (Samuel Walker 1958)

Moorman, J., *The Franciscans in England* (Mowbrays 1974)

Franciscan Sites and Images

Baldyga, S. M., *The San Damiano Cross* (Portiuncula Press 2005)

Bellucci, G., *Assisi: Heart of the World* (Portiuncula Press 2001)

Benedict XVI, *The Pardon of Assisi* (Portiuncula Press 2006)

Dean, J., *Every Pilgrim's Guide to Assisi* (Canterbury Press 2002)

Desbonnets, T., *Assisi: In the Footsteps of St Francis: A Spiritual Guidebook* (Portiuncula Press 2003)

Guinan, M., *The Franciscan Vision and the Gospel of John: The San Damiano Crucifix* (FIP 2006)

Saint Sing, S., *Francis and the San Damiano Cross: Meditations on Spiritual Transformation* (SAM 2006)

Simpson, C., *Message of Assisi* (Catholic Truth Society 2002)

Franciscans and art

Arnold, L., *Princely Gifts and Papal Treasures: The Franciscan Mission to China and Its Influence on Art in the West 1250–1350* (Desiderata 1999)

Casciani, S., *Dante and the Franciscans: Medieval Franciscans*, Vol. 3 (Brill, Leiden 2006)

Derbes, A., *Picturing the Passion in Late Medieval Italy: Narrative Painting, Franciscan Ideologies and the Levant* (Cambridge University Press 1996)

Kaftal, G., *St Francis in Italian Painting* (Allen and Unwin 1950)

Lunghi, E., *The Basilica of St Francis in Assisi* (Riverside 1997)

Moleta, V., *From St Francis to Giotto: The Influence of St Francis on Early Italian Art and Literature* (FP 1999)

Romanini, A. and Romanini, M., *Assisi: The Frescoes in the Basilica of St Francis* (Rizzoli 1998)

Wright, T., *The Hymn of the Sun* (Hymn of the Sun Productions 1991)

Periodicals and Series

Franciscan Studies (FIP)
Greyfriars Review (FIP)
The Chord (FIP)

Audio Cassettes

Bodo, M., *A Mosaic of Francis: Making His Way Our Own* (SAM 1986)

Chesterton, G., *St Francis of Assisi* (read by B. Mayes) (Blackstone Audio 1992)

Videos

Batty, P., *Il Poverello: Story of St Francis of Assisi* (1985)
Cavani, L., *Francesco* (1989)
Curtis, M., *Francis of Assisi* (1961)
Francis of Assisi (Ignatius Press 1998)
Francis, The Knight of Assisi (CCC Publications 1991)
Glavich, K., *Francis of Assisi* (Twenty-Third Publications 1997)
Rossellini, R., *Francesco, Giullare di Dio (Flowers of St Francis)* (1950)
Webb, R., *Seven Cities of Gold* (Life of Junipero Serra) (1955)
Zeffirelli, F., *Brother Sun, Sister Moon* (1971)

15

Websites

www.ciofs.org
The website of the Secular Franciscan Order.

www.fmdminternational.co.uk
The website of the Franciscan Missionaries of the Divine Motherhood (Sisters).

www.fmm.org
The international website of the Franciscan Missionaries of Mary (Sisters).

www.franciscaneweb.com
The Franciscan Wikipedia, containing information about Francis and Clare of Assisi and their followers through the centuries.

www.franciscans.ac.uk
The website of the Franciscan Study Centre at Canterbury, with news and information about the centre.

www.franciscans.ie
The website of the Order of the Friars Minor in Ireland.

www.franciscansinternational.org
The website of Franciscans International, a non-governmental organization at the United Nations, which includes news and information about world issues.

www.franciscans.org
The website of the Conventual Franciscans in the USA but with general Franciscan information and links to other websites.

www.franciscans.org.uk
Temporarily at www.sidings.org/franciscans
The website of the European Province of the Anglican Society of St Francis, which includes First Order Brothers and Sisters, the Community of St Clare (Second Order) and links to the Anglican Third Order.

www.franciscantradition.org
The website, initiated by leaders of the English-speaking OFM provinces, for those concerned with the Franciscan Intellectual Tradition, which provides a community forum and resources.

www.friar.org
The website of the English province of the Order of the Friars Minor.

www.ofm.org
The international website of the Order of the Friars Minor.

www.ofmcap.org
The international website of the Order of the Capuchin Friars Minor.

www.ofmconv.org
The international website of the Order of Friars Minor Conventual.

www.poorclaresarundel.org
The website of the Poor Clares at Arundel. This site includes links to other Poor Clare websites, as well as a website dedicated to the TV programme made at Arundel, entitled *The Convent*.

Websites

www.s-f-o.org
The website of the Secular Franciscan Order, both for members and for those seeking information.

www.tssf.org.uk
The website of the European Province of the Third Order of the Society of St Francis.

Index